Passive Patient Culture in India

In a society shaped by deep inequalities, where healthcare and legal systems often reinforce class, caste, religion, and gender hierarchies, this book offers a powerful examination of patienthood in India. Through its critical approach, it seeks to disrupt binaries—such as universalistic and particularistic values and data versus theory—while decentering normative discourses by foregrounding lived experiences within the context. It offers philosophical and conceptual insights that extend far beyond local variations and contexts, challenging dominant narratives in global discourses on medical decision-making and concepts such as informed consent, autonomy, and respect.

This book critiques the archetype of the "passive patient" entrenched in both medicine and law in India—an image that undermines agency, diminishes self-respect, and sustains a culture of disrespect. Chapters of the book unpack the intersections of power, social categories, and patienthood, exposing how marginalized communities face everyday indignities in healthcare and law. It explores law and medicine's role in maintaining presumed 'passive patient' archetype, especially through legal judgements and healthcare encounters. This book advocates for reimagining patienthood as centered on self-respect, recognition, and agency, arguing that the "passive patient" is not an isolated phenomenon but an outcome of broader, oppressive structures.

Contributing to robust debates in medical sociology, bioethics, and social justice, this book is essential reading for those interested in the intersections of these fields, along with applied ethics, health services research, and law.

Supriya Subramani is Lecturer at Sydney Health Ethics, School of Public Health, Faculty of Medicine and Health, University of Sydney. She explores ethics, embodied emotions, and the politics of knowledge. Employing critical philosophical ethnography and a phenomenological approach, she critically examines structural injustice in health, disrespect and othering, the ethics of belonging, and the intersections of paternalism, respect, and agency.

Routledge Research in Health Law

Workplace Mental Health Law
Comparative Perspectives
Takenori Mishiba

Mental Health Law in China
A Socio-legal Analysis
Bo Chen

International Human Rights Law and the Framework Convention on Tobacco Control
Lessons from Africa and Beyond
Edited by Ebenezer Durojaye and Lucyline Nkatha Murungi

Patient Autonomy and Criminal Law
European Perspectives
Edited by Paweł Daniluk

Regional Cooperation, Intellectual Property Law and Access to Medicines
A Holistic Approach for Least Developed Countries
Tolulope Anthony Adekola

Passive Patient Culture in India
Disrespect in Law and Medicine
Supriya Subramani

For more information about this series, please visit:
www.routledge.com/Routledge-Research-in-Human-Rights-Law/book-series/RRHL

Passive Patient Culture in India

Disrespect in Law and Medicine

Supriya Subramani

Routledge
Taylor & Francis Group
LONDON AND NEW YORK

First published 2025
by Routledge
4 Park Square, Milton Park, Abingdon, Oxon OX14 4RN

and by Routledge
605 Third Avenue, New York, NY 10158

Routledge is an imprint of the Taylor & Francis Group, an informa business

The author gratefully acknowledges the financial support from her research allocation under the Start-up Faculty Grant at the School of Public Health, University of Sydney, and the Brocher Foundation, which enabled the Open Access publication of this book.

British Library Cataloguing-in-Publication Data
A catalogue record for this book is available from the British Library

Library of Congress Cataloging-in-Publication Data
Names: Subramani, Supriya, author.
Title: Passive patient culture in India: disrespect in law and medicine / Supriya Subramani.
Description: Abingdon, Oxon [UK]; New York, NY : Routledge, 2025. | Series: Routledge research in health law | Includes bibliographical references and index.
Identifiers: LCCN 2024053988 | ISBN 9780367655365 (hardback) | ISBN 9780367655372 (paperback) | ISBN 9781003129998 (ebook)
Subjects: LCSH: Patients–Legal status, laws, etc.–India. | Medical care–Law and legislation–India. | Public health laws–India. | Right to health–India.
Classification: LCC KNS1520.5 .S83 2025 | DDC 344.5404–dc23/eng/20241114
LC record available at https://lccn.loc.gov/2024053988

ISBN: 978-0-367-65536-5 (hbk)
ISBN: 978-0-367-65537-2 (pbk)
ISBN: 978-1-003-12999-8 (ebk)

DOI: 10.4324/9781003129998

Typeset in Galliard
by Deanta Global Publishing Services, Chennai, India

To my mother,
To those who live at the margins,
To those who defy and resist,
To those who teach us the strength of love and liberation,
To those through whom we learn joy in the struggle and reclaim freedom,
To every liminal space of existence.
To bell hooks,
As I unlearn, lean, and find my freer self

Contents

Copyright Permissions and Acknowledgements

I would like to thank publishers for granting permission to include portions of my previously published work in this book. This book refers and/or extends arguments and material that first appeared in the following publications:

Subramani, S. (2018). The moral significance of capturing micro-inequities in hospital settings. *Social Science & Medicine*, *209*, 136–144. Permission was kindly granted by PERGAMON.

Subramani, S. (2019). Practising reflexivity: Ethics, methodology and theory construction. *Methodological Innovations*, *12*(2), 2059799119863276.

Permission was kindly granted by SAGE Publications Ltd.

Subramani, S. (2019). The rhetoric of the 'passive patient' in Indian medical negligence cases. *Asian Bioethics Review*, *11*(4), 349–366. Permission was kindly granted by NUS Press.

Subramani, S. (2020). The social construction of incompetency: moving beyond embedded paternalism toward the practice of respect. *Health Care Analysis*, *28*(3), 249–265. Permission was kindly granted by KLUWER ACADEMIC PUBLISHERS (DORDRECHT).

Subramani, S. (2022). Moral habitus: An approach to understanding embedded disrespectful practices. *Developing World Bioethics*, *22*(2), 94–104. Permission was kindly granted BLACKWELL PUBLISHING LTD.

Subramani, S., & Biller-Andorno, N. (2022). Revisiting respect for persons: conceptual analysis and implications for clinical practice. *Medicine, Health Care and Philosophy*, *25*(3), 351–360. Permission was kindly granted by KLUWER ACADEMIC PUBLISHERS (DORDRECHT).

I appreciate the opportunity to revisit and extend these ideas within the context of this book.

Preface

Finding Voice

This book is my sincere attempt to center the voices and experiences that have been dismissed, silenced, disregarded, and oppressed. In my previous efforts, I failed to convey, as fully as I intended, why we must center these voices and experiences, and why resisting the passive patient culture in medicine and law in India is morally urgent. I do not claim this attempt will be flawless, but I promise it is an honest effort to mirror and confront the taken-for-granted nature of our culture of disrespect and to demonstrate why it's necessary to resist the oppressive structures that sustain it. Finding your voice when you've been taught to please, when you lack the social capital or the right language and tools to unpack complex ideas—especially when the issues cut so deeply and intimate—is no easy task. It's painful, messy, and requires years of unlearning. For instance, it took me years to embrace my fractured identities and the way I experience and understand the world I live in. I can't claim to have arrived at the end of this process; instead, I see it as a journey, one rooted in resistance to dominant ways of knowing and in the struggle to find a language that can hold and mirror the truths of this self, in this moment. I hope this book captures that journey, my attempt to become a 'sutradara' (storyteller or narrator) and hold space for ways of resistance, sharing and knowing.

This book is based on my doctoral and postdoctoral research, conducted between 2013 and 2021, and much has changed in both India and the world since then, and I have changed, and continue to change. Through unlearnings and relearnings, I found myself questioning the relevance of this work in the face of collective mourning and grief, spurred by the visual witnessing of violence against Palestinians, Sudanese, Ukrainians, and mass systematic violations of dignities and dehumanization. The diminishing optimism and hope during this moment of polycrisis is a painful realization that the patterns of structural injustice remain as persistent as ever. The systems of domination continue to reproduce and normalize themselves, woven into the very fabric of our everyday lives. What I had hoped might feel outdated instead serves as a painful reminder of how power, privilege, and oppression still shape our world in ways we cannot ignore. For instance, the COVID-19 pandemic and the recent rape and murder of a junior doctor at RG Kar Medical College, followed by strikes by doctors, underscore the persistent failure to address the structural and everyday violence faced by socially marginalized communities, and how those in power and institutions sustain inequalities and inequities through the privileged gaze. What I aim to show in this book is that the treatment of people—shamed, humiliated, silenced and disregarded in India, whether in medicine, law, or public and private institutions like banks or schools—stems from deeply ingrained assumptions about citizens, often viewed as "incompetent, passive, ignorant, stupid, arrogant, naïve". The construction of the "passive patient", as I demonstrate, strips away self-respect, humanitiy, and agency, and is deeply rooted in colonial continuities, upper-caste-class, and gendered hierarchies that continue to perpetuate injustice and shape both the Indian healthcare and legal systems.

I am part of a community that the Indian state classifies and categorizes as "Backward". Who would want to identify or be categorized as "Backward"? This categorization is a legacy of British colonialism, which established social identities for administrative convenience and created new boundaries. In contemporary India, these designations aim to recognize communities that have historically endured disadvantages, facilitating access to educational and employment opportunities through affirmative action policies. The Badaga and Kota communities, to which I am socially and politically connected and belong, are identified as a hill tribe or "Adi Dravidar", or Indigenous communities.

The Hatti (village) from which my father is from, along with other socio-economically marginalized groups within the Tribal Welfare community, self-recognize as tribal communities. These groups seek cultural recognition to protect their culture, language, and identity, and they seek support from the state. Since the 1990s (and even earlier, due to colonial categorizations), there has been a persistent push for recognition of our indigenous status, including legal appeals to the High Court and the Supreme Court of India. The question of who is considered indigenous in India and how one experiences othering due to categorization are two different but overlapping issues. I will not explore both here, but these are areas I hope to explore into as part of my learning and unlearning journey in the future. In the rural community where I grew up, we were migrants in a strange township surrounded by villages. People from my mom's family or others in our community often referred to my father and us as "kadjana" (forest people), which immediately placed us in a marginalized category within the social world. Most of my education took place in schools and colleges (except maybe IIT Madras, which was a random chance) that few have heard of, unless they are from my village or the nearby town outside Bangalore. My education was primarily aimed at securing a job and earning money to support my family. But as life unfolded, I went along with the paths that opened up before me. After completing my master's, I found myself working at IIT Madras as a project associate on a Wellcome Trust, UK based funding organization, grant focused on patient autonomy.

In that role, I was largely seen as a "data collector" with the assumption that I wasn't equipped to contribute theoretically or conceptually. Despite the challenges I faced during that fieldwork, the experience played a crucial role in shaping my decision to pursue a doctoral degree when the opportunity presented itself two years later. I took the University Grants Commission junior research fellowship exam in social work, passed it, and began my doctoral studies.

Being who I am, from where I came, with unsophisticated English, was incredibly difficult in Brahminical, upper-caste-class-gendered institutions, where fluency in English is often seen as a marker of intellect. What made it worse was that even those who identified as "left" contributed to the hostility, alongside others in positions of power. Some of my peers, shaped by their classist-casteist biases about what constitutes knowledge, saw me as incapable and incompetent simply because I couldn't express my thoughts in the polished academic language and refined English, they deemed essential for intellectual contribution. Rather than recognizing my potential and offering support, those years became suffocating and painful, devoid of the mentorship and kindness one so desperately needs in academic spaces. It took at least a year away from India to begin recovering from the depression those experiences caused. I won't get into the details of my experiences in upper-caste-class and white-dominated spaces, where trust was broken and my ideas were taken without citation—that's perhaps for future writings, or perhaps not.

For those of us who experience marginalization and social exclusion within oppressive structures, the culture of disrespect and violence in our everyday lives is all too familiar—how we are humiliated, shamed, silenced, disregarded, and dismissed. Learning from and being influenced by critical scholars, particularly bell hooks—whose work, regrettably, I discovered quite late—has been transformative for me. I often wish I had encountered her writings in my teens or 20s, but as they say, it's never too late. Her work, along with Dalit, Black, and Indigenous autobiographies and critical scholarship, and the writings of insurgent decolonial scholars, has shown me the importance of centering marginalized voices, experiences, and emotions. These thinkers have helped me channel my rage and find my voice to join liberation struggles, urging us to free ourselves from these oppressive structures which sustain social inequalities, as Dr. B. R. Ambedkar, Savitribai Phule, and Periyar E. V. Ramasamy emphasized through self-respect movements.

This book, while aimed at a specific audience such as health researchers, healthcare professionals, and applied ethicists in the health space, is also intended to contribute to patient rights movements, anti-caste and anti-class struggles, and the resistance against oppressive structures. As bell hooks powerfully expressed in Feminist Theory: From Margin to Center, "We looked both from the outside in and from the inside out. We focused our attention on the center as well as on the margin. We understood both. This mode of seeing reminded us of the existence of a whole universe, a main body made up of both margin and center. Our survival depended on an ongoing public awareness of the separation between margin and center and an ongoing private acknowledgment that we were a necessary, vital part of that whole". We are those at the margins.

I hope this work offers a glimpse into how structural forces sustain the passive patient culture in India, along with the pervasive culture of disrespect that silences, marginalizes, and rejects our voices. By exposing the structural violence and the quiet struggles we endure, I aim to highlight that these struggles themselves are acts of resistance—fights for self-respect, agency, self-love, dignity, and integrity. By centering recognition and self-respect, this book seeks to amplify our voices in the effort to dismantle the culture of disrespect in India. I am fully aware of the relative privilege I now hold, and I understand the responsibility that comes with it. My hope is to use this privilege as a tool to center our voices, and to challenge structural violence in every way I can, with the capacities I have. I am realizing the fight and resistance, and survival in these spaces, particularly academic spaces, is not neat! I know there will be times when I may fail or fall short. In those moments, I call on my peers—those in communities of resistance and rebellion, those who practice every day—to guide me, to help me remain true to my values. This journey is about turning privilege into purpose and commitment, a constant choice, ensuring that our presence in these spaces becomes a force to resist and challenge the very systems that oppress. I often wonder if I will ever be able to translate this entire book into my mother tongue or discuss the ideas I have learned, in my fading, broken language, in Kannada, Tamil, or even Badaga (one of the unscripted languages of the Nilgiris), trying to keep the learning alive, so I can share these reflections with my communities and with those whose first language is not English. Still, my hope is that if someone who contributed their time and perspectives to this project were to read this book one day, they would feel that their time was not wasted.

I hope this book offers even a small glimpse into the immense suffering of those who are marginalized, and provides insight through both my perspective and the experiences of those I engaged with. The analysis and ethnographic descriptions I present, particularly around indignities and the construction, maintenance, and normalization of the passive patient archetype, are only a partial view. There is much more to be explored—such as the de-prioritization and corporatization of health, violence against patients and doctors, workplace violence, the need for training healthcare professionals in humane and respectful practices, and the state's role in shaping health policy and patient rights, and many more aspects to achieve transformative, just, and respectful care. Through the rhetoric, narratives, reflections, and experiences I've illustrated in this book, I hope we remain critical of whom we imagine when we talk about patients, and what the passive patient archetype achieves, or not, in our moral, ethical, legal, and political discourse.

To the Many Whom I Thank!

Growing up at the intersections of multiple marginalized identities, it has taken—and continues to take—time for me to learn, unlearn, and resist the dominant ways of thinking, doing, and being in academic spaces. I never imagined I would find myself in academia, and even now, I'm uncertain how long I will stay. But I want to thank those who made this journey possible, those who made it difficult, and those who supported me in ways I needed—and sometimes in ways I didn't. If not for my parents and the many strangers who helped me along the way, I might have ended up working in a garment factory or as a bus conductor—alternate realities that are now something we joke about in my family! If it weren't for my parents, particularly my ಅಮ್ಮ (mom), who sacrificed so much for my education—selling what little gold they had, taking loans from ruthless local lenders, and refusing to marry me off, even after I got "caught" with my boyfriend—I wouldn't be where I am today. ನನ್ನ ಅಮ್ಮನಿಗೆ ಎಲ್ಲಕ್ಕೂ ನಾನು ಋಣಿಯಾಗಿದ್ದೇನೆ! (I am grateful and indebted to my mom for everything). For all the freedom, support, and opportunities to resist and rebel, for not holding me back from attending university, and for encouraging me to move out and pursue my education at 21, supported by government fellowships throughout my master's and doctoral studies—I am deeply grateful! I am grateful for all the opportunities and support I've had throughout my life—gaining wisdom over everyday life being at the margins, from being a bookseller in K.R. Market, a dance teacher in my strange township in a village, a chemist trainee in an industrial estate, a telecaller for a bank on commission, and after precarious postdoc gigs, now a lecturer at a university. While I've recently gained some relative privilege, I remain thankful for the journey.

To Aditya Narayanan, my partner—thank you for being such an amazing partner, and to believe in me and reassure when needed. Together, we've gone through so much learning and unlearning, and we continue to grow. Our inter-caste-class marriage added a new layer to the questions I was already pondering about identity and how to navigate a culture of disrespect and violence. I am thankful to you for being there during my ups and downs, for listening to my ideas and arguments, and for your constant support that helped my confidence. To my brother, Sujay, who sees "something" in me to admire—I'll do my best to live up to it! And to my in-laws, thank you for your encouraging words.

This work would not have been possible without the support of many patients and their family members, doctors, nurses, hospitals, and ethics committee members. I am deeply grateful to all of you for sharing your views, experiences, opinions, and beliefs—especially the patients, caretakers, and healthcare professionals. A special thanks to the many anonymous reviewers for their critical and constructive feedback while I was working to get my papers published. Their engagement with my ideas—rather than focusing on my imperfect non-native English—and their unflinching yet gentle honesty gave me confidence and helped shape my work. I'd like to thank my editor, Kendrick Loo, for encouraging me to write this book and for his incredible patience. He graciously accommodated all my "just a little more time" requests, and, well, five years later, here we are! Although academia often feels like a gatekeeping industry, I was fortunate to receive varying degrees of support along the way. Thanks to many friends and peers, especially from South Asian Bioethics Community, Department of Humanities and Social Sciences, and Department of Physics, IIT Madras.

I am thankful to Prof. Nakkeeran who made my introduction to qualitative research both insightful and engaging, and P. Sivakumar for their support throughout various learning journeys. I also want to acknowledge V R Muraleedharan, John Bosco Lourdusamy, Parivalavan Rajavelu, Kathy Charmaz, Vijay Gopichandran, Amar Jesani, Girija Suresh, Gowri Shankar, Ludwig Siep, Shingo Segawa, Michael Kühler, James Childress, Sreeparna Chattopadhyay, Nikola Biller-Andorno, Sreekumar N, Sunita Bandewar, Luna Dolezal and Peter Schaber for their support and engagement with my work at different phases of my doctoral and postdoctoral work. My sincere gratitude to Prof. Joga Rao and Dr. Suresh V for helping me understand how courts function and how the law operates through "cases". Prof. Joga Rao graciously supported me during a short internship at his law firm, providing me with access to the NLSIU library and the opportunity to work on a medical negligence case. This experience gave me valuable insight into court proceedings and judgments in the Indian context. I would also like to thank the librarians at Tamil Nadu Ambedkar Law University for their support.

Despite facing many othering experiences during my doctoral work, I was fortunate to receive opportunities to go to Germany for short visiting fellowships. I am grateful to Prof. Thomas Gutmann for offering me a Junior Fellowship at the Centre for Advanced Study in Bioethics, University of Münster, Germany. I sincerely thank Prof. Gutmann for his encouraging words and for continued belief in my approach and support since then! The overall experience at the Centre—through weekly seminars, and both formal and informal interactions with fellows—made me realize how academic culture can nurture scholarship and motivated me to strive towards becoming a researcher.

My experience in Münster brought me immense joy. People took me seriously, even when I presented fragmented thoughts and broken ideas. They listened, allowed me to finish my imperfect English statements, and treated me as an early-career researcher, offering guidance on readings and learning, which was a huge challenge during my doctoral work. Those experiences helped me grow. They opened the door to literature that was difficult to access and comprehend due to its complex vocabulary and obscure language, but I was given the time, mentorship, and space to reflect and learn. For few who were keen to listen, for few who encouraged and those supported, especially anonymous reviewers and editors of journals where I published my earlier works and sample chapters of this book—thank you!

I must say, my doctoral study was greatly enriched by many fellow peers during my PhD journey. I want to thank particularly Aditya Narayanan, Samik Malla, Aniket Nandan, William K. Moses Jr., and Avinash Hariharan for the late-night talks, concerts, debates, trips, fights, and dinners that gave me cherished experiences and shaped my ideas and reflections throughout my time at IITM. To my Chennai Trekking group friends, thank you for the surfing, trekking, dancing, and cooking, which helped me stay connected to the fun side of life! A big thank you to my friends from the engineering departments for showing interest in my research, patiently listening, attending my talks and seminars, and asking engaging questions. You helped me learn how to interact with scholars and peers from diverse disciplines. To my peers in the Humanities and Social Sciences department, IITM, thank you for attending my talks and seminars, and for ensuring I wasn't speaking to an empty room and for the corridor and lab interactions that added to my experience. Thanks to the many peers and friends from various universities who have listened to my work, including the Institute of Biomedical Ethics and History of Medicine at the University of Zurich, the Department of History at the University of Exeter, and colleagues from Sydney Health Ethics at the University of Sydney, for their support with timetabling, helping me to complete this work as well as engagement with my work. Thanks so much for Seye Abimbola and Alice Bayingana to engage with my thoughts and reflections on this work, and to Niro Kandasamy and Michael McDonnell for their support, encouragement, and for reading sections of my work as I navigate these new academic spaces.

I extend my gratitude to many institutions and fellowships that supported and funded the writing of this book: the University Grants Commission (UGC) Junior/Senior Research Fellowship; the Visiting Research Fellowship at the Centre for Advanced Study in Bioethics, University of Münster, Germany; the Swiss Excellence Government Postdoctoral Fellowship; the Stehr-Boldt Fellowship at the Institute of Biomedical Ethics and History of Medicine, University of Zurich; the Writing Residency Fellowship at the Brocher Foundation; and School of Public Health, Sydney Health Ethics, University of Sydney.

Introduction

The Silent Struggle

It's not often just physical pain that patients and family members complain about the most, especially those who are from marginalized and minoritized communities. It's the treatment—yelling, abusing, shaming, humiliating, invisibility, ignoring, and not acknowledging. As Vani, who was taking care of her mother during her mother's hospitalization, put it to me:

> I keep following them [the doctors] from the ward to their offices and back. They don't even bother to stop for a second and listen to me. I don't know what is wrong with my mother. We have been here for the past 15 days. Some days back, the junior nurses told me that it is some infection. They performed surgery again but did not tell me anything about it—why or what. As everywhere else, we are made to keep waiting.

Marginalized, subordinated, and disadvantaged people are routinely met with condescension, disdain, and degradation—a reality that must be recognized as unjust. This is what I mean by a culture of disrespect: a system that normalizes the denial of self-respect, dignity, and agency for marginalized individuals and communities. It is crucial that we resist this structural violence and stand with those already leading the fight to dismantle it, embracing the political and moral commitments that such resistance demands. For those familiar with critical scholarship including Dalitbahujan works and our everyday experiences, ಆತ್ಮ ಗೌರವ (*Ātma gaurava*, self-respect) and ಮಾನವೀಯತೆ (*Mānavīyate*, humanity) are central to human relationships and our sense of self. In oppressive structures, self-respect and humanity are often targeted, stripping away our agency and dignity. Liberation of the self is key, and centering how these oppressive structures strip away one's agency and dignity becomes essential. For instance, if you read Dalit scholar, Siddalingaiah's poems, particularly ಇಕ್ರಲಾಒದೀರ್ಲಾ (Ikrala Vadirla), one can immerse ourselves in how he uses anger, satire, humor and rage to capture how the culture of disrespect targets the humanity and self-respect of the socially marginalized, while at the same time resisting the gaze of the privileged.

Language carries rich ethical meanings in our everyday lives, and while this book may not fully capture the depth of these nuances, it's important to

DOI: 10.4324/9781003129998-1

acknowledge them. Translating words like dignity and respect (or any moral and social concepts) into our languages brings multiple layers of meaning, and these words often don't hold a single interpretation. In Kannada, for example, dignity and respect can serve to highlight both self-respect and humanity, though they may also be interpreted in ways that reinforce power dynamics. ಘನತೆ (*Ghanate*, dignity) can refer to prestige, honor, or esteem, often linked to social status when separated from concepts like self-respect and humanity. For instance, someone might say that marrying within one's caste preserves the family's dignity (in this case, honor). Similarly, ಗೌರವ (*Gaurava*, respect) can also mean deference, such as when my mother asks me not to sit cross-legged in front of elders as a gesture of respect.

Reflections on and references to self-respect are central to many critical scholars, including B. R. Ambedkar's work, and it's important to think critically about how we use and understand these terms and how we center self-respect in our social, political, and cultural discourse. In this book, by critically engaging with the passive patient culture in medicine and law, I emphasize why it is crucial to take recognition and self-respect seriously in our conversations—through the lens of affective and epistemic injustice—and to reimagine the world we want to live in, where *true dignity* (*self-respect* + *humanity*) is realized.

In the Indian healthcare system, individuals with caste, class, gender, religion, geographical location, and able-bodied privilege, coupled with luck and social capital, are better positioned to obtain information, access healthcare, and receive attention from professionals. This advantage allows a select few to navigate and secure quality and dignified healthcare. Those lacking these privileges often bear the weight of everyday epistemic and embodied injustices in various encounters, whether in healthcare settings or public spaces. Faced with this indignities, they either distance themselves from modern healthcare institutions or enter the system fully aware of their presumed "passive patient" roles as patients, a choice made without much agency. Persons, here patients and family members, on margins are acutely aware of how these interactions bring about shame, humiliation and everyday indignities. Those who choose to "complain" or express their frustrations to those in power, particularly in healthcare settings, often find themselves reduced to just another "annoying patient" or "difficult patient", rather than being treated as agents. Some of them become "frustrated patients" who empathize with the overburdened system, "angry patients" who acknowledge the uncertainty of medical conditions, or "arrogant patients" whose curiosity is met with dismissal and skepticism. In this bureaucratic healthcare system, often they become invisible, longing not to be seen merely as patients but as persons deserving of self-respect and recognition.

In a society characterized by dominant upper-caste-class patriarchal values, the doctor–nurse–patient relationship thrives on a cultivated interpretation of respect, synonymous with "deference". Everyday interactions, including those in healthcare settings, are governed by a prevailing moral framework that emphasizes "deference", perpetuating the influence of authority figures. Here is an excerpt from a practicing general surgeon at a private hospital to elucidate this point: Kumar asserted, "Our job is to give quality care to them, and theirs is to respect us and listen to us...these days people don't do that; they think they know because they have Google". Kumar operates within a value system wherein the fundamental archetype of the patient is one who "listens" and "respects" medical authority and knowledge, casting the doctor in the role of protector. This has become part of visible norms and expectations within healthcare spaces, particularly in private practice. For instance, billboards or posters with statements in hospitals like "Please Do Not Confuse Your Google Search With My Medical Degree" or "Trust Me, I'm Way Better Than the Internet" reflect the growing tensions between healthcare professionals and patient communities, as well as the increasing lack of trust within the healthcare system.

Similar to the value system of doctors, the nurse–patient relationship is grounded in caregiving and protective moral norms, such as "doctors know best" and "the best interests of patients". Based on the observation, which you will learn more about in following chapters, nurses primarily function as bridges or mediators, either enhancing or mitigating the power asymmetry between doctors and patients. This dynamic often involves perceiving patients in a more passive role, with the overarching objective of maintaining the "quality of care" provided. The underlying ideology and normative assumptions regarding patients are deeply embedded not only in routine healthcare interactions but also within legal frameworks. An illustrative example can be observed in the 2008 Supreme Court of India case, *Samira Kohli v. Dr. Prabha Manchanda* (Subramani, 2019). The judgment reinforced the prevailing archetype of the "passive patient" in the Indian context, stating, "They are passive, ignorant, and uninvolved in treatment procedures". Critical analysis of landmark decisions allows us to dissect the language of patienthood, which you will see in Chapter 2, unveiling the construction and moral narratives that are intimately connected to specific social and moral concepts of what it means to be a patient.

In the ever-evolving Indian healthcare, characterized by advancing medicalization, technological developments, increasing privatization, and rising inequalities, the question arises: what does it mean to be a patient in India? Who is considered a "good" patient? Who is labeled as "difficult" or "bad" or "deviant"? What kind of patient embodies an active or passive archetype? These questions reflect the changing dynamics and perceptions within the healthcare system, which are crucial for understanding patient–provider relationships and the broader culture within the healthcare system. These patient archetypes represent different unconscious meanings and normative assumptions associated with specific groups or individuals. The term "archetype" I use here is to capture the characteristics of these varied identities. Each archetype carries with it certain normative expectations within relationships, encounters, and institutions. When applied within medicine and law, these archetypes become crucial in establishing and reproducing social and normative practices. The underlying normative assumptions of these archetypes underscore the importance of social identities in defining who constitutes an "active patient" or "passive patient".

Recognizing that these archetypes should not be seen as rigid categories, I view them as existing on a spectrum and socially constructed. For instance, a patient may be "active" in some respects and "passive" in others due to various factors such as changes in health status, education, support systems, or intersectional experiences with the healthcare system. In this book, my aim is not only to illustrate the underlying constructions of "passive patienthood" within medicine and law but also to critically examine the unacknowledged assumptions, oversimplified binary oppositions, and power dynamics embedded in legal texts, ethical concepts, and social practices. Furthermore, I engage in a critical analysis of how healthcare professionals and legal texts construct representations of specific patient archetypes and how these contribute to the construction of patient imaginaries within broader political and social contexts. The underlying normative assumptions and archetypes of patients significantly shape interactions between healthcare professionals and their patients, as well as influence medical decision-making. These assumptions, rooted in our moral economy, reflect deep-seated values, expectations, societal norms, and ethical principles. They play a crucial role in defining how patients are perceived and treated within the healthcare system, impacting both the quality and culture of care they receive.

Contextualizing Passive Patient Discourse

In this book, I explore the evolving narratives of patienthood within the Indian healthcare system, focusing on how historical, social, and cultural forces have shaped the archetype of the passive patient. Through a series of interconnected chapters, I examine the emergence of the "passive patient" archetype, the rhetoric of passivity in legal and medical discourses, and the everyday indignities faced by patients and family members, especially those who are marginalized, in a system where deep inequalities persist. My aim is to argue for a reimagining of patienthood that centers self-respect, recognition and agency. As I show in the following chapters, the passive role of patients is not merely the result of isolated interactions but is perpetuated by the very oppressive structure of the healthcare system and the broader societal, cultural and political context. The hierarchical nature of medical institutions entrenched upper-class-caste-gender norms in India, which impacts both healthcare providers and patients, and cultural expectations surrounding authority, all contribute to an environment where passivity is normalized. This larger humiliating structure has been discussed by scholars from varied perspectives, which gives us a glimpse of everyday political and social realities for those who are at margins in India (see Ambedkar, 2020; Das, 2015; Drèze, 2019; Drèze & Sen, 1991; Teltumbde, 2010, 2020; Guha, 2011; Guru, 2009; Guru & Sarukkai, 2018, 2019; Ilaiah, 2010; Rege, 1998, 2014; Sen, 1983; Paik, 2014). In this moral and political climate, patients, particularly those from marginalized backgrounds, quickly learn that being a "good" patient means being a quiet one, someone who does not disrupt the flow, challenge the status quo, or demand too much attention. The consequences of this enforced passivity are far-reaching. Patients who adopt a passive role are less likely to seek clarification, question their treatment, or express concerns about one's care. This passivity can lead to poorer health outcomes, as critical information may be overlooked or misunderstood, disrespected through everyday indignities, dismissed and silenced, and it perpetuates a cycle of disregard where patients feel increasingly incapable of advocating for themselves within the healthcare system. Thus health inequalities and inequities has both epistemic and affective injustice. This cycle is not merely an individual failure but a structural problem, deeply rooted in the power dynamics that govern medical and legal institutions. In this book, I do not want to restrict my argument solely to its relation to overall health and health outcomes—many across disciplines have been establishing these connections for years. Instead, by acknowledging and centering the lived experiences of patients and their family members, particularly those who are marginalized, we begin to see the profound relationship between knowing and caring. Treating individuals with true dignity becomes central, highlighting the need to address epistemic and affective injustices. This approach not only builds trust, respect, care, and belonging within the healthcare system but also facilitates better medical decision-making and improves overall health outcomes. Moreover, this recognition has the potential to disrupt and transform how we think about medical education, health systems' approaches to inequities, and health policies and programs.

Influenced by various critical theorists (Ambedkar, 1990; Fanon, 2010; Honneth, 1995, 2014a; hooks, 2014, 2015; Rodrigues, 2024; Yancy, 2008), I employ a framework of self-respect and recognition, as it provides a valuable lens through which to understand the implications of passive patienthood—especially how it disregards one's true dignity, and why it should matter to us. Recognition is a fundamental human need, essential for the development of a person's identity and self-respect, and social recognition—being seen, acknowledged, and respected by others—is crucial for individuals to view themselves as full members of society. It is essential to distinguish between the concept of social recognition as framed by Honneth (1995) and the discourse of respect for autonomy in bioethics, which often centers around the narrow conceptions of capacity, competency, and personhood. In bioethics, respect for autonomy is frequently interpreted narrowly, focusing on the patient's ability to make informed decisions, often reduced to a clinical assessment of their capacity and legal assessment of competency (Beauchamp & Childress, 2013; Faden et al., 1986). This approach tends to prioritize cognitive abilities and decision-making capacities, sometimes overlooking the broader social context in which these decisions are made or takes for granted the context and social recognition. While increasingly scholars has been questioning this narrow approach from various perspectives (Childress, 2017, 2020; Lysaught,

2004; Mackenzie & Rogers, 2013; Mackenzie & Stoljar, 2000; Zeiler & De Boer, 2020), social recognition is a more expansive concept that encompasses not only the individual's cognitive abilities but also their social identity, relational standing, and the respect they command within their community. Social recognition acknowledges the person as a whole, embedded in their embodied social and political realities, which are often marked by structural injustices.

Self-respect, as it is often understood in much of the philosophical literature (Dillon, 2015), is conceptualized as an individual's inherent sense of worth—something that is self-contained and largely detached from the social context in which a person lives. This traditional view suggests that self-respect is primarily a personal quality, cultivated internally and independently of external forces or societal conditions. However, this perspective overlooks the profound ways in which social structures, norms, and systems of power shape an individual's ability to recognize and affirm their own worth. Learning from critical scholarship (Ambedkar, 1991; Mills, 2000; Wilson, 2012), I approach self-respect through a social lens, understanding it as a construct that is deeply embedded within and influenced by the social world. In this view, self-respect is not merely an individual trait but a relational and structural phenomenon that is contingent on the conditions of the society in which one exists.To understand self-respect, we have to look at the systems of power, domination, and oppression that structure our lives. These systems tell us who we are and who we can be. They whisper to the oppressed that their voices don't matter, that their agency isn't real, and that their worth depends on conforming to standards set by those in power. But self-respect cannot flourish in these conditions. It cannot grow when the world is constantly sending messages of disregard, devaluation, and erasure.

Oppressive systems—casteism, sexism, racism, classism—don't just threaten our sense of worth; they work to rewrite who we are, reshaping our sense of self in ways that break us down, making us believe we are less than. This is where resistance must begin: with the rejection of these false narratives and the reclamation of our dignity. In the context of healthcare, the archetype of the "passive patient" is one of the most insidious ways this erasure plays out. Expected to submit, to comply, to shrink ourselves into silence so that the "experts" can take over. This archetype tells us that patients—especially those from marginalized groups—don't deserve to have agency, that their voices are not worth listening. For the poor, for women, for those living under the shadow of caste, who are marginalised, this dynamic becomes even more brutal. Healthcare systems that embrace this archetype dehumanize, stripping away the power of individuals to assert themselves, to say, "I matter". It is a violence against the soul as much as it is a violation of the body. When patients internalize this archetype, it becomes a barrier to self-respect. Over time, repeated experiences of dismissal and disrespect teach people to doubt their own worth, to question their right to speak, to demand care, or even to be seen as fully human. This is why we must challenge these systems, because self-respect does not grow in environments of domination. It grows where there is recognition, care, and love. It grows when we honor the humanity in each other, not as an abstract idea, but as a lived reality.

I believe, to create a just society, we have to build systems—of healthcare, of education, of community—that nurture self-respect by affirming social recognition and true dignity. It is not enough to remove barriers; we must actively create spaces where people can thrive, where they can speak, where they can exist fully as themselves. Self-respect is not an individual act of will—it is born in the spaces between us, in the ways we care for one another, in the ways we resist the systems that tell us we are unworthy. A truly just society must dismantle the archetype of the "passive patient" and replace it with a vision of respectful care that sees every individual as whole, as valuable, as deserving of love and respect. Resistance to systems of domination begins with this self-respect and recognition: we are all worthy, we are all capable of reclaiming our power, and we are all deserving of the conditions that allow self-respect to grow. Our liberation depends on it, in healthcare and beyond.

In a context where everyday indignities are commonplace—due to one's marginalized identities due to religion, caste, gender, ethnicity, language, class, and other social groups/categories/identities—respect for autonomy as narrowly defined in bioethics can seem insufficient. It fails to address the pervasive and everyday experiences of disrespect that many patients endure. These experiences are not just about the individual's ability to make decisions; they are about whether the individual is even seen as a person worthy of making decisions. The bioethical discourse on autonomy often presupposes a level playing field, where all individuals are afforded the same social standing and respect, which is far from the reality in deeply unequal societies. In our context, countries like India, where caste-class-based discrimination, gender inequities, religious marginalization, and social disparities are entrenched, the question is not just about whether a patient can make autonomous decisions, but about how we can respect a patient as a person in a context where their very social, relational, and political self/person is under constant threat. I am not referring here to debates about who is considered a person and the related narrow concepts of rationality, reasoning, and autonomy, but rather to how our existence is mutually and experientially recognized in intersubjective spaces. Every day, social recognition is something we fight for, moving through a world that constantly undermines our sense of self and worth. In a society that devalues our very being, self is never just an abstract idea—it's deeply tied to the social and political realities shaping our lives. To speak of respecting patients without confronting the epistemic and embodied injustices we endure is to overlook the heart of the issue.

For persons from marginalized backgrounds, social recognition is not a given; it is something that must be fought for continuously. Every interaction, whether in a hospital, at work, or in the community, carries the risk of further disrespect, dehumanization, and devaluation. This ongoing struggle for recognition is fundamentally linked to patients' experiences within the health and legal system. When a patient from a marginalized community enters a healthcare setting, they do so not just as a "patient" in the abstract sense, but as a person whose identity is deeply intertwined with the social injustices one endures. Therefore, moving beyond the "passive patient" archetype and towards a model of self-respect and recognition in healthcare requires a broader understanding of what it means to recognize someone as a person. It involves acknowledging the social and political realities that shape a patienthood and ensuring that healthcare interactions do not perpetuate the very injustices that patients face outside of the hospital. This shift in perspective is critical for creating a healthcare system that does not merely respect autonomy in a narrow sense through bureaucratic informed consent forms but respects the embodied humanity and recognizes self-respect of each patient, to practice true dignity within the given context. It calls for a recognition of the person not just as a legally competent decision-maker, but as a social being whose self-respect, dignity and worthiness are continually negotiated within a landscape of structural inequalities. Only by integrating this deeper understanding of social recognition into our healthcare practices can we begin to dismantle the structures that sustain passive patienthood and move towards a system that truly respects persons.

In recent years, in health ethics discourse, relational autonomy is discussed to emphasize that individuals are embedded within a web of relationships and social structures that significantly influence their capacity for autonomous decision-making. This approach has been particularly valuable in recognizing that autonomy is not exercised in a vacuum but is shaped by interpersonal and social dynamics, which is especially relevant in healthcare settings. Relational autonomy, as a thick conception, acknowledges that individuals' decisions are influenced by their relationships, social conditions, and cultural contexts. It challenges the notion of the atomistic self, suggesting instead that autonomy is relationally constituted and dependent on the supportive or oppressive nature of these relationships and contexts. This perspective is important in recognizing that a patient's capacity to make autonomous decisions is influenced by their interactions with healthcare providers, family members, and the broader socio-political environment. However, most relational autonomy discourse still largely focuses on the capacity to make decisions and the ways in which relationships support or hinder this capacity. It tends to center on the individual's ability to navigate these relationships and contexts to assert their autonomy, with few exceptions. However, while relational autonomy offers a more nuanced understanding of how autonomy is exercised, I think, it may still fall short in addressing the deep-seated issues of recognition and self-respect that are central to dismantling the "passive patient" archetype, especially in contexts marked by systemic inequalities. As I understand, in both thick and thin version of autonomy discourses, social, moral, and political recognition is assumed to be often given or taken for granted, but employing self-respect and recognition framework helps us to account the material, political, and social inequities, and embodied injustices within intersubjective spaces and interactions.

In contexts like India, where systemic inequalities related to caste, class, gender, and religion are pervasive, relational autonomy may overlook the fundamental problem that many individuals are not granted social recognition as persons with equal moral worth and their agency is not acknowledged within oppressive conditions. For marginalized patients, the issue is not just whether they can make decisions within a network of relationships, but whether they are seen as full embodied agents as well as deserving of self-respect and recognition in those relationships and social-political realities. That is lack of social and political recognition. The passive patient archetype is a manifestation of this lack of recognition, where patients, especially from marginalized backgrounds, are often seen as less capable, less deserving of respect, and therefore more likely to be treated as passive recipients of care. Taking forward critical scholarship, influenced by self-respect movements by Dr. B. R. Ambedkar and Periyar, and in particular Honneth's (1995, 2014) theory of recognition, this book offers a profound critique of the "passive patient" archetype by emphasizing that recognition respect is foundational to one's sense of embodied self and agency. It is not merely about the capacity to make decisions but about being *seen* and *respected* as someone who is morally and politically worthy, and as an agent even within oppressive conditions. This kind of respect is essential for persons to develop and maintain a positive sense of self-respect, and to feel that we are full members of the community, especially at our most vulnerable times and spaces such as healthcare settings.

Disrespect is not just a failure to support someone's autonomy; it is a failure to recognize their self-respect, humanity and true dignity. This disrespect manifests in social exclusion, devaluation, and the denial of agency, all of which are central to the passive patient archetype. Patients who are not recognized as persons with moral worth are systematically devalued and disempowered, which goes beyond the relational challenges highlighted by relational autonomy. This lack of recognition leads to the internalization of passivity, where patients may come to see themselves as less capable of making decisions or as unworthy of respect sometimes. Critical scholars who work around recognition and respect (Honneth, 2007, 2014b; Honneth & Margalit, 2001) emphasize recognition also bringing to light different conceptions of the self that are often overlooked in normative discourses in health, for instancebio/medical/public health ethics. As I understand recognition respect, it acknowledges that the self is not only relational but also socially and politically embedded and constructed. This means that the self is shaped by broader structures of power and inequality, and these structures deeply influence whether individuals are recognized and respected as persons, as we are evalulative beings.

Breaking free from this cycle of passive patienthood is crucial for creating a healthcare system where patients are not merely passive recipients of care but engaged embodied agents in their own health and well-being, and to be treated respectfully. It is also important to acknowledge that often patients do resist, question, and exercise their agency, even within a system that discourages such behavior. I acknowledge that, the act of sharing their perspectives and experiences, and being aware of the hierarchical structures that constrain them, is itself a form of resistance and a desire for change. Recognizing one's social position, and being aware of oppressive conditions, and acknowledging the need for systemic transformation reflects one's agency and push toward reform. I would see that, based on my analysis, to move beyond passive patient culture in India, healthcare providers and institutions must engage in self-reflection and critically examine the power dynamics that shape their interactions with patients and their family members, and how they normalise and sustain everday indignities, and ways patients voices could be facilitated. Healthcare institutions must work to dismantle the paternalistic and authoritative values that underlie the passive patient archetype and instead foster an environment where patients are encouraged to voice their concerns, ask questions, and engage fully in their health and care. This requires not only changes in individual attitudes but also broader systemic reforms that address the structural inequalities that perpetuate disrespect and passivity.

Creating a healthcare system that values self-respect and recognition is not just about improving patient health outcomes—it is about affirming the dignity of every person, regardless of their socio-economic and intersectional background. It is about ensuring that all patients are treated, especially marginalised communities, with the respect they are owed, as moral and political agents capable of making decisions about one's own health and lives. Only then can the necessary disruptions and ruptures occur to resist dominant values and move toward true dignity. Only by moving away from the passive patient archetype and embracing a model of healthcare grounded in self-respect and recognition respect can we begin to create a system that is truly just and humane, and vision a culture of respect in our societies. Taking forward key critical theorists works, when individuals are denied this recognition, they experience "disrespect", which can manifest in various forms, including social exclusion, devaluation, and the denial of agency. As I will show in this book, the passive patient archetype is a form of institutionalized disrespect, which is sustained, reproduced and normalized in the culture of disrespect. Patients are not recognized as agents and are disrespected by seeing them socially and politically as "incompetent" or "passive", as well as treating them with discrimination in everyday encounters through epistemic and affective dispositions. In societies like India, where social hierarchies are deeply entrenched, the conception of the self is often fractured by the intersection of caste, class, gender, and religion. These intersections shape individuals' experiences of respect and disrespect. As discussed briefly earlier, for many marginalized individuals, the self is continually negotiating in an oppressive environment that denies self-respect and recognition. The passive patient archetype is thus not just a matter of relational dynamics within a healthcare setting but a reflection of these broader social forces that deny certain individuals, who are at the margins, social and political recognition. Thus, experiential lens of how one experiences disrespect matters to our lived social reality, whether as a patient in healthcare institutions or otherwise as persons in an unequal world.

Mapping the Journey: Reimagining Ethics Through Critical Philosophical Ethnography

This book is a reflection of many years of work since my doctoral and postdoctoral research, which explored the "essence" of informed consent in medicine and law and its implications in India. I employed an ethnographic approach and socio-legal analysis to understand this concept, during my doctoral work. I have published parts of my doctoral and postdoctoral work in various established journals, but I increasingly feel that, although the central argument has remained the same, I want to tell a coherent story that centers on how the culture of disrespect has sustained, reproduced, and normalized the passive patient rhetoric and archetype in India. The methodology of my doctoral study is not merely a series of techniques used to gather data; it is a critical act of engagement with the structures of power that permeate healthcare spaces, doctor–patient relationships, and the broader legal systems. Drawing inspiration from critical scholars of situated knowledge (Haraway, 1988), this work is shaped by my intimate connection to the experiences of being both a patient and a caretaker from the margins within the very system I was studying. My personal history, social location, and the lived realities I carry have profoundly influenced the way I approached this work.

Even though, almost seven years ago, I lacked the vocabulary or language I have now, I maintained a reflexive stance throughout the research process, continually interrogating how my own social position and personal experiences influenced my work (Subramani, 2019). As I write this book, my identities have been shifting, and also very well aware that identities are not static. I come from the Badaga hill tribe (father) and Gowda (mother) family ties. The Badaga are a community whose indigenous identity is contested within India's state's political discourse, and institutionally categorized as a 'Backward Community'. Raised in a lower-caste and class background, with phases of poverty I have some intimate knowledge of what it means to navigate spaces marked by gender, ethnic, caste, class, and racial discrimination. I am not suggesting I have an epistemic authority because of my identity, but I certainly have some partial knowledge and experience being on the margins and I share this to contextualise my work, and for readers to situate my work within this vast literature. I was never entirely comfortable being vulnerable about my social location and identities. Now, I am becoming more comfortable sharing my intersecting and shifting identities, embracing my conception of authenticity and voice, and contextualizing my work to make sense of theorization in an academia that still feels a bit alien to me. Sharing glimpses of my stories and experiences helps contextualize why this work is so important to me and to others who sit at the margins—not as epistemic authority, but as epistemic resistance, vulnerability, and insight. These experiences have profoundly shaped my epistemic practices—both theorizing and praxis—where questions of knowing and being are deeply interconnected. During my doctoral work, I was in an elite upper-caste-class institution where I often experienced caste, class, and gender discrimination—experiences that, over the course of my life, had become normalized. These encounters, along with many I had with medical authorities and hospitals—both public and private—have made me acutely aware of how gender, class, caste, and able-bodiedness, shape how we access healthcare and experiences of care. These experiences have informed my understanding and approach to the ethical concepts discussed here, not just as a legal or ethical obligation, but as a reflection of broader socio-political realities. Rather than retelling the methods and methodology in a narrow sense, I take this opportunity to reframe the way I view my approach to "doing research" and critically reflect on how I situate my work. While much of my research reflects and engages with bioethics, medical sociology, and health services research, I have been hesitant to label myself as a philosopher, bioethicist, or anything in particular. The varied questions and diverse disciplines that center on human suffering, the way institutions facilitate this suffering, and how experiences of othering influence our perceptions of self, others, and the world around us have always been my primary interests. Some friends and colleagues refer to me as a 'field philosopher' or encourage me to simply call myself a philosopher. Whatever the label ascribed to me or that I choose to embrace, I remain deeply intrigued by moral inquiry as it is embedded in the moral life. While decades of debate between universalists and relativists persist, my journey of unlearning has led me to the understanding that any form of knowing and moral inquiry must take everyday experiences and encounters seriously. Ethnographic work and philosophical inquiry, as interpretative exercises, help advance the discourse on how we can better live, engage, and be in this world. Much of this work is rooted in my doctoral research, drawing on philosophical inquiry and ethnography, in South India alongside critical analysis of legal texts. However, the analysis and rewriting in this book have been shaped by years of learning, unlearning, distancing, revisiting, and intimate experiences, which have helped me retell the narrative, I hope, with better language and framing. If you are interested in learning more about my methods and methodology from earlier work, you can refer to my published papers (Subramani, 2018, 2019, 2020, 2022; Subramani & Biller-Andorno, 2022).

I have always been drawn to the spaces where theory meets life, where abstract ideas collide with the everyday struggles of being. Growing up, I learned early that knowledge is not neutral. It does not hover above us, untouched by the hands and hearts that create it. Knowledge emerges from lived experience—sometimes painful, sometimes joyous, always real. bell hooks taught us that theory must serve life, that it must heal, resist, and transform. Otherwise, what good is it, right? To theorize the world is one thing. To live in it, to sit with its discomfort, to bear witness to the struggles and joys that shape lives, is another. When I started reading philosophical text, in all its diversity, I believed in the promise of understanding—understanding justice, equity, and how we might live ethically together. But too often, I saw philosophy abstracted, reduced to words on a page that never touched the ground. It became a language of exclusion, a discourse of detachment.

Philosophy—especially moral philosophy, except few—has too often stayed locked in the ivory tower, far from the spaces where people fight to be seen, heard, and valued. It has turned its back on the messiness of life, clinging instead to neat binaries: descriptive or normative, objective or subjective, theory or practice. These divisions are illusions, distractions from the real work of understanding the world and the ethics that shape it. When we look closely, when we listen deeply, we see that ethical reasoning is never abstract. It is relational. It is situated. It is lived. To sit with ourselves, to sit with people—to hear their stories, to witness their lives—is to understand that ethics cannot be in a vacuum.

Being familiar with ethnography and moral philosophy, and working at margins, I think, this is where critical philosophical ethnography begins. It is a practice of being present, of engaging with the lived realities of moral life. It refuses the philosopher's gaze that observes from afar. Instead, it invites us to be with people—in their world, in our world, with all its beauty, contradictions, and struggles. Learning from situated knowledge discourses and critical moral epistemologies, knowledge from the margins is not supplemental—it is foundational. The voices of those on the periphery tell us something the center cannot. They teach us what justice really looks like, what moral agency feels like, what recognition, self-respect and care demand of us. In this way, critical philosophical ethnography does not simply describe what is; it reveals what has been silenced and invites us to imagine what could be. Situated knowledges call for an end to the lie of objectivity that erases bodies, histories, and power. I see critical philosophical ethnography carrying this call forward. It asks us to see ourselves within the work—to acknowledge our positionality, our limitations, our complicity. There is no moral philosophy without reflexivity, without asking, who am I in this space? What power do I hold? Whose lives am I engaging, and what do I owe them? This work is not comfortable, but it is necessary. It is the work of accountability, and sometimes being vulnerable and sharing partial knowledge and perspectives, and stories of my own is a way I try to hold myself accountable. I am hoping this approach refuses the old binaries. It does not split the descriptive from the normative. To describe the struggles of a patients and family members, especially those marginalised, fighting for true dignity is already a normative act.

Critical philosophical ethnography teaches us that describing the world—as it is—and imagining a better one are not separate tasks. They are intertwined. I think of my current and earlier work around marginalized communities, forced to navigate in oppressive healthcare systems while creating spaces of care and belonging. Sitting with their stories, seeing how they sustain oneself and one another, I am reminded that moral reasoning is not abstract. It is embodied. It is relational. It is to make visible what systems of power obscure and to demand that our ethical theories be accountable to the lives they claim to understand. Learning from bell hooks theory is a tool—a map, a lantern, a lifeline. But she also reminded us that theory must be accessible and rooted in the realities of people's lives. Critical philosophical ethnography carries this spirit. It does not shy away from the complexities of lived experience. It does not ask people to fit their stories into pre-made boxes. Instead, it listens. It learns. It sits with the contradictions, knowing that ethical life is messy and unfinished. In this way, philosophical ethnography transforms moral philosophy. It shifts our gaze away from abstract universals and toward the richness of lived experience. It centers the voices of those often excluded from ethical theorization—Adivasis/Adi Dravidar, queer, women, migrants, the poor, those deemed "other". It asks us to rethink our concepts: whatdoes respect, care, and dignity mean here, in this place, for this community? What does autonomy look like when survival is at stake? These are not hypothetical questions. They are urgent, pressing, real. To engage in critical philosophical ethnography is to take a stand. It is to recognize that ethical theorization cannot be neutral. It is always situated, always political, always accountable to the world it seeks to understand. In doing so, philosophical ethnography reminds us that theory—like ethics—is a living thing. It breathes. It moves. It resists. In traditional, narrow understanding, philosophy, describing ethical and moral practices is seen as separate from evaluating them. But this separation is false. To describe is to reveal. To reveal is to unsettle. We are confronted with the inadequacies of dominant ethical theories, with their inability to account for the moral agency that emerges from struggle. Rather than impose external ideals or prescribe universal frameworks, it attends to the ways ethical life emerges from situated conditions, and resistance towards oppressive condition. It asks us to learn from the lives of others, especially marginalized—to listen to their struggles, to recognize their resistance, and to let their experiences shape our understanding of ethics itself.

To practice critical philosophical ethnography is to move away the easy answers of abstraction. It asks us instead to sit with the discomfort of the world as it is, to see its beauty and its violence, its struggle and its resistance. It asks us to learn from those who live at the margins, to honor their knowing and being, and to allow their experiences to reshape how we understand ethics itself. I understand, this is the work of critical philosophical ethnography: to bridge the gap between theory and life, between knowing and being. And in this practice, we find the radical possibility of ethics—an ethics that is not abstract but alive, not universal but situated, not imposed but acknowledging the moral life. Aligned with this book's focus, I remain committed to its goals and aim to explore these questions further in my ongoing methodological work.

My doctoral study, influenced by situated knowledge epistemologies, employed a constructivist grounded theory approach (Charmaz, 2006), recognizing that knowledge is not neutral or objective but shaped through our interactions, identities, histories, and power relations. The conception of "passive patients" in Indian healthcare settings is not just a theoretical construct; it is a lived experience, one that I, like many others, have felt deeply in moments of vulnerability and care. My positionality—the intersection of caste, class, and gender—inevitably informs the kinds of questions I ask and the ways I interpret perspectives and experiences. Rather than distancing myself from these factors, I lean into them as a critical tool for understanding how power is negotiated. I have elsewhere elaborated more on how ethics, methodology and theory construction are intertwined, and practicing reflexivity helps us demystify it (Subramani, 2019).

As a patient and caretaker navigating a system that often silences and disregards, and as a caretaker witnessing the ways my family members were treated with varying degrees of disrespect, my personal encounters could not be easily separated from the questions and analysis that began to emerge. The authority and paternalism of medical professionals in India were not abstract concepts but lived realities. These experiences pushed me to critically engage with the concept of informed consent—not as a mere formality, but as a relational and ethical interaction shaped by power dynamics. I knew that to study informed consent in Indian hospitals, I could not merely examine it as a bureaucratic or legal formality. Instead, I had to explore how the concept of consent was lived, understood, and practiced by patients, doctors, nurses, and caretakers. This required me to engage with both the structural inequalities of the healthcare system and the micro-level interactions that often reveal how power operates on an intimate scale.

Growing up amidst experiences of disrespect —trying to assert one's place in a world that often refuses to *see* or respect you—has deeply influenced how I theorize and make sense of concepts and meanings such as disrespect, othering, and belonging. My personal experiences of being labeled as "backward" and navigating an Indigenous identity, alongside varied intersectional experiences—as a scholar with limited social capital and academic networks in India and elsewhere, a recent migrant and person of color in settler-colonial societies such as Australia, a cisgender woman questioning heteronormativity, now racialized as a "Brown", and being categorized as part of the "Global South"—position me in complex and multifaceted ways within academia. Being in upper-caste-class and white-dominant spaces, my lived experiences of exclusion and marginalization have fueled my drive to understand the process of theorization and question the value of normative concepts and values, while at the same time aspiring for hope and change in the way we understand worlds and ways we can reimagine.

Embracing the margins, as hooks (2014) often writes about, has grounded me in openness and reflexivity, particularly in how I produce knowledge. The experiences have shaped how I see the world, how I experience, how I theorize, how I write, and why I write, and to whom. These experiences have taught me that recognition is not just about being seen but about being seen with true dignity. For communities like mine and many others, who have long been relegated to the margins, the question of self-respect and recognition is about challenging the very structures that deem us "uncivilized" or unworthy of respect. These are not easy questions. They are personal, political, and deeply intertwined with my own ambivalence about how my work will be received—not just by the academic world but by the very people whose lives

I write about and people who I love and care about. For now, I continue to embrace the complexity of these questions, understanding that the act of writing is also an act of navigating these tensions, a practice of making visible what has long been hidden.

As this book unfolds, you will see how I weave together the critical insights from my doctoral and postdoctoral work, continually returning to one core question: what does it mean to truly respect persons, who are patients, within a culture so deeply marked by disrespect? I hope this work extends beyond the confines of academic inquiry, and contributes toward transformative justice within patients' rights and dignity discourse in India. It is an invitation to rethink how we recognize, respect, and engage with individuals, especially those who have long been silenced and marginalized. In centering self-respect, recognition, and true dignity, I strive not to treat it as an abstract ideal but as a lived, embodied practice of liberation within intersubjective spaces—one grounded in self-respect and recognition, and the unwavering belief that every person deserves to be truly seen. This is not just about generating knowledge; it is about healing the structures that withhold recognition and self-respect from those who need it most.

Book Overview: Toward Dismantling Passive Patienthood

To dismantle the passive patient archetype, it is crucial to move beyond the narrow framework of autonomy, and recognize self-respect and recognition as I see it as a precondition for any autonomy, capacity or competency discourses in health, medicine, and illness. In Chapter 1, "Situating Patienthood", I map the emergence of the archetype of the "active patient" from the traditional "sick role" within healthcare discourses, while situating the historical and sociocultural dimensions of patienthood. It emphasizes how patient archetypes and narratives of patienthood are shaped by broader social, cultural, political, and historical factors. Additionally, the chapter discusses the early narratives of modern medicine, which viewed patients as passive subjects, in contrast to the evolving concept of the "active or engaged patient" who proactively engages in their healthcare decisions. Through an engagement with various historical, philosophical, and sociological literature, this chapter illustrates the envisioning of the "active patient" and the preconditions necessary for its realization, particularly within contexts such as the Indian law and clinical practice. The chapter concludes by suggesting that the social recognition of persons within the socio-cultural-political and historical context is a precondition for actualizing active patienthood in everyday healthcare encounters, especially in societies plagued by deep inequalities and inequities.

In Chapter 2, "Rhetoric of Passive Patient in Indian Legal Discourse", I critically examine the implications of legal judgments in India that construct the archetype of the "passive patient" within the context of medical negligence cases. Building on the understanding that legal decisions are shaped by underlying ideologies and values, it explores how this constructed narrative reinforces paternalistic values, often rooted in dominant social norms, which marginalize patients' agency in the Indian context. This chapter illustrates how the rhetoric of the "passive patient" sustains domination, exclusion, and marginalization within legal frameworks, reflecting the broader social inequities perpetuated by elite values. Through critical reflection, it argues for the necessity of shifting the legal perspective to recognize patients as persons with agency in their healthcare decisions and to transcend the limiting rhetoric of the "passive patient" and the dichotomy between health/care and choice, ultimately challenging the hegemonic influence of upper-caste, class, and gendered values in legal judgments.

In Chapter 3, "Construction of the Incompetent Patient", I build on the discussion of passive patienthood in legal discourse by exploring how healthcare professionals, particularly doctors and nurses, perpetuate the image of the "incompetent patient". In a society like India, where many cannot afford to "be sick" and are often socially and politically marginalized within a rigid positivist paradigm of biomedicine dominated by upper-class-caste heterosexual norms, the routine moral evaluation of patients is expected within healthcare spaces. Building on the discussion from Chapter 2 about the rhetoric of the passive patient within the legal system, this chapter illustrates how healthcare professionals, particularly doctors and nurses, create the dominant archetype of "incompetent patient" based on their perceived social categories and identities—especially class, caste, and gender. Through their subjective assessments and by labeling patients as "incompetent" or "troublemakers", healthcare professionals justify their often paternalistic and authoritative actions, behaviors, and practices, that often normalizes disrespectful attitude and behavior. This chapter demonstrates how patients' social and political recognition is routinely called into question in healthcare encounters and care contexts, showing how this process targets self-respect, and humiliates them, and disregards the agency of patients and their families by upholding the archetypal image of the passive patient.

In Chapter 4, "Everyday Indignities: Institutionalizing Passive Patienthood", I turn to the everyday indignities within healthcare settings that perpetuate the culture of passivity and disrespect. In Indian society, where no institution is exempt from the class-caste-gender hierarchy and power dynamics, including healthcare, those who exist on the margins have become adept at navigating structures designed to shame, disdain, and humiliate. For the marginalized, everyday indignities, through othering, when interacting with these institutions, healthcare encounters become another arena where inequalities and inequities are deeply entrenched and felt at the most personal levels. This chapter shows the ways in which doctors and nurses often disregard patients and family members. Through the experiences of patients and family members, as well as the perceptions of doctors and nurses, the chapter reveals how healthcare settings become spaces where a culture of disrespect is not just present but normalized, perpetuated, and reproduced. This culture is sustained through everyday moral and social evaluative judgments, reinforcing an institutional ethos that upholds the archetype of the "passive patient". These everyday indignities are not isolated incidents but part of a broader institutional culture that legitimizes the dismissive attitudes of healthcare professionals. By maintaining the image of the passive patient, the system not only strips individuals of their agency but also justifies the continuation of these harmful practices.

In Chapter 5, "Towards Self-Respect and Recognition in an Unequal World", which serves as the book's conclusion, I reflect on the ethical and political implications of the archetype of the passive patient in Indian society. In contemporary India, where everyday acts of othering and indignities are embedded within social, economic, political, and cultural realities—including within the healthcare system—the "passivity" of citizens, epitomized by the archetype of the "passive patient", is often both expected and perpetuated by individuals and institutions. This compels one to center affective and epistemic injustice, where shame and humiliation are integral to the lives of marginalized individuals. Viewed through the lens of indignities, the ethical and political question arises: why is the archetype of the "passive patient" morally wrong? Building on the analysis from the previous four chapters and drawing from philosophical, phenomenological, and sociological literature on relational conceptions of self within oppressive socio-historical political conditions, this chapter argues that self-respect and recognition are a necessary precondition for patient rights, decision-making, autonomy, and informed consent discourses. This recognition is also a pathway toward reimagining the archetype of the patient as a social and political agent. Such an approach moves beyond mere narrow discussions of autonomous decisions and informed consent within healthcare ethics, instead centering recognition, self-respect and justice against the background of structural injustice. This chapter seeks to reflect on these questions by foregrounding the indignities that target one's epistemic, affective, and social self, which disrupt the conception of self and undermine true dignity. It aims to serve, as the conclusion to this book, as a critical reminder to reflect on the moral world we aspire to in the unequal societies we inhabit and to move away from the archetype of the "passive patient".

Why Dismantle?

The recognition of patients as social, moral and political agents challenges the status quo, demanding a shift in how we think about agency. It requires us to confront the deeply ingrained prejudices that shape our interactions with patients and to dismantle the structures that perpetuate disrespect. Through this book, I argue that the reimagining of patienthood—away from passivity and towards recognition—is not just a theoretical exercise but a moral and practical necessity. It is a prerequisite for creating a healthcare system that is not only effective but also just and humane, particularly in societies where the legacies of colonialism and the dominance of upper-caste-class-gendered values continue to shape every aspect of life.

The passive patient archetype, deeply embedded in the fabric of Indian healthcare, sustains and legitimizes a culture of disrespect and paternalism, where patients—particularly those from marginalized communities—are denied self-respect and agency. The persistence of this archetype reflects and reinforces broader social hierarchies, particularly those rooted in colonial continuities and the entrenched values of the upper-caste-class-gendered order. These colonial continuities have long upheld a view of the patient as a subject to be controlled, a vestige of a system that prioritized authority and control. The passive patient archetype perpetuates these legacies by marginalizing those who do not conform to the dominant social norms—norms that are often defined by upper-caste, upper-class, and patriarchal values. Central to the experience of being cast as a passive patient is the profound sense of shame and humiliation that patients and their families often endure. In healthcare settings where patients are seen as passive, incompetent, and/or ignorant, one's social and moral worth is constantly called into question. These labels, imposed by professionals and institutions who operate within a framework of paternalism, strip patients of their dignity and reinforce the power imbalances that pervade the system.

For marginalized patients—those who are socio-econmically marginalized, an ethnic minority, from lower castes, and women and queer communities—this experience of shame and humiliation is exacerbated by one's social and political positioning. They are often seen incompetent and socially inferior, their voices dismissed and their concerns trivialized. The humiliation that accompanies this treatment is not merely an emotional response; it is a reflection of the deeper structural inequalities that shape their interactions with the healthcare system. This shame is felt acutely by families as well, who are often made to feel responsible for their loved one's perceived failings. Families, especially those from marginalized communities, are frequently subjected to the same dismissive attitudes and judgments, reinforcing their exclusion from meaningful participation in care decisions. The persistence of these attitudes is not an isolated issue; it is a symptom of the broader social and political context in which healthcare is situated. Recognition is not merely about acknowledging the existence of patients; it is about affirming one's agency, self-respect, and dignity, and one's right to participate in interaction, care, and decisions that affect one's lives. The social and political recognition of individuals as persons is foundational to dismantling the passive patient archetype. Without this recognition, any discussion of rights or ethics is hollow, failing to address the root causes of inequalities and injustice within the healthcare system.

Recently, as I write this Introduction, my cousin in Thoraihatty, a small village near the Nilgiris, has begun experiencing severe respiratory issues. After consulting multiple doctors in the main town of Ooty, he, along with his brother, my dad, and my aunt, decided to seek help at the government hospital there. The doctors at the hospital, however, informed them that he needed to be taken to Coimbatore, which is almost a 6-hour bus journey from our village. Given our family's financial constraints, they made the difficult decision to leave his brother to stay with him at the hospital, while my dad and aunt went to a relative's house nearly two hours away, so they could visit him occasionally. Days passed with little information. When my dad visited, all that the nurse could tell him was that they needed to keep my cousin there. Despite the severity of the situation, no doctors had yet spoken with my family or discussed the diagnosis. My dad started to sense that things were critical. He confided in me, saying in Badaga, "Ava pova, irakamma", meaning "He's going (dying), it's almost certain". The sight of medical students and doctors treating my cousin as a mere case study deepened his despair. He felt as though my cousin had become a living cadaver for their training, stripped of dignity and humanity. As my dad grappled with the reality that his nephew might not survive, he found himself humorously lamenting in frustration, "Naman noddre helangilaa!?" (when they see us they don't want to share!?). It was a bitter joke, born out of helplessness and anger, but not new for us, as he watched his loved one fade away without so much as an explanation from those who were supposed to care for him. As we talked, I shared my frustration about trying to explain what I am writing in this book. They asked, "What would your book do? Would it help us, people like us, at least in the distant future?" And, of course, being my *appaji* (father), he encouraged me by saying later, "I hope it does something".

I see this book as a retelling that had to happen—a gesture of hope, a spark for conversation, a space where rage and grief find voice, and perhaps a testament to the deep suffering and humiliation within our health and legal system. My hopes and desires are that one day, it will contribute for a conversation and nurture a culture of respect, not just in healthcare, but across all of Indian society. For me, this work is an act of ethical imagination, a way to shed light on how the process of othering unfolds, and to remind us that disrespect is not a distant issue to be dealt with later, but an urgent moral crisis, a barrier to live with self-respect and true dignity. I call upon those in power—healthcare professionals, judges, and others whose authority stems from unearned privilege—to look inward, to reflect on the overt and hidden ethos one contributes to the institutional ethos that perpetuates culture of disrespect. It is only through this reflection that we can begin to break the cycles of harm that continue to marginalize and dehumanize.

References

Ambedkar, B. R. (1990). *Dr. Babasaheb Ambedkar: Writings and speeches,* Vol. 2. Government of Maharashtra, Bombay.

Ambedkar, B. R. (1991). *What Congress and Gandhi have done to the untouchables,* BAWS, Vol. 9, Bombay: Education Department, Government of Maharashtra.

Ambedkar, B. R. (2020). *Beef, Brahmins, and broken men.* Columbia University Press. https://doi.org/10.7312/ambe19584

Beauchamp, T. L., & Childress, J. F. (2013). *Principles of biomedical ethics.* Oxford University Press.

Charmaz, K. (2006). *Constructing grounded theory: A practical guide through qualitative analysis.* Sage.
Charmaz, K. (2008). Constructionism and the grounded theory method. In Holstein, J. A. & Gubrium, J. F. (Eds.), *Handbook of constructionist research* (Vol. 1, pp. 397–412), Guilford Publications.
Childress, J. F. (2017). Needed: A more rigorous analysis of models of decision making and a richer account of respect for autonomy. *The American Journal of Bioethics, 17*(11), 52–54. https://doi.org/10.1080/15265161.2017.1382168
Childress, J. F. (2020). Respecting personal autonomy in bioethics: Relational autonomy as a corrective? In J. F. Childress & J. F. Childress (Eds.), *Public bioethics: Principles and problems.* Oxford University Press. https://doi.org/10.1093/med/9780199798483.003.0002
Das, V. (2015). *Affliction: Health, disease, poverty.* Fordham University Press. https://doi.org/10.5422/fordham/9780823261802.001.0001
Dillon, R. S. (2015). Self-respect in Kant and Hill. Reason, value, and respect: Kantian themes from the philosophy of Thomas E. Hill, Jr., 42.
Drèze, J. (2019). *Sense and solidarity: Jholawala economics for everyone.* Oxford University Press.
Drèze, J., & Sen, A. (1991). *Political economy of hunger: Volume 1: Entitlement and well-being.* Clarendon Press.
Faden, R. R., & Beauchamp, T. L. (1986). *A history and theory of informed consent.* Oxford University Press.
Fanon, F. (2010). The lived experience of the Black man. In Imre Szeman, & Timothy Kaposy (Eds.), *Cultural theory: An anthropology* (pp. 422–431). John Wiley & Sons.
Guha, R. (2011). *Makers of modern India.* Harvard University Press.
Guru, G. (2009). *Humiliation: Claims and context.* Oxford University Press.
Guru, G., & Sarukkai, S. (2018). *The cracked mirror: An Indian debate on experience and theory.* Oxford University Press.
Guru, G., & Sarukkai, S. (2019). *Experience, caste, and the everyday social.* Oxford University Press.
Haraway, D. (1988). Situated knowledges: The science question in feminism and the privilege of partial perspective. *Feminist Studies, 14*(3), 575–599. https://doi.org/10.2307/3178066
Honneth, A. (1995). *The struggle for recognition: The moral grammar of social conflicts.* Polity Press. http://ebookcentral.proquest.com/lib/usyd/detail.action?docID=4029984
Honneth, A. (2007). Recognition as ideology. In *Recognition and power: Axel Honneth and the tradition of critical social theory* (pp. 323–347). Cambridge University Press.
Honneth, A. (2014a). *Disrespect: The normative foundations of critical theory.* John Wiley & Sons.
Honneth, A. (2014b). *The I in we: Studies in the theory of recognition.* John Wiley & Sons.
Honneth, A., & Margalit, A. (2001). Recognition. *Proceedings of the Aristotelian Society, Supplementary Volumes, 75*, 111–139. JSTOR.
hooks, bell. (2014). *Feminist theory: From margin to center* (3rd ed.). Routledge. https://doi.org/10.4324/9781315743172
hooks, bell. (2015). Choosing the margin as a space of radical openness. In *Women, knowledge, and reality* (pp. 48–55). Routledge.

Ilaiah, K. (2010). *The weapon of the other: Dalitbahujan writings and the remaking of Indian nationalist thought.* Pearson Education India.

Lysaught, M. T. (2004). Respect: Or, how respect for persons became respect for autonomy. *Journal of Medicine and Philosophy, 29*(6), 665–680. https://doi.org/10.1080/03605310490883028

Mackenzie, C., & Rogers, W. (2013). Autonomy, vulnerability and capacity: A philosophical appraisal of the Mental Capacity Act. *International Journal of Law in Context, 9*(1), 37–52.

Mackenzie, C., & Stoljar, N. (2000). *Relational autonomy: Feminist perspectives on autonomy, agency, and the social self.* Oxford University Press.

Mills, C. W. (2000). Race and the social contract tradition. *Social Identities, 6*(4), 441–462.

Paik, S. (2014). *Dalit women's education in modern India: Double discrimination.* Routledge.

Rege, S. (1998). Dalit women talk differently: A critique of'difference'and towards a Dalit feminist standpoint position. *Economic and Political Weekly*, WS39–WS46.

Rege, S. (2014). *Writing caste/writing gender: Narrating Dalit women's testimonies.* Zubaan.

Rodrigues, V. (2024). *Ambedkar's political philosophy: A grammar of public life from the social margins.* Oxford University Press.

Sen, A. (1983). Poor, relatively speaking. *Oxford Economic Papers, 35*(2), 153–169.

Subramani, S. (2018). The moral significance of capturing micro-inequities in hospital settings. *Social Science & Medicine*, 209, 136–144.

Subramani, S. (2019). Practising reflexivity: Ethics, methodology and theory construction. *Methodological Innovations, 12*(2), 2059799119863276. https://doi.org/10.1177/2059799119863276

Subramani, S. (2019). The rhetoric of the 'passive patient'in Indian medical negligence cases. *Asian Bioethics Review, 11*(4), 349–366.

Subramani, S. (2020). The social construction of incompetency: Moving beyond embedded paternalism toward the practice of respect. *Health Care Analysis, 28*(3), 249–265.

Subramani, S. (2022). Moral habitus: An approach to understanding embedded disrespectful practices. *Developing World Bioethics, 22*(2), 94–104.

Subramani, S. & Biller-Andorno, N. (2022). Revisiting respect for persons: conceptual analysis and implications for clinical practice. *Medicine, Health Care and Philosophy, 25*(3), 351–360.

Teltumbde, A. (2010). *The persistence of caste: India's hidden apartheid and the Khairlanji murders.* Zed Books.

Teltumbde, A. (2020). *Dalits: Past, present and future.* Routledge India.

Wilson, W. J. (2012). *The truly disadvantaged: The inner city, the underclass, and public policy.* University of Chicago Press.

Yancy, G. (2008). Elevators, social spaces and racism: A philosophical analysis. *Philosophy & Social Criticism, 34*(8), 843–876. https://doi.org/10.1177/0191453708094727

Zeiler, K., & De Boer, M. (2020). The empirical and the philosophical in empirical bioethics: Time for a conceptual turn. *AJOB Empirical Bioethics, 11*(1), 11–13.

1 Situating Patienthood

Contextualizing the "Active Patient"

When does a person become a patient? Throughout my life, I observed my parents self-medicating for minor ailments like the common cold, and even for serious conditions like diabetes. Whether it was my brother or me falling ill during our childhood, the response was usually to drink ತಿಳಿ ಸಾರು (*Tiḷi sāru*, a kind of soup) or ಗಂಜಿ ganji (Porridge) or take a couple of paracetamols, avoiding a visit to the clinic. Not because my parents didn't believe in modern scientific medicine, but because they couldn't afford to take us to the nearby clinic, coupled with my mother's core practice that "unless it's an emergency, you don't meet a doctor". It was only when my dad had a heart attack and needed bypass surgery when I was 19 that I truly understood the meaning of being a patient and/or caretaker in the Indian healthcare system when you can't afford a private hospital. This experience introduced me to the realities of being a patient and family member, especially when financially constrained. It also revealed the roles and moral norms embraced by us as patients and family members, and witnessing how healthcare professionals embrace their roles and norms. Moreover, I became familiar with what it means to be a "good patient and caretaker", or conversely, not.

Decades of literature in medical sociology, anthropology, and other health research fields have greatly contributed to our understanding of illness behaviors, highlighting how patient responses to sickness are influenced by broader social, cultural, political, and historical factors. Health, disease, and illness, therefore, are social phenomena, shaped and influenced by the prevailing socio-cultural-political-historical norms and practices (Arnold, 1993; Das, 2015; Zola, 1973). For example, in Orissa at the turn of the century, a patient undergoing variolation is "humoured, dealt gently with, and never scolded, even if fractious, as it is believed that the deity presiding over small-pox is present in the child's system" (Arnold, 1993). Additionally, the representation of patients (and populations) through a racial colonial gaze, where depictions of Indian women as plague victims (or corpses), or as just female relatives by a hospital bed next to patient are common, illustrates another dimension of this social aspect of health (Arnold, 2023). Influenced by Talcott Parsons's "sick

DOI: 10.4324/9781003129998-2

role" (Parsons, 1975), many significant works have explored these dynamics through the lens of ethnicity, gender, class, and power structures to understand patient behavior and practices (Armstrong, 2014; Burnham, 2012; Frank, 2016; Shilling, 2002).

While the concept of the "sick role" has been referenced in the past, there has been a significant shift away from this paradigm in health literature over the past few decades. This transition has been driven by several structural factors, such as advancements in medical technology, the privatization of healthcare services, and an increase in health literacy. Furthermore, there is an ethical imperative to give precedence to patients' values, beliefs, and experiences. Consequently, the focus has shifted to the idea of the "active patient" in the age of new medicine. In this chapter, rather than exploring the regimes of patienthood—a topic that other scholars have extensively explored to understand illness and health narratives (Jeske et al., 2023; Joyce et al., 2020), I focus on examining the underlying moral construction of "active patient". I believe this will help us to critically understand the reference to "passive patient" signifies within the Indian context, and ways one can move against this paradigm.

Death of "Sick" Patienthood?

Understanding patienthood—how an individual becomes a patient, how they perceive themselves in that role, and how this relates to their identity and relationships with others—is crucial for situating and unpacking the moral aspects of health and illness within any socio-cultural and political context. In an ancient Indian medical literature, which includes storytelling, mythology, oral traditions, and sometimes in contemporary illness narratives, there is a notable tendency to intertwine a patient's physical suffering, and illness experience with moral self-blame. Concepts like "karma", "sins", and "fate" are often linked to illnesses such as leprosy, elephantiasis, or medical conditions like infertility, blindness, deafness, etc. In this context, the concept of patienthood and the understanding of illness and disease are seen through a lens of predetermination, where individuals suffer and become patients due to their past and present "moral actions". For instance, in the 'Caraka Samhita on the Doctrine of Karma', Weiss (1980) illustrates how in Caraka Samhita the relationship to one's karma, fate and present moral (in)actions to diseases in Puraryas and Dharmasastras is discussed.

> Thought, word, deed (karma) properly bound,
> Cleary-headed with sparkling judgement,
> Intent in his practice of austerities and knowledge-
> diseases do not befall such a man as this.
>
> (p. 92)

Modern medicine and everyday clinical practices, in contrast, tend to view the patient more as a "case" or a "workable object", moving away from this predetermined, morally intertwined understanding of illness. However, larger social categories continue to influence the idea of patienthood, and this is often overlooked. In this contemporary understanding, the medicalization and institutionalization of health and illness play significant roles in shaping patienthood, and patient's experiences are also deeply informed by their cultural background, personal beliefs, and social and ecological environment.

In a letter to the editor, a few doctors (Pandey & Sharma, 2018, p. 1), on the occasion of National Doctors Day, emphasized the importance of building trust and faith in the doctor–patient relationship amidst the evolving consumerist landscape of Indian society. They reminisced about the past, referring to it as a "golden era", and mentioned:

> Sadly, doctors do not hold the same respect as they did during the time of Dr. B. C. Roy and there is a steadily declining mutual trust and erosion of the sanctity of doctor–patient relationship. While patients often complain that doctors are proud, indifferent, do not give them expected care, charge hefty fees, are dominating, and confuse them with medical jargon; doctors are also bitter about the increasingly aggressive attitude of patients who do not respect doctors or their work, blame doctors for suboptimal outcomes, and indulge in litigation, without understanding the disease and its consequences.
>
> (p. 1)

The statement reflects certain expectations of patients and the sacred role of the doctor in their relationship. Patients are often perceived as "complainers" rather than fulfilling the role of the desired "passive patient" who trusts and respects doctors. Based on the narratives which I will illustrate in next chapters, similar to the tone of this above statement, from the perspective of healthcare professionals in India, patienthood is typically associated with being a "passive patient" who blindly trusts doctors and does not, or should not, question medical authority. This statement hints at the larger structural concerns such as literacy, privatization and corporatization of healthcare, where lack of trust in doctors has been compounded, along with how medical authority needs to be upheld or resistant to patients concerns. Scholarship in health studies indicates that within the Indian context, from the healthcare professionals' perspective, the role of the "sick" is predominantly one of "passivity". Patients are often expected to revere their doctors as "gods", especially in situations of medical uncertainty, or show deference without posing threat to medical authority (Bharadwaj, 2006; Fochsen et al., 2006; K. Kumbhar, 2023; Subramani, 2020).

Much of the early health literature within the Anglo–American tradition, particularly before the 1990s, focused on the "sick role" of the patient. This concept was first developed by Talcott Parsons (1975), who noted that individuals are biologically predisposed to become sick and that society recognizes and accepts this predisposition. His sociological analysis suggested that individuals have a social responsibility to fulfill the role of a sick person, which includes adhering to the doctor's orders, seeking treatment, and relinquishing certain activities. While Parsons' analysis primarily characterized illness as not just an "organism's condition" but as an institutionalized role, and the sick role as a form of social deviance where sick persons are unable to fully participate in other relationships and roles, such as family and job, he also emphasized the patient's role in therapeutic interactions. Parsons outlined three criteria for accepting the social role of being sick: first, both the individual and others must accept that being ill is not the sick person's own fault; second, the individual is exempt from ordinary daily obligations and expectations in the role of the sick; and third, there is an expectation to seek help from some kind of institutionalized health service agency (Parsons, 1975). Thus, the patient engages in roles that are aimed at maximizing the chances of facilitating recovery and contributing to society.

In his analysis, Parsons emphasized that healthcare professionals have a fiduciary responsibility towards the sick, and this duty to recover should also be shared by the sick persons. For example, when discussing the role of the patient, he mentions,

> The acceptance of the role of patient, that is, participation in interaction with the healthcare agency, may be said to impose a definite responsibility on the patient in working toward the common goals of the system as a whole. The first of the obligations thereby assumed seems to me to consist in the commitment to cooperation in the healthcare therapeutic or management functions of the system. This commitment may, in certain cases, be confined to the patient exposing himself as a passive object to the manipulations of healthcare personnel. It may not, however, be confined to this passive level. In many different degrees and respects, patients are asked to, and they often do, take the initiative in assuming the responsibility for a more active role in the care of their own health.
> (p. 267)

He goes on to address misinterpretations of his work, stating that the role of the sick person is not merely that of a purely passive object of manipulation or treatment. He argues that even the acceptance of such treatment constitutes a form of active participation by the sick person. In this analysis of the construction of the patient, he situates the role of the patient within an "inherent built-in unequal asymmetrical relationship" in the medical institutional hierarchy (Parsons, 1975).

Parsons' concept of the "sick role" highlights not only its potentially manipulative nature in creating a "sick" identity but also acknowledges the sick as individuals needing attention and care, often reliant on their immediate family and support system. This concept centers on the illness-health-medical complex, where patients assume the "sick" role to be excused from their usual societal functions, and doctors are responsible for legitimizing this role. Parsons, in his analysis, identified the sick role as a social role, but his primary interest lay in exploring the doctor–patient relationship as a social system, emphasizing the significant role of the doctor in maintaining the institutionalized system.

Growing up, when my mother's grandmother was sick, it was a moral duty and expectation for our family to visit or when she was at our place to care for her. For instance, my grandmother, even though not fully bedridden, she had the role expectation of sick to just lay on bed and every need would be served or cared need on bed. For Parsons, the "sick role" provided insights into how individuals are exempted from their normal duties when ill, similar to my experience of skipping school or while my mother took leave from work to care for my grandmother. However, these behaviors and actions should be contextualized within the cultural and social settings they occur in. This cultural perspective deepens our understanding of illness behaviors and the social roles people adopt. It also sheds light on moral roles and obligations, demonstrating how relationships become interdependent during the recovery process, shaping both the experience and role expectations of being a patient.

Initially, Parsons perceived the "sick role" as a "universal" concept. However, in his later works, and through further development by other scholars, it became clear that this concept varies across different cultures and historical periods (Segall, 1976; Williams, 2005). This variation highlights not just the subjective experiences of illness by patients but also the specific cultural and moral norms that influence relationships and caregiving practices in different societies. While many scholars have expanded upon the understanding of the "sick role" to explain how individuals adapt to culturally prescribed roles during illness, others had engaged with social role theory even before Parsons (Burnham, 2012, 2014; Frank, 2016). Additionally, some scholars, although not directly engaging with the "sick role" concept post-Parsons, have nonetheless explored the social roles of patients and healthcare professionals, and health behaviors (Hydén, 1997; Kleinman, 1980, 2020). Recently scholars illustrate that the "sick role" concept has seen a shift in its reception and interpretation within medical sociology and anthropology (Shilling, 2002; Varul, 2010). Scholars like Gerhardt (Gerhardt, 2015) have critically examined and clarified misconceptions surrounding this concept.

Many criticized Parsons' concept for being overly narrow, reinforcing social control mechanisms, adhering to a notion of "normalcy", and failing to account for a diverse range of illness experiences (such as chronic illnesses), thereby resisting the structural-functionalist approach to understanding illness and the patient's role. Due to these criticisms and the shifting social and political landscapes in the study of societies, especially institutions, the concept of the sick role gradually lost prominence in health literature, with a greater focus on health and illness behavior instead. Concurrently, the emergence of individualistic values and a belief in effecting social change, coupled with an emphasis on the individual's role in managing their health behaviors and maintaining "healthiness", have been influenced by capitalist ideals. This change in outlook has led to the emergence of a new interpretation of the patient role, emphasizing personal responsibility and agency. This evolution marks the birth of a new patient archetype: the active, empowered patient.

Welcoming "Active Patient" in New Medicine

Before exploring the "active patient" archetype narrative here, let me briefly explain what I mean by "modern medicine" and "new medicine". With advancements in science and the development of innovative medical technologies and interventions for understanding the human body, diseases, and illnesses, modern medicine has embraced scientific and evidence-based practices. In "The Birth of the Clinic", Foucault (1977) critically examines how modern medicine, with its focus on positive knowledge and rationality, approaches the human body and disease. He suggests that medicine's significance in shaping the sciences concerning humans is profound, affecting not just methodology but also our ontological understanding—how we perceive human beings as subjects of positive knowledge. Foucault delves into the social experiences of diseases and the institutionalization of modern medicine, highlighting its impact on medical practice and the patient experience. Particularly, he discusses how poor patients are subjected to the "medical gaze", leading to the objectification of their bodies. He underscores the crucial role of societal ideologies in either advancing or impeding medical practices, suggesting that the values and beliefs of society deeply influence the development and execution of medical knowledge and treatment.

In modern medicine, the prevailing archetype of the patient is characterized by passivity, with individuals being objectified by disease and the medical gaze. He reflects on how this perspective shapes the understanding of doctor–patient interactions within hospital and clinic. For instance, Foucault (1977) illustrates this point by stating: "Doctor and patient are caught up in an ever-greater proximity, bound together, the doctor by an ever-more attentive, more insistent, more penetrating gaze, the patient by all the silent, irreplaceable qualities that, in him, betray—that is, reveal and conceal—the clearly ordered forms of the disease…In the hospital, the patient is the subject of his disease, that is, he is a case; in the clinic, where one is dealing only with examples, the patient is the accident of his disease, the transitory object that it happens to have seized upon" (p. 16 and 71). While critical reflection on the history of modern medicine is essential from the European discourses, we must also consider how the narrative of "modern medicine" is perceived in non-Western contexts. Recognizing that the modernization of medicine is documented in the history of "modern medicine", especially in non-European scholarship, few scholars have challenged the dominant narrative that modern medicine was primarily a Western invention exported to colonies, and the colonial influence on the narrative framing of modern medicine (Ebrahimnejad, 2009). For example, medical historian Mark Harrison (Harrison, 1992, 2009), in his discussion on tropical medicine in British India, notes:

> But the European perspective of existing histories of 'tropical medicine' has obscured important developments in the understanding of diseases in the tropics which took place prior to 1890; most of which occurred in the colonies themselves – and especially in India....
>
> (Harrison, 1992, p.12)

In modern medicine, influenced by principles such as those in the Hippocratic Oath, the doctor is seen as the authoritative figure in medical knowledge. This perception, based on years of medical training and expertise, implies on one hand the idea that "the doctor knows best" and on the other, that the doctor has a fiduciary duty to act in the best interests of the patients and their well-being. In India, these values are not only present in modern medicine but also echo the commitments found in traditional medicine, which similarly underscored the values and roles of physicians (Arnold, 2000; Pati & Harrison, 2009). During the colonial period, the intertwining of medical education with the prevailing gender, caste, and class hierarchies further reinforced and practiced the "doctor knows best" approach within healthcare settings.

Medicine served as one of the technologies for imperial control and understanding of the Indian environment and its people. In the 19th century, medical interventions were not solely pursued for scientific interest but also acted as a means to fulfill cultural and political agendas benefiting the colonial state. The institutionalization of "modern medicine", exemplified by the Indian Medical Service—an archetypal "colonial service" intertwined with the military and administrative needs of the colonial state and initially staffed almost exclusively by Europeans—highlights this point (Arnold, 1993; Ruddock, 2021; Sen, 2010). The push for medical education aimed to serve the Company's interests, where the values of objectivity and evidence in modern medicine were promoted. Colonial authority also established a medical hierarchy that mirrored and reinforced existing caste, class, and gender hierarchies, fostering institutional conformity. In the early post-independence period, scholars have noted that rural patients often avoided doctors due to lack of access or conflicting values and belief systems (Harrison, 2009; Kumbhar, 2023; Kumbhar, 2022; Pati & Harrison, 2009). Additionally, many history of medicine literature suggest that modern medicine was predominantly accessed by the highly educated, urban, upper-class, and caste populations.

Since the early post-independence period to the present, socio-economic inequalities and inequities have shaped healthcare culture and influenced interactions within it. Particularly in public hospitals, it is the socio-economically disadvantaged who predominantly utilize the services, with some people spending their savings to afford care, while the privileged opt for private and corporate hospitals. Thus, the structure of post-colonial society, along with the inherent class-caste-gender hierarchy, sustains modern medicine in India, which relies on the value system of a benevolent, trusting physician. However, increasing health literacy, the patient rights movement, and patient dissatisfaction with their doctors are driving the Indian healthcare system towards "new medicine".

Amidst critique of bioethics' foundational narrative, which suggests that patient autonomy was historically compromised by paternalistic practices for clinical benefit—an approach once standard in Western medical ethics and widespread until bioethics reformed ethical standards and medical practice—dominant scholarship in the US underscores paternalism as a hallmark of early modern medicine, epitomized by the "doctor knows best" attitude. This concept is increasingly deemed outdated in the context of "new medicine", where there's no place for such paternalism. Critics, for instance, have challenged the Hippocratic Oath for its paternalistic undertones, arguing it neglects patient values and preferences. Robert Veatch (2008), a prominent bioethics scholar in the US, articulates a vision for a new medicine:

> A medicine in which patients will recapture responsibility for their own health choices—including choosing their own therapies based on their own beliefs and values. It will be a world in which patients will, in a very real sense, have to heal themselves...Physicians no longer can be expected to be able to do what is in their patients' interest just because they are competent physicians. They cannot be expected to do what best serves patients' interests because they cannot be expected to know what patients' interests are. The new medicine will be one that focuses on the value choices that have to be imposed on the facts of medicine in order to decide what is good practice. The new medicine rejects the old slogan, Doctor knows best.
>
> (p. 4)

In the above passage we witness a transformative shift in medical paradigms towards prioritizing the patient at the core of "new medicine". This transition in values, observable across various spheres—be it legal frameworks in certain countries, large medical institutions, individual physician practices, or influenced by the patient's rights movement—prompts a reevaluation of traditional notions of expertise and authority over a patient's body, health, and well-being. In this evolving landscape of "new medicine", the question isn't about diminishing the doctor's role due to their medical knowledge; rather, it's an invitation to critically examine how this expertise intersects with, and is contextualized by, the patient's knowledge and values. Particularly in technologically advanced countries, with growing health literacy and greater access to healthcare, these considerations become central to the practice of medicine, whether in biomedical research or clinical settings. Moreover, the rise in medical malpractice and negligence cases has further propelled the discourse towards embracing "new medicine". We can see how modern medicine reflects neoliberal and capitalist ideologies, particularly by perpetuating market logics and prioritizing individual choice without much acknowldeging larger inequalities and determinants of health.

While discussions surrounding the Hippocratic Oath traditionally centered on the "sick patient", emphasizing the physician's duty to benefit the sick according to the physician's ability and judgment, the new medicine paradigm shifts focus away from the "sick" patient. This change might stem from the increasing discourse on liberal individualism across various domains and institutions. However, it's also noticeable that the social and cultural dimensions of the "sick patient" seem to fade from these discussions. Reviewing literature from medical humanities, bioethics, and qualitative health research, it's evident that in the discourse on "new medicine", scholars utilize diverse social theories and ethical arguments to better integrate the social aspect of the "sick" patient. This approach moves beyond viewing the patient as "passive, ignorant, and incapable of making choices", and the physician as solely benevolent, paternalistic, or, in some cases, authoritarian. Instead, as I observe, dominant bioethics literature and medical debates increasingly advocate for the notion of "patient knows best", transitioning the archetype from the "sick patient" to the "active patient", but with limited attention to social, cultural and political realities.

As mentioned in earlier discussions and this section, the decline of the "passive patient" narrative, along with the "sick patient" concept in health discourse, is attributed not only to the shifting social, historical, and political landscapes but also to the rise of an individualistic value system that stresses personal responsibility and choice. This shift is further propelled by capitalism, through which privatization and deregulation have enabled certain patient demographics to become consumers actively involved in their health decisions, supported by the patients' and consumer rights movement. Additionally, the emergence of chronic illnesses and advancements in information technology have improved access to information, setting the expectation for patients to be "nformed and active". Therefore, the normative expectation for patients to be "active" was inevitable in the current socio-economic and political climate. In the following section, I will review and critically analyze the genealogy of the moral construction of the "active patient" in medical ethics debates, highlighting how ethical and legal concepts have significantly influenced this transition, and outline the normative characteristics of the "active patient" archetype.

Normative Expectations of "Active Patient"

Having outlined the key transitioning conceptions of patient roles from "passive" to "active" within health discourse and the impact of the broader socio-political environment on these archetypes, this section will explore the normative expectations of the "active patient" in the ethical discourse. I will examine how these ethical underpinnings influence the current debates in medical ethics and the expectations placed on patients and doctors in today's healthcare interactions. Before presenting the dominant patient archetype in India from legal and clinical perspectives, I aim in this section to lay the groundwork for envisioning and actualizing how the 'situated agent' archetype can become a possibility in our moral imaginations and be practiced in everyday healthcare and legal contexts. I envision, without succumbing to binaries of passive versus active or compliant versus resistant, a patienthood that is deeply relational, contextually embedded, and grounded in a commitment to justice and collective transformation. The 'situated patient' is not merely a recipient of care or an autonomous decision-maker navigating a marketplace of health options. Rather, this archetype embodies a form of agency that emerges through interconnectedness—recognizing the social, economic, cultural, and political contexts that shape health and healthcare. In this vision, the patient is not isolated but engaged within a web of relationships, including with caregivers, healthcare providers, and the broader community. The 'situated patient' actively collaborates in their care but also critically engages with the structures and power dynamics that influence their healthcare experiences. This archetype insists that we look beyond simplistic frames of power and resistance to engage with the complex, often contradictory, realities of agency and healing. Then, as I see, for the situated patient archetype, this means their health and agency are not isolated phenomena but deeply connected to the lives of others and the structural forces that shape their existence. Agency here is not just about asserting individual autonomy; it is about reclaiming power in relational, ethical, and systemic ways.

Dare I say, then, the situated patient is a subject of their own story, actively shaping their healthcare experience, but also a participant in collective struggles to make healthcare systems more just and humane. This archetype rejects the neoliberal myth that individuals are solely responsible for their health while also refusing the disempowering narratives that position patients as mere victims of systems beyond their control. Instead, the situated patient occupies a space of possibility—a site where personal agency and systemic critique coexist. They bring their lived experiences, cultural knowledge, and relational ties into healthcare encounters, demanding recognition, self-respect and true dignity. If we take this archetype seriously then the healthcare relationship becomes a site of liberation—a space where patients and providers come together to co-create new ways of understanding care. Healthcare, like any institution, is a space of power, and power can be contested and reimagined. The situated patient archetype is grounded in this vision of contestation, where patients challenge the silences and erasures that devalue their voices and experiences. Whether it is the marginalized woman confronting caste and gender bias in a clinic or the rural laborer demanding access to equitable care, the situated patient embodies a refusal to be invisibilized. Their agency is not an abstract ideal but a lived practice that emerges through resistance and negotiation to receive care which they deserve within the healthcare spaces.To bring this archetype into practice, we must center dialogue. In healthcare, dialogue means that patients and providers engage in relationships that prioritize listening, understanding, and mutual respect. It means acknowledging that healing is not simply a technical or biomedical process but a deeply human one, shaped by histories, emotions, and social conditions.

Similarly, in the legal context, the situated patient archetype disrupts paternalistic and disempowering frameworks. The law must move beyond the narrow focus on individual rights to embrace a vision of justice that recognizes collective suffering and collective healing. The situated agent does not navigate the legal system alone—they do so as part of a broader community that insists on structural accountability and systemic change. The situated patient actively navigates safety, quality of care and risk, resisting narratives that flatten their experiences into compliance or defiance. Their choices—whether to resist, comply, or negotiate—are made within the constraints of structural injustice but also with the recognition of their own power to transform those constraints. Ultimately, envisioning the situated patient is an act of hope, in the power of love, respect, care, and resistance to transform oppressive systems. It asks us to imagine healthcare and law not as spaces of domination but as sites of possibility, where patients, providers, and communities can collectively work toward liberation. By grounding this archetype in relationality and justice, we take a step toward dismantling the dominant patient archetypes and building culture of respect that honor the full humanity of all who enter them. I will reflect back to this archtype in Chapter 5 to explore further.

Against the backdrop of significant human experimentation abuses and a burgeoning civil rights movement in the United States, the National Commission for the Protection of Human Subjects of Biomedical and Behavioral Research was established in 1974 (Cassell, 2000). This commission's landmark publication, the Belmont Report, issued in 1979, laid down three foundational ethical principles that would anchor discussions in biomedical research ethics: respect for persons, beneficence, and justice. The principle of respect for persons, as articulated in the Belmont Report, encapsulates two critical ethical convictions. The first conviction is that individuals should be treated as autonomous agents, capable of making their own decisions based on personal deliberation and goals. The second conviction is that those with diminished autonomy, due to age, condition, or circumstance, warrant additional protections. To respect an individual's autonomy, according to the report, means to seriously consider their opinions and choices, avoiding any actions that might obstruct these choices unless such actions could harm others. A lack of respect for an autonomous individual is seen as a denial of their ability to make considered judgments, either by ignoring these judgments, restricting their freedom to act upon them, or by failing to provide necessary information for making informed decisions, barring any compelling reasons to do so.

Over the years, within the evolving discipline of bioethics, the concept of "respect for persons" underwent a significant transformation. The emphasis gradually shifted towards prioritizing the respect for patient autonomy (Lysaught, 2004). This shift was paralleled by the growing importance of informed consent (Faden et al., 1986; Manson & O'Neill, 2007; Wear, 1998), which emerged as a fundamental mechanism to protect and facilitate patients' autonomous choices. Informed consent serves not only as a procedural requirement but as a moral cornerstone, ensuring that patients are fully aware of, and agree to, the procedures and treatments they undergo, thus embodying the principle of respecting patient autonomy. This evolution reflects the dynamic nature of bioethics as it continues to adapt to changing societal values, medical advancements, and the complex landscapes of patient care and research ethics.

The ethical landscape of medical ethics has significantly shifted from the paternalistic "doctor knows best" model towards a more patient-centered approach that values and incorporates patients' values and beliefs in medical decision-making. This transition is fundamentally rooted in the principle of respect for patient autonomy, a concept that has become central to contemporary medical ethics, emphasizing the protection and support of autonomous choices as articulated by Beauchamp and Childress (2013). The discourse in moral philosophy is rich with discussions on autonomy, derived from the Greek words "auto" meaning "self" and "nomos" meaning "rule", encompassing a range of moral concepts such as individual choice, self-governance, self-determination, authencity, and liberty. While theories of autonomy are diverse, the dominant discourse focus is on personal autonomy, highlighting psychological attributes like self-knowledge, self-control, and reflective capacity as crucial. Despite the variations in how autonomy and its relation to the self are conceptualized—be it through subjectivist, social relational, or narrative accounts of self, where the essence of "who a person is, and how one relates to one self and others" remains pivotal—all interpretations fundamentally agree that autonomy involves the capacity to act or live freely from unwarranted impediments within socially embedded context.

Applied in the context of healthcare interactions and taking forward the analysis of respect for patient autonomy, as expressed in Kantian philosophy, "to respect an autonomous agent is to recognize with due appreciation that person's capacities and perspective, including his or her right to hold certain views, to make certain choices, and to take certain actions based on personal values and beliefs. Such respect has historically been connected to the idea that persons possess an intrinsic value independent of special circumstances that confer value. As expressed in Kantian philosophy, autonomous persons are ends in themselves, determining their own destiny, and are not to be treated merely as means to the ends of others" (p. 8). Classic bioethics literature on autonomy, especially in relation to biomedical context, moves away from the idea of autonomous individuals as "ideal choosers"—an aspirational yet often unattainable standard. Instead, the focus shifts towards "normal choosers", emphasizing actions based on "substantially autonomous decisions". This perspective recognizes the practical realities of patient decision-making, acknowledging that while the ideal of complete autonomy may guide principles, the application in healthcare must account for the varied and complex nature of autonomy.

Beauchamp and Childress (2013), define "normal choosers" as individuals who act 1) intentionally, 2) with understanding, and 3) without controlling influences that determine their actions (p. 69). In their book 'A History and Theory of Informed Consent', Faden and colleagues (1986) elaborate on these three essential conditions for autonomous action. They note that while intentionality is not a matter of degree—actions being either autonomous or not—the conditions of understanding and freedom from controlling influences vary in degree. According to prevailing theories of personal autonomy, the normative expectation for a patient, or any person, is to be independent, free from coercion and undue influence (whether from healthcare professionals, family members, or societal pressures), and in control. This entails being a rational agent capable of analyzing information, understanding, and weighing the costs and benefits of decisions, thereby making informed choices that reflect their values, beliefs, and preferences. Patients are thus expected to actively seek, receive, and comprehend relevant information about their health conditions and proposed medical treatments, including understanding the risks, benefits, and alternatives.

Active participation in the decision-making process is also expected, involving questioning, expressing concerns, and discussing preferences with healthcare providers to ensure decisions align with their values and wishes. Moreover, making informed decisions about their health and care, consenting to or refusing treatments based on provided information and in accordance with their personal beliefs and values, is a key expectation. Effective communication with healthcare providers is seen as a normative expectation, implying that health literacy among patients is considered standard. The fundamental normative expectation is for patients to clearly and assertively communicate their understanding, preferences, and decisions, ensuring their autonomy is respected and upheld. Informed consent, as a legal and moral requirement, necessitates that patients not only respect the process but actively engage with it to become informed and involved in their decision-making, moving beyond mere bureaucratic compliance.

Actualizing "Active Patient"?

Within the domain of bioethics, while the prevailing discourse tends to champion the ideal of the "active patient" as one who is "independent", "rational", and "in control", capable of making decisions that resonate with their authentic sense of self, this perspective is primarily anchored in a relatively narrow conception of personal autonomy. However, some scholars challenge this viewpoint, introducing a nuanced discussion around the "thin" and "thick" conceptions of autonomy in bioethics (Childress & Quante, 2021; Fateh-Moghadam & Gutmann, 2014; Gutmann, 2022). The "thin" conception of autonomy is characterized by a focus on the minimal requirements for autonomous action, such as the absence of coercion and the presence of basic rational capacities. This perspective often emphasizes the importance of non-interference and the individual's right to make decisions independently, aligning with the traditional emphasis on informed consent as a mechanism to safeguard autonomy. Conversely, the "thick" conception of autonomy emphasizes the conditions that foster truly autonomous choices. This broader interpretation advocates for a positive obligation on the part of healthcare providers, not just to refrain from coercive practices but to actively facilitate the patient's ability to make autonomous decisions. This involves disclosing information comprehensively and creating an environment that promotes effective communication and comprehension.

One of the presumed assumptions of the thick conception of autonomy, including relational autonomy discourses (Childress, 2020; Mackenzie & Stoljar, 2000), is that it acknowledges the complex interplay between individuals and their social, cultural, and relational contexts, recognizing that autonomy is not merely about making decisions in isolation but about doing so in a way that is informed, supported, and understood within a broader context. This critical examination of autonomy underscores the importance of considering the relational and fiduciary relationship between healthcare providers and patients. It suggests that respecting patient autonomy, particularly in its thick conception, encompasses a positive duty to disclose information and to cultivate conditions conducive to autonomous choices and actions. Such an approach challenges healthcare professionals to go beyond mere non-interference, advocating for active engagement in enhancing patient autonomy through promoting communication and ensuring comprehension, thereby enriching the ethical foundation of patient care and decision-making processes.

The critique of the liberal conception of personal autonomy, particularly its emphasis on self-sufficiency and "atomistic individualism", has been a point of contention among several scholars. These critics argue that the hyperfocus on autonomy as independence overlooks the fundamentally social nature of individuals and their decision-making processes. Charles Taylor's (1989) assertion, "One cannot be a self on one's own", (p. 36) encapsulates the critique against the notion of atomistic individualism, emphasizing the intrinsic social dimension of autonomy. Many scholars who argue that the self is inherently situated within a social context, positing that the existence and significance of the self emerge from social interactions (Abbott, 2020; Alcoff, 2012; Anderson & Honneth, 2005; Kühler & Jelinek, 2013; Meyers, 2005, 2018; Zahavi, 2008). These varied perspectives and approaches of understanding self suggests that self-reflection, choice, and action gain meaning through engagement with the social world, where language and emotions—rooted in sociocultural contexts—are crucial. I would understand that, thus, intersubjective recognition becomes a key aspect of understanding autonomy, especially the thick conception.

Similarly, in response to thin conception of autonomy and narrow conceptions of doing bioethics, particularly empirical research, the concept of relationality has gained traction among bioethicists and critical theorists (Childress, 2017; Childress & Quante, 2021; Mackenzie & Stoljar, 2000; Subramani, 2019; Subramani & Biller-Andorno, 2022; Zeiler, 2014; Zeiler & De Boer, 2020). This approach challenges the atomistic view of personhood, situating autonomy within the broader socio-cultural and historical contexts where intersectional factors significantly influence individuals' autonomy. Relational autonomy acknowledges that people's decisions, values, and actions are deeply embedded in their relationships and social networks, thereby advocating for a more nuanced understanding of autonomy that incorporates the roles of community, social structures, and cultural norms. This shift towards relational autonomy represents a significant departure from traditional views that prioritize individual independence. It underscores the importance of acknowledging the interconnectedness of individuals and the impact of social and cultural environments on their ability to make authentic, autonomous decisions. By emphasizing the social nature of autonomy, scholars advocate for a more context-specific approach to understanding decision-making processes.

In extending the discussion on the archetype of the patient within the framework of relational autonomy, it becomes clear that patients are deeply embedded in and influenced by their social relationships and contexts. Autonomy is exercised within this social and relational sphere, recognizing the critical role of interpersonal interactions in decision-making processes. Thus, decision-making is inherently contextual, with decisions emerging co-constructively within a network of relationships. This perspective shifts the normative expectation of the "active patient" towards one who actively engages in the shared decision-making process with healthcare providers.

Under the relational autonomy model, patients are expected to proactively seek out and utilize support, be it emotional, informational, or practical, from their family network or within the healthcare system. Recognizing and navigating one's vulnerability becomes a normative expectation of the "active patient". Patients are encouraged to articulate their values and goals concerning healthcare decisions, which is essential for respecting the relational autonomy of the patient. Effective communication, including self-advocacy, is pivotal in making informed care decisions and ensuring respect for patient autonomy. Within this relational framework, the ethical principle of informed consent gains additional significance. It acts as a foundational element for shared decision-making, facilitating patient-centered care practices. This approach underscores the importance of informed consent not merely as a procedural formality but as a dynamic, interactive process that embodies the principles of relational autonomy. It ensures that healthcare decisions are not only informed by medical knowledge and expertise but are also aligned with the patient's values, preferences, and social context.

In these accounts, the ideal of the active patient is envisioned as someone whose emotional needs are acknowledged and whose self-respect remains intact during healthcare interactions, as they exercise autonomy. In both thick and think conceptions of autonomy, the normative assumption underlying the archetype of the "active patient" is that the patient is regarded as "socially and politically worthy". Recognition and self-respect is assumed in these discourses. But what happens when the foundational precondition—that one is recognized as a person, socially and politically worthy of self-respect, recognition, and dignity—is not only absent but actively challenged, ignored, or disregarded? Given that our self-respect is influenced by the way others treat us, in socio-cultural and political contexts where there is inherent struggle for recognition, how can "active patient" be actualized? How can the autonomy of an "active patient" be actualized in a socio-political environment where feelings of injustice and experiences of disrespect related to caste, gender, class, ethnicity, and other intersectional factors are entrenched and normalized through socialization, impacting one's self-respect?

Without confronting the absence of this recognition, health and legal systems as I show in next chapters, perpetuate harm by overlooking the experiences of those who are seen as "less worthy" of care, recognition and dignity. It becomes moral necessity to first illustrate how the lack of recognition is perpetuated and normalized, and it is not just about reforming systems but about fostering the conditions for self-respect, recognition, and true dignity. And liberation. Only when individuals are recognized as worthy—socially, politically, and emotionally—can they truly exercise their autonomy. This is transformative, as it reclaims one's self-respect and it demands that institutions, medicine, and law begin with the acknowledgement of social and political recognition, not as an afterthought, but as the very foundation upon which justice and care are built.

In the next three chapters, I will illustrate the prevalent archetype of patients in India as the "passive patient", highlighting a culture of disrespect and how the socio-political-cultural and economic conditions within the Indian context shape this archetype. This examination aims to demonstrate why both the narrow conception of autonomy and the discourse on relational autonomy fall short in progressing towards the archetype of the 'situated patient' which engages with the precondition of recognition, as it is a moral and political necessity. In the final chapter, building upon existing philosophical and sociological literature about relational conceptions of self and others within a socio-historical political context, I argue for social recognition as a precondition for autonomy discourses, including patient rights and medical decision making, and a pathway towards the archetype of the 'situated patient' who is perceived to be worthy and respected agent within the realities of structural injustice and collective struggles. This approach transcends narrow discussions on autonomous actions and informed consent within the domain of healthcare ethics, and centers on social justice.

References

Abbott, O. (2020). *The self, relational sociology, and morality in practice* (1st ed. 2020.). Springer International Publishing. https://doi.org/10.1007/978-3-030-31822-2

Alcoff, L. M. (2012). Gender and reproduction. In S. Gonzalez-Arnal, G. Jagger, & K. Lennon (Eds.), *Embodied selves* (pp. 12–28). Palgrave Macmillan UK. https://doi.org/10.1057/9781137283696_2

Anderson, J., & Honneth, A. (2005). Autonomy, vulnerability, recognition, and justice. In *Autonomy and the challenges to liberalism: New essays.* Cambridge University Press.

Armstrong, D. (2014). Actors, patients and agency: A recent history. *Sociology of Health & Illness, 36*(2), 163–174. https://doi.org/10.1111/1467-9566.12100

Arnold, D. (1993). *Colonizing the body: State medicine and epidemic disease in nineteenth-century India.* University of California Press.

Arnold, D. (2000). *Science, technology and medicine in colonial India.* Cambridge University Press.

Arnold, D. (2023). Dr Hunter's plague: Gender, race and photography in British India. *Indian Journal of Gender Studies*, 09715215231210522. https://doi.org/10.1177/09715215231210522

Beauchamp, T. L., & Childress, J. F. (2013). *Principles of biomedical ethics.* Oxford University Press.

Bharadwaj, A. (2006). Sacred conceptions: Clinical theodicies, uncertain science, and technologies of procreation in India. *Culture, Medicine and Psychiatry, 30*(4), 451–465. https://doi.org/10.1007/s11013-006-9032-0

Burnham, J. C. (2012). The death of the sick role. *Social History of Medicine, 25*(4), 761–776. https://doi.org/10.1093/shm/hks018

Burnham, J. C. (2014). Why sociologists abandoned the sick role concept. *History of the Human Sciences, 27*(1), 70–87. https://doi.org/10.1177/0952695113507572

Cassell, E. J. (2000). The principles of the Belmont report revisited. How have respect for persons, beneficence, and justice been applied to clinical medicine? *Hastings Center Report, 30*(4), 12–21.

Childress, J. F. (2017). Needed: A more rigorous analysis of models of decision making and a richer account of respect for autonomy. *The American Journal of Bioethics, 17*(11), 52–54. https://doi.org/10.1080/15265161.2017.1382168

Childress, J. F. (2020). Respecting personal autonomy in bioethics: Relational autonomy as a corrective? In J. F. Childress & J. F. Childress (Eds.), *Public bioethics: Principles and problems.* Oxford University Press. https://doi.org/10.1093/med/9780199798483.003.0002

Childress, J. F., & Quante, M. (2021). *Thick (Concepts of) autonomy: Personal autonomy in ethics and bioethics* (1st ed. 2022, Vol. 146). Springer Nature. https://doi.org/10.1007/978-3-030-80991-1

Das, V. (2015). *Affliction: Health, disease, poverty.* Fordham University Press. https://doi.org/10.5422/fordham/9780823261802.001.0001

Ebrahimnejad, H. (2009). *The development of modern medicine in non-western countries.* Routledge.

Faden, R. R., Beauchamp, T. L., & King, N. M. (1986). *A history and theory of informed consent.* Oxford University Press.

Fateh-Moghadam, B., & Gutmann, T. (2014). Governing [through] autonomy. The moral and legal limits of "soft paternalism." *Ethical Theory and Moral Practice, 17*, 383–397.

Fochsen, G., Deshpande, K., & Thorson, A. (2006). Power imbalance and consumerism in the doctor-patient relationship: Health care providers' experiences of patient encounters in a rural district in India. *Qualitative Health Research, 16*(9), 1236–1251. https://doi.org/10.1177/1049732306293776

Foucault, M. (1977). *The birth of the clinic.* Routledge. https://doi.org/10.4324/9780203406373

Frank, A. W. (2016). From sick role to narrative subject: An analytic memoir. *Health*, *20*(1), 9–21. https://doi.org/10.1177/1363459315615395

Gerhardt, U. (2015). The return of the ghost of utilitarianism: Talcott Parsons and the theory of George C. Homans in the 1960s. In *George C. Homans* (pp. 229–254). Routledge.

Gutmann, T. (2022). Is "Autonomy Talk" misleading? In J. F. Childress & M. Quante (Eds.), *Thick (Concepts of) autonomy: Personal autonomy in ethics and bioethics* (pp. 117–133). Springer Nature.

Harrison, M. (1992). Tropical medicine in nineteenth-century India. *The British Journal for the History of Science*, *25*(3), 299–318. Cambridge Core. https://doi.org/10.1017/S0007087400029137

Harrison, M. (2009). Medical experimentation in British India: The case of Dr Helenus Scott. In H. Ebrahimnejad (Ed.), *The development of modern medicine in non-western countries* (pp. 37–55). Routledge.

Hydén, L. (1997). Illness and narrative. *Sociology of Health & Illness*, *19*(1), 48–69.

Jeske, M., James, J., & Joyce, K. (2023). Diagnosis and the practices of patienthood: How diagnostic journeys shape illness experiences. *Sociology of Health & Illness*, *n/a*(n/a). https://doi.org/10.1111/1467-9566.13614

Joyce, K. A., James, J. E., & Jeske, M. (2020). Regimes of patienthood: Developing an intersectional concept to theorize illness experiences. *Engaging Science, Technology, and Society*, *6*, 185–192.

Kleinman, A. (1980). *Patients and healers in the context of culture: An exploration of the borderland between anthropology, medicine, and psychiatry* (Vol. 3). University of California Press.

Kleinman, A. (2020). *The illness narratives: Suffering, healing, and the human condition*. Basic Books.

Kühler, M., & Jelinek, N. (2013). *Autonomy and the self* (1st ed. 2013.). Springer Netherlands. https://doi.org/10.1007/978-94-007-4789-0

Kumbhar, K. (2023). Doctor sahab: Doctors and the public in the 'golden era' of the Indian medical profession. *Sociology of Health & Illness*, *n/a*(n/a). https://doi.org/10.1111/1467-9566.13630

Kumbhar, K. S. (2022). *Healing and harming: The "Noble Profession" of medicine in post-independence India, 1947–2015*. Harvard University.

Lysaught, M. T. (2004). Respect: Or, how respect for persons became respect for autonomy. *Journal of Medicine and Philosophy*, *29*(6), 665–680. https://doi.org/10.1080/03605310490883028

Mackenzie, C., & Stoljar, N. (2000). *Relational autonomy: Feminist perspectives on autonomy, agency, and the social self*. Oxford University Press.

Manson, N. C., & O'Neill, O. (2007). *Rethinking informed consent in bioethics*. Cambridge University Press.

Meyers, D. T. (2005). Decentralizing autonomy: Five faces of selfhood. In J. Christman & J. Anderson (Eds.), *Autonomy and the challenges to liberalism* (pp. 27–55). Cambridge University Press.

Meyers, D. T. (2018). *Feminists rethink the self*. Routledge.

Pandey, S. K., & Sharma, V. (2018). July 1 is National Doctors' Day: How to regain the lost public trust in healthcare? *Indian Journal of Ophthalmology*, *66*(7). https://journals.lww.com/ijo/fulltext/2018/66070/july_1_is_national_doctors__day__how_to_regain_the.46.aspx

Parsons, T. (1975). The sick role and the role of the physician reconsidered. *The Milbank Memorial Fund Quarterly. Health and Society*, *53*(3), 257–278. JSTOR. https://doi.org/10.2307/3349493

Pati, B., & Harrison, M. (2009). *The social history of health and medicine in colonial India*. Routledge.

Ruddock, A. (2021). *Special treatment: Student doctors at the All India Institute of Medical Sciences*. Stanford University Press. https://doi.org/10.1515/9781503628267

Segall, A. (1976). The sick role concept: Understanding illness behavior. *Journal of Health and Social Behavior*, *17*(2), 162–169. JSTOR. https://doi.org/10.2307/2136342

Sen, I. (2010). Memsahibs and health in colonial medical writings, c. 1840 to c. 1930. *South Asia Research*, *30*(3), 253–274. https://doi.org/10.1177/026272801003000303

Shilling, C. (2002). Culture, the 'sick role' and the consumption of health. *The British Journal of Sociology*, *53*(4), 621–638. https://doi.org/10.1080/0007131022000021515

Subramani, S. (2019). Practising reflexivity: Ethics, methodology and theory construction. *Methodological Innovations*, *12*(2), 2059799119863276. https://doi.org/10.1177/2059799119863276

Subramani, S. (2020). The social construction of incompetency: Moving beyond embedded paternalism toward the practice of respect. *Health Care Analysis*, *28*(3), 249–265. https://doi.org/10.1007/s10728-020-00395-w

Subramani, S., & Biller-Andorno, N. (2022). Revisiting respect for persons: Conceptual analysis and implications for clinical practice. *Medicine, Health Care and Philosophy*. https://doi.org/10.1007/s11019-022-10079-y

Taylor, C. (1989). *Sources of the self: The making of the modern identity*. Cambridge University Press.

Varul, M. Z. (2010). Talcott Parsons, the sick role and chronic illness. *Body & Society*, *16*(2), 72–94. https://doi.org/10.1177/1357034X10364766

Veatch, R. (2008). *Patient, heal thyself: How the new medicine puts the patient in charge* (1st ed.). Oxford University Press, Incorporated.

Wear, S. (1998). *Informed consent: Patient autonomy and clinician beneficence within health care*. Georgetown University Press.

Weiss, M. (1980). Caraka Samhita on the doctrine of karma. In W. Doniger & W. D. O'Flaherty (Eds.), *Karma and rebirth in classical Indian traditions*. University of California Press.

Williams, S. J. (2005). Parsons revisited: From the sick role to...? *Health*, *9*(2), 123–144. https://doi.org/10.1177/1363459305050582

Zahavi, D. (2008). *Subjectivity and selfhood: Investigating the first-person perspective*. MIT Press.

Zeiler, K. (2014). A philosophical defense of the idea that we can hold each other in personhood: Intercorporeal personhood in dementia care. *Medicine, Health Care and Philosophy*, *17*(1), 131–141.

Zeiler, K., & De Boer, M. (2020). The empirical and the philosophical in empirical bioethics: Time for a conceptual turn. *AJOB Empirical Bioethics*, *11*(1), 11–13.

Zola, I. K. (1973). Pathways to the doctor—From person to patient. *Social Science & Medicine (1967)*, *7*(9), 677–689. https://doi.org/10.1016/0037-7856(73)90002-4

2 Rhetoric of Passive Patient in the Indian Legal Discourse

Contextualizing Patient Rights and Consent Debates in India

Categorizing patients is a value-laden and socially constructed process that carries significant implications for their agency, rights and beingness. I will show, in this chapter, legal reasoning and standards adopted that are legitimized on the conceptually problematic archetype of "passive patient". The below excerpt is from the Supreme Court of India's landmark case, *Samira Kohli v. Dr. Prabha Manchanda & Anr*, dated 16 January 2008.

> In India, majority of citizens requiring medical care and treatment fall below the poverty line…Poor patients lying in the corridors of hospitals after admission for want of beds or patients waiting for days on the roadside for an admission or a mere examination, is a common sight. For them, any treatment with reference to rough and ready diagnosis based on their outward symptoms and doctor's experience or intuition is acceptable and welcome so long as it is free or cheap; and whatever the doctor decides as being in their interest, is usually unquestioningly accepted. They are a passive, ignorant and uninvolved in treatment procedures. The poor and needy face a hostile medical environment - inadequacy in the number of hospitals and beds, non-availability of adequate treatment facilities, utter lack of qualitative treatment, corruption, callousness and apathy. Many poor patients with serious ailments (eg. heart patients and cancer patients) have to wait for months for their turn even for diagnosis, and due to limited treatment facilities, many die even before their turn comes for treatment. What choice do these poor patients have? Any treatment of whatever degree, is a boon or a favour, for them. The stark reality is that for a vast majority in the country, the concepts of informed consent or any form of consent, and choice in treatment, have no meaning or relevance. The position of doctors in Government and charitable hospitals, who treat them, is also unenviable. They are overworked, understaffed, with little or no diagnostic or surgical facilities and limited choice of medicines and treatment procedures. They have to improvise with virtual non-existent facilities and limited

DOI: 10.4324/9781003129998-3

> dubious medicines. They are required to be committed, service oriented and non-commercial in outlook. What choice of treatment can these doctors give to the poor patients? What informed consent they can take from them?

In this chapter, I will explore this case and its implications for the discourse on patient agency and dignity in India in detail. But before that, take a moment and picture the "patient" to whom the judges are referring in the above excerpt. What does this archetype or image capture? As I interpret the excerpt and critically read the judgment, along with many other cases I explored in my doctoral work that reference this precedent case, the central image of the patient is one who is "passive, ignorant and uninvolved". The patient here is portrayed as a "passive person"—someone who doesn't actively engage, is poor, uneducated, unable to comprehend, blindly trusting, and lacks access to quality healthcare they deserve. I see this image of the "passive patient" as evoking a particular stereotype and identity in the minds of many upper-class-caste-patriarchal individuals in India. It is shaped by narratives from the upper-middle class and caste (the elite), which draw on the stereotype of the "Indian patient" who accesses the public healthcare system and is situated at the intersection of marginalized identities, who are imagined as poor vulnerable victims. We know that such archetypal images, shaped by norms conditioned by historical, socio-cultural contexts, and experiences, become central to any law, legal reasoning, and public policy. For instance, as noted by Schneider & Ingram (1993), most policies reinforce certain social constructions of specific groups, with target populations often being based on "popular images of the persons or groups", which are typically rooted in stereotypes about particular individuals, communities and groups. It becomes a moral imperative because labeling or categorizing patients as "passive" provides the state, institutions, and healthcare professionals with legal and moral justification to deny them rights and agency.

Scholars and activists have consistently showed us how the discourse of protection, especially when framed around shielding women and marginalized communities from violence, is frequently employed to reassert colonial agendas and justify new ways of domination, infused by upper-caste-class values and ideologies by institutions, even legal (Baxi, 1982; Chattopadhyay, 2017; Dhagamwar, 2006; Kannabiran, 2013; Kapur, 2013; Kotiswaran, 2017; Madhok, 2014). Baxi also emphasized, "in a highly unequal society the exploiters will always have an edge over the exploited and that the legal system will, more or less, act as a resource for the dominant interests as a pliant agency of repression of the vulnerable people" (Baxi, 1982, p. 5). Thus the legal system becomes a space to critically understand how dominant interests and values are repressing and marginalizing vulnerable individuals experiences and agency. While scholars have extensively debated medical and legal standards for determining patient incompetence in the US and UK, there has been limited exploration of this discourse within its social and political context both in those countries as well as in India.

Some scholars frame the right to healthcare within the broader context of citizenship crises and their implications for social justice and health justice (Parmar & Wahi, 2011; Pinto, 2021). In India, legal provisions related to patients' rights are scattered across various legal documents. These include the Constitution of India (1950), the Indian Medical Council (Professional Conduct, Etiquette, and Ethics) Regulations (2002), the Drugs and Cosmetics Act (1940), the Clinical Establishment (Registration and Regulation) Act (2010), the Indian Penal Code (1860), the Code of Criminal Procedure (1973), as well as various judgments from the Supreme Court of India and decisions from the National Consumer Disputes Redressal Commission. These laws guide healthcare professionals in maintaining standards of patient care and treatment. However, due to the absence of a dedicated law specifically addressing patient rights, the Ministry of Health and Family Welfare, in collaboration with the National Human Rights Commission, introduced the Charter of Patient Rights, through citizenship justice. Given that health is a state subject in India and regulations vary widely, it is impossible to refer to a single law or regulation when discussing patient rights. Therefore, it is essential to contextualize each regulation or law to fully grasp its background and significance. Given the breadth of these laws and regulations, and the lack of comprehensive literature that explores their nuances concerning patient rights, I focus on Supreme Court and High Court judgments that set precedents for informed consent in the Indian healthcare context. These judgments provide insight into how the judiciary perceives and constructs the archetype of the patient in India—often depicted as "passive".

The language of human rights in the 21st century, which seeks to address power imbalances, emphasizes the importance of individual rights in all areas of human life (Baxi, 1986a). Within health discourse, health has been a part of the human rights tradition, with self-determination and opportunities for health and well-being central to equity and social justice discourse as well (Anand et al., 2006; Sen, 2001; Venkatapuram, 2013; Venkatapuram & Marmot, 2009). The concept of self-determination, often rooted in libertarian philosophy, plays a dominant role in the contemporary doctor–patient relationship. The growth of scientific and medical knowledge, advances in medical technology, variations in expert advice, and medical uncertainties all reinforce the need for decision-making by the person directly affected—namely, the patient. As a result, patient autonomy and rights discourse within law, both thick and think conceptions, have become a central principle in both legal and philosophical analyses of medical decision-making, across different countries (Childress, 2017; Schermer, 2002; Childress & Quante, 2021). Informed consent, which stems from the principle of autonomy, is a concept shaped by the culture of consumerism, intertwined with human rights and liberal values, particularly in American society. It refers to the duty of physicians to explain the procedure to the patient and to warn them of any material risks or dangers inherent in or collateral to the procedure, enabling the patient to make an informed and intelligent choice about whether to undergo treatment. The primary purpose and justification of informed consent is to empower individuals to make autonomous choices and protect their decisions (Beauchamp & Childress, 2013; Faden et al., 1986). The ethical imperative to respect for patient autonomy has shifted the focus of authority in medical decision-making from the physician to the patient. Moral principles are thus enforced by law in the form of rights and duties.

While human rights have been integrated into the health discourse internationally, for instance through WHO and UN policies, the legal doctrine of informed consent to emphasis patient's self-determination within the healthcare context was first established in the 1972 US case of *Canterbury v. Spence*, influenced by the historical and political climate. It was later recognized in the UK through cases such as *Sidaway v. Board of Governors of the Bethlem Royal Hospital and The Maudsley Hospital and Others* in 1985, and *Chester v. Afshar* in 2004, though not precisely in the same way it was applied in the US. In the US and many other developed countries, obtaining a patient's informed consent is both a moral and legal obligation in healthcare practice (Berg et al., 2001). This is increasingly true in contemporary India as well. However, the interpretation of consent, whether as informed consent (as understood in US law) or valid consent (as understood in UK jurisprudence), carries specific implications within the Indian context. The Indian legal system, with its Anglo-Saxon roots inherited from the British legal framework, upholds a common law model similar to that of the British courts. As Upendra Baxi (2000) notes, postcolonial law "registers breaks as well as continuities" (p. 543). It has continued to retain till today the normative and institutional structures of the British Indian Legal System (Baxi, 1982). This reflects how the Indian judiciary, influenced by its colonial past, along with nationalism, navigates the application and evolution of legal principles such as informed consent within the healthcare sector.

Indian courts frequently refer to British court cases when dealing with medical negligence cases, where the current rulings do not require disclosure of risks and information by physicians as a duty to patients, based on what patient needs. However, the Charter of Patient Rights in India lists the "Right to Information" as its foremost right. According to the Charter, patients have the "right to adequate and relevant information about the nature, cause of illness, provisional/confirmed diagnosis, proposed investigations and management, and possible complications, which should be explained at their level of understanding in a language they know. The treating physician is obligated to ensure that this information is provided in simple and intelligible language, either communicated personally by the physician or through qualified assistants" (p. 3). These provisions are also outlined in Annexure 8 of the standards for Hospital Level 1 by the National Clinical Establishments Council, established under the Clinical Establishment Act of 2010, the Medical Council of India Code of Ethics, the Patients Charter by the National Accreditation Board for Hospitals (NABH), and the Consumer Protection Act of 1986.

In the UK, the duty to disclose full material risks was traditionally declined, with the standard for information disclosure being based on the medical professional standard, unlike in the US. This approach led to debates that highlighted the reaffirmation of a paternalistic attitude in the courts, which had largely protected the medical profession until the landmark *Montgomery v. Lanarkshire Health Board* case in 2015. After this case, the so-called Bolam test, which determined a doctor's negligence by referring to a responsible body of medical opinion, was no longer applicable to the issue of consent in UK jurisdiction. The law now requires doctors to consider and ensure that patients are aware of any material risks, based on the reasonable person standard. In contrast, Indian courts in present-day medical negligence cases continue to refer to and align with UK court judgments on information disclosure from before the *Montgomery* case, such as in the *Samira Kohli v. Dr. Prabha Manchanda* case of 2008. As a result, the Bolam test, originating from the 1957 *Bolam* case, continues to be applied in medical negligence cases in India.

Scholarly debates on the concept of informed consent within clinical context have started to gain traction among Indian practitioners and hospitals, marking an important step toward deeper engagement with doctor–patient relationship in current social and political climate. While these discussions are still in the early stages, and critical engagement is needed, they represent a valuable beginning in addressing the nuances of informed consent within the Indian healthcare context. For instance, an empirical study in South India revealed that patients were often unfamiliar with the information provided in the informed consent form, and the decision-making about surgery was largely left to the doctor (Kumar et al., 2012). It has also been observed that patients in India generally tend to place the responsibility for care and trust on the doctor, and account for larger context (Gopichandran, 2019). Few others show how doctors take informed consent as part of defensive practice (Fochsen et al., 2006) and in other studies the healthcare professional did not share or discuss any information, and patients were perceived as passive observers (Madhivanan et al., 2014). While a few studies have provided an overview of consent and the legal paradigm in India, they have also highlighted the need for a more detailed examination of consent process, laws and guidelines in biomedical context (Agrawal, 2016; Jacob, 2014; Paramasivan et al., 2021; Sanwal et al., 1996).

Judges and legal scholars have long emphasized the importance of patient autonomy, and self-determination, in medical decision-making. The *locus classicus* for this principle remains the judgment of Justice Cardozo in *Schloendorff v. Society of New York Hospital* (1914), where it was stated that "every person of adult years and sound mind has a right to determine what shall be done with their own body". Autonomy has been recognized as a legally protectable interest and has been vindicated as a byproduct of protection for two interests—bodily security, as protected by rules against unconsented physical contact, and bodily well-being, as protected by rules governing professional competence. These interests, in short, can be termed as bodily integrity and individual self-determination, which reflect the dominant narrow conception of the principle of patient autonomy. The right to bodily integrity is embodied in common law through civil and criminal laws on assault and battery (Berg et al., 2001; McLean, 2009). There are also constitutional underpinnings to this right, and to the right to individual self-determination. Informed consent has evolved through lawsuits and this concept will be evolving, as jurisprudence grows under common law. We can trace the transition from simple, voluntary to informed consent. In *Slater v. Baker and Stapleton* in 1767, the surgeon had to obtain consent from the patient before beginning the treatment; and in *Schloendorff v. Society of New York Hospital* in 1914, voluntary consent was emphasized, i.e. the patient had to give permission for a specific procedure. In the *Salgo v. Leland Stanford Junior University Board of Trustees* case (1957), it was held that physicians had an affirmative duty to disclose information. We can see how the doctrine of informed consent has evolved over a period.

According to the current understanding of the doctrine of informed consent, practitioners must fully inform patients about the risks, benefits, and other aspects of a proposed treatment, as well as provide information on the option of receiving no treatment. The widely accepted components of informed consent—competence, disclosure, understanding, voluntariness, and consent (Faden et al., 1986)—are grounded in the value of patient autonomy. In the cases mentioned and in related lawsuits, the focus has shifted from merely obtaining consent for treatment to emphasizing the physician's duty to disclose information. As a result, the disclosure of information has become a critical element in cases involving consent. To analyze the legal and ethical foundation of the concept of consent, it is important to understand the existing legal protections that safeguard patient autonomy. Here, when I refer to existing legal protections, I mean whether they fall under the theories of battery or professional negligence.

In India, laws governing medical negligence are largely based on English common law. Individuals affected by medical negligence or malpractice can seek legal recourse through the Civil Procedure Code, the Criminal Procedure Code (Section 304A of the Indian Penal Code), the Consumer Protection Act (CPA) of 1986, or the Code of Medical Ethics Regulations of 2002 for disciplinary action. Jurisprudentially, there is no fundamental distinction between negligence under civil and criminal codes; the key difference lies in the determination of liability. In tort law, the extent of liability is determined by the amount of damages incurred, while in criminal law, it is the degree of negligence that matters. Those seeking financial compensation typically file cases against medical professionals under the CPA, as it offers a more accessible avenue for grievance redressal and compensation unless there is battery or assault is involved.

I assume that language within legal texts carries the imprint of social meaning, allowing for the interpretation of constructed concepts and ideas (Baxi, 1986b, 2000; Goodrich, 1984a, 1984b). It is widely acknowledged among legal scholars that judgments often reflect the "post-hoc justifications of those writing a decision in a particular case and do not fully capture the judicial decision-making process" (Gatowski et al., 2001). While analyzing and interpreting court judgments, I remained acutely aware of this limitation, understanding that written judgments may not fully disclose all the values and influences that shaped the decision-making process. Nevertheless, I treated these judgments as final texts that serve as influential tools, representing the constructed ideas, values, and assumptions that underpin the judicial reasoning.

While some scholars challenge the persistence of power asymmetry in clinical interactions, others have argued that it should be understood within social and organizational embeddedness (Pilnick & Dingwall, 2011; Shim, 2010). Additionally, scholars have suggested that this asymmetry reflects the exercise of power and existing medical authority, positing that medicine operates as a normative, order-maintaining enterprise that results in patients adopting a "sick role" and "illness behavior" (Collyer, 2018; Hahn & Kleinman, 1983; Parsons, 1975). Other studies have critiqued the concept of the "sick role", arguing that it promotes conformity and passivity while undermining the importance of individual agency (Burnham, 2012; Frank, 2016; Sakalys, 2000). The conception of the patient and role expectations is shaped by perceptions, assumptions, and the inherent asymmetry in the doctor–patient relationship within particular social and political context. The portrayal of the patient as "passive", "ignorant", "helpless", and "vulnerable", and of the doctor's role as one of restoring "health" in the "best interests of patients", has been observed and discussed in legal contexts dominantly in US and UK too, especially when engaging with women patients (Hoffmann & Tarzian, 2001; Montgomery, 2017; Secker, 1999). Amsterdam and Bruner (2009) remarked:

> familiarity is dulling—that when our ways of conceiving of things become routine, they disappear from consciousness and we cease to know that we are thinking in a certain way or why we are doing so…to make the familiar strange again, to rescue the taken-for-granted and bring it back into mind…The practice of law is full of such dissociated routines, of canonical ways of proceeding "scarcely worth a moment's thought".
>
> (p. 1)

This understanding underscores the complex dynamics at play in the doctor–patient relationship, where the traditional view of patient passivity is increasingly being challenged in both medical and legal spheres. The concept of autonomy is a central moral justification in contemporary bioethics debates, particularly in discussions about moving away from paternalism. Informed consent is crucial to respecting autonomy and the autonomous choices of patients in both the US and UK (Berg et al., 2001; Faden et al., 1986; McLean, 2009). With this context in mind, I now turn to the legal judgments to explore the dominant narratives and rhetoric within court decisions, specifically examining the roles and assumptions tied to the notion of "patienthood" as it is discursively constructed in India. As discussed in Chapter 1, these debates often hinge on the underlying perception and archetype of a patient as a "competent adult who can make autonomous choices".

Analyzing how the concept of consent is understood and applied by the judiciary in various court judgments related to medical negligence cases in India provides crucial insights into the underlying meanings, assumptions, and ethical values embedded in the Indian context. This chapter builds upon my doctoral work, where, guided by a literature review and discussions with lawyers specializing in health law in India (during my internship and pilot study), I identified *Samira Kohli v. Dr. Prabha Manchanda* as the landmark case on consent in India. Through my research and literature review, it became clear that the *Samira Kohli* case remains a foundational precedent in the Indian legal landscape today. The *Samira Kohli* case is particularly important because it set a precedent for defining the nature of real or valid consent and discussed the standards for information disclosure. This case has continued to be cited in subsequent judgments, including the recent cases.

Considering the vast number of negligence cases, I strategically selected cases that cited the *Samira Kohli* case as a precedent in their judgments. To do this, I conducted a review using Manupatra, an online legal information database. Initially, I included cases from August 2008 to July 2016, identifying 137 cases that referenced *Samira Kohli*. I then refined my selection to focus on cases that not only mentioned the term "consent" and cited *Samira Kohli*, but also engaged in in-depth discussions on consent. In this chapter, I analyze how the patient is "imagined". The broad framework for analyzing these legal judgments is based on a critical hermeneutic approach, grounded in interpretivism. This approach aids in understanding the context necessary to interpret court judgments, while also examining the relationship between the application of norms and the selection of facts in each case. Numerous socio-legal studies have shown that political ideology, values, beliefs, and attitudes of decision-makers play a heuristic role in the judicial decision-making process (Baxi, 2013; Baxi, 1982, 1986b, 1986a; Gillman, 2001; Goodrich, 1984b; Rhode, 2013). Goodrich, (1984b) aptly states:

> [A]ny legal philosophy worthy of the name should first begin to concentrate its attention upon the precise analysis of the social, political, and ideological values existent throughout the syntactic and discursive processes of law.
>
> (p. 534)

However, in the Indian context, research on these factors remains relatively sparse, especially from patient autonomy and agency perspective. Given this background, I utilize the *Samira Kohli v. Dr. Prabha Manchanda* (2008) case to explore the conception and portrayal of a patient in Indian court judgments, particularly in relation to the concept of consent, to illustrate how these ideas shape legal reasoning. In the next section, I will provide a brief background on the *Samira Kohli* case, as it represents the current precedent in cases involving medical negligence, consent, and information disclosure.

Samira Kohli Case—Exposing Gendered and Poverty Rhetoric

Outline of the Case

Samira Kohli, an unmarried woman aged 44, consulted Dr. Manchanda on 9 May 1995, for prolonged menstrual bleeding. She was admitted to the hospital, and consent forms for admission, medical treatment, and surgery were signed. The surgery consent form specified "diagnostic and operative laparoscopy" and noted that a laparotomy might be necessary. During the laparoscopic examination, performed under general anesthesia, Dr. Lata Rangan, another doctor involved in the case, sought consent from Samira's mother for a hysterectomy while Samira was unconscious. With her mother's consent, Dr. Manchanda proceeded to remove Samira's uterus (abdominal hysterectomy), ovaries, and fallopian tubes (bilateral salpingo-oophorectomy). On 19 January 1996, Samira Kohli filed a complaint with the National Consumer Disputes Redressal Commission, seeking Rs 25 lakh in compensation from Dr. Manchanda. She claimed that the doctor had been negligent and that the radical surgery, which involved removing her reproductive organs, had been performed without her consent. The compensation she sought was for the loss of her reproductive organs, diminished prospects of matrimony, irreversible damage to her body, loss of the opportunity to become a mother, and the resulting emotional trauma.

The National Commission dismissed her complaint, stating that the hysterectomy had been performed with adequate care and that the patient had voluntarily sought treatment at the clinic. However, when the case was appealed to the Supreme Court, the order of the National Consumer Dispute Redressal Commission was overruled, and Dr. Manchanda was held liable for negligence. The Supreme Court's decision was rooted in the principle of assault and battery, as the physician had performed an unauthorized abdominal hysterectomy–bilateral salpingo-oophorectomy (AH-BSO) without obtaining Samira's specific consent. Although the physician had obtained consent from the patient's mother, this was not considered valid, as it violated the patient's bodily integrity and constituted a deficiency in service. The right to self-determination and fiduciary duty protects patients from unwarranted intrusions, such as surgery without consent. Initially, the judges discussed the breach of duty under the battery theory, but the case was later evaluated under the negligence theory of liability, where compensation is awarded to the plaintiff. This shift in focus from battery to negligence in medical consent cases highlights that "unintentional or careless" action, such as performing surgery without consent, itself constitutes negligence, making the physician liable.

The judgment in the Samira Kohli case not only clarified the requirements for specific consent to additional surgery but also elaborated on the broader meaning of consent and the nature of information disclosure in Indian context.

The case set guidelines for these issues in the Indian context, drawing on precedents from British court decisions. Understanding the meaning of consent and the standards for information disclosure is crucial for examining the roles and authority of physicians and patients, evaluating the degree of respect for a patient's agency, and reflecting the judicial stance on the importance of material information within the doctor–patient relationship.

Unpacking Gendered Assumptions

When closely examining the judgment, several significant issues arise concerning consent, autonomy, medical paternalism, and the underlying gendered assumptions about women's bodies and health, along with the narrative of the patient as a "passive" recipient of care. The doctor "acted in excess of consent" by performing the hysterectomy, which raises critical concerns about whether the patient was fully informed of all available options, risks, and consequences. The judgment frequently emphasizes that the doctor's decision to proceed was "in good faith and for the benefit of the appellant (patient)", which exemplifies a paternalistic approach where the medical professional assumes the authority to decide what is best for the patient. This "doctor knows best" attitude reinforces the notion of passive patienthood, effectively reducing the appellant to a passive recipient of care rather than an active participant in her health decisions. This approach undermines the patient's agency, in particular women's bodily autonomy and agency, as it assumes that the medical professional's judgment supersedes the patient's right to make informed decisions about her own body and health. The judgment thus highlights the tension between medical paternalism and patient autonomy, particularly in the context of gendered assumptions that influence the perception and treatment of women's health in medical and legal settings. How law often fails women's agency in the legal system is not new; it frequently fails to support women's agency because it operates within patriarchal norms that shape its rules and judgments. Many scholars have shown and critically engaged with how legal avenues may reinforce traditional gender roles through violence against women, such as sexual harassment, domestic violence, and rape (Basu, 2015; Baxi, 2013; Chattopadhyay, 2017; Gangoli, 2016; Kapur & Cossman, 1996; Narain, 2001; Sircar et al., 2016). For example, using rape law to secure marriage or domestic violence law for alimony perpetuates women's dependence on marriage and economic support rather than offering them true autonomy. These legal strategies often compel individuals who are often marginalised to conform to societal expectations rather than challenge the structures that oppress them, thus limiting their ability to fully exercise agency. By prioritizing conformity over resistance, law can obscure the deeper inequalities women face.

The narratives in this judgment pathologize natural processes such as menstruation and menopause, using the patient's menorrhagia and pre-menopausal status to justify the hysterectomy. This perspective aligns with the respondent's claim that "hysterectomy was not an unreasonable option as there was no scope left for fecundability in a woman aged 44 years suffering from endometriosis". Analyzing this through a feminist lens, it is evident that such medicalization reinforces harmful stereotypes about women's bodies and normal physiological changes. This approach raises important questions about whether the hysterectomy was presented as the only viable solution, potentially sidelining other treatment options that could prioritize the patient's quality of life and personal preferences. By framing the hysterectomy as a necessity, the judgment distanced the patient from involvement in her treatment plan and decision-making process. The respondent's statement that "there was no scope left for fecundability" in a 44-year-old woman with endometriosis reflects ageist and sexist assumptions. Many feminist studies and literature challenge the notion that a woman's health and worth are intrinsically tied to her reproductive capacity, advocating for a holistic understanding of women's health beyond fertility. The passage implies that because the appellant was "fast approaching the age of menopause", her menstrual problems were less significant or warranted drastic measures. A critical analysis scrutinizes this logic, questioning why a menopausal status should diminish the importance of addressing menstrual health with sensitivity and respect for the patient's preferences. This perspective also examines the long-term consequences of the appellant having to undergo hormone therapy post-hysterectomy. The passage downplays this by stating "no other serious repercussions are made out as a result of the removal", but the analysis emphasizes the need for a thorough discussion of hormone replacement's long-term requirements. Ensuring that the risks and benefits are clearly communicated is crucial for respecting the patient's right to be fully informed about all aspects of her treatment.

Overall, this case highlights how the archetypal image of the passive patient is deeply entrenched in multiple ways, particularly impacting marginalized groups at various intersections. This perception underscores systemic issues within healthcare, where women's health concerns are frequently dismissed or inadequately addressed. The narrative portrays how doctors providing "permanent relief" through surgical removal, deemed to be "in their best interest", represents a narrow and paternalistic approach to patient care that denies patients' agency, particularly undermining women's agency and bodily integrity. This reflects and parallels broader discourses surrounding women's reproductive autonomy, illustrating the pervasive nature of these issues within both medical practice and legal frameworks. Furthermore, one can observe how negative stereotypes of women, combined with ageist biases, often contribute to the construction of a "passive patient" archetype. This categorization renders women more likely to be deemed "incompetent", reinforcing the idea that doctors are better positioned to make decisions in their "best interest". In this way, the way we perceive and construct reality—particularly through the lens of judges—plays a crucial role in determining who is labelled as a "passive patient" and how that categorization becomes an archetype.

Unmasking Poverty-Induced Shame Rhetoric

Questions about who is poor often provoke indignation among economically vulnerable communities, especially when one's situations and voices are not centered in discussions. Relationship of poverty and shame is intertwined and has been a significant topic of conversation in India and other countries (Gubrium & Pellissery, 2013; Guru, 2009; Guru & Sarukkai, 2018; Walker et al., 2013). Having experienced phases of poverty where I had to ask my neighbor for 5 rupees to buy milk for my brother, or request an extension on debt at the nearby grocery store while waiting anxiously for the owner to just make any eye contact, and creditors coming to our home, with my mother and I trying to offer excuses and explain our situation, only to be dehumanized in front of all the neighbors with every slur a woman in India might hear, and wearing torn clothes from cousins who thought I was only worthy of wearing such hand-me-downs. All of these moments, and many more, of deep shame and dehumanization, caused by phases of poverty and the social categories we lived in, are nothing compared to the suffering endured by many poor marginalized communities in India. Yet, this poverty-shame is familiar to those who have lived and continue to live it, but this does not mean that one cannot be recognized as an agent with self-respect and dignity. Despite India's economic growth, which benefits only 2% of elite, it remains home to the largest number of poor. The lack of focus on marginalized voices can be attributed to India's patriarchal and hierarchical social structure, which is shaped by caste, gender, class, geography, religion, and other intersecting factors. People are frequently shamed and stigmatized for their poverty, both in everyday interactions and at institutional levels. For example, one can observe how shaming occurs in national anti-poverty interventions, such as the food security policy under the Public Distribution System (PDS) and the income-maintenance policy through the National Rural Employment Guarantee Act (NREGA) (Pellissery, 2008; Pellissery & Mathew, 2013). These programs often reinforce the rhetoric of poverty shame and shape how marginalized communities are perceived by state policies and programs. This has contributed to the creation of "passive poor" narratives in public and institutional discourse. This "passive poor" rhetoric is evident in legal judgments, where poor patients are perceived as lacking decision-making capacity, being intellectually incompetent, and relying on doctors while blindly trusting the system because "they don't have options". Such narratives not only diminish the agency of the poor but also reinforce a paternalistic approach that fails to respect their self and dignity.

When examining legal judgments, including those of the Supreme Court, the rhetoric of poverty is often normalized and justified within legal reasoning. This construction of "poor Indians" as a distinct category reinforces the perception of their lack of agency. Various studies illustrate how the poor are often viewed as morally weak, lazy, and unintelligent. However, I argue that the rhetoric of "poor patients" in these judgments serves to justify actions taken in their "best interests". This narrative perpetuates paternalistic attitudes, where decisions are made on behalf of the poor under the assumption that they are incapable of making informed choices for themselves. The separation and stigmatization of people in poverty is deeply ingrained in India, where the poor are often categorized by class and caste, particularly those from marginalized communities such as scheduled castes, tribes, and backward communities. In both everyday narratives and institutional contexts, the poor are frequently portrayed as deviant, weak, and morally deficient. The "us" versus "them" narrative is prevalent, especially in legal judgments where the poor are viewed as individuals needing state care. While the state has obligations and duties, such as implementing social welfare schemes and programs to support impoverished communities, it must fulfill these responsibilities without perpetuating stigma or shame.

In the *Samira Kohli* case judgment, the judges acknowledge poverty as a social issue, yet they portray individuals as helpless rather than considering how their judgments could embody a political imagination that centers the concerns and voices of the vulnerable. Legal rhetoric often mirrors dominant cultural assumptions, and when judges construct their arguments, they rely on assumptions that are widely accepted within society. These assumptions lend power and influence on their arguments. Moreover, as members of the same society, judges are likely to hold these beliefs themselves. It is crucial to recognize the significance of one's social position—whether it be gender, class, caste, or religion—in the context of India, where judges often come from upper-class-caste communities. The rhetoric surrounding poverty in legal judgments demands us to examine how culturally ingrained, stereotypical assumptions about the poor, shape our broader perceptions. These assumptions prevent judges from recognizing the poor as agents who make decisions in everyday life. Instead, the narrative often reduces them to passive, helpless figures, reinforcing a limited and paternalistic view that fails to acknowledge their agency. Thus, it becomes moral necessity for a more nuanced and empathetic approach in legal reasoning, one that challenges ingrained stereotypes and supports the marginalized.

Denial of Patient Agency

In Samira Kohli case, the judgment not only outlined the specific consent that should be obtained before surgery but also expanded on the meaning of consent and the nature of information disclosure that should be practiced in the Indian context. These guidelines drew on precedents from the UK, specifically the *Bolam v. Friern Hospital Management Committee* (1957) and *Sidaway v. Board of Governors of the Bethlem Royal Hospital* (1985) cases, as cited in the *Samira Kohli* case. The judgment deliberately favored the concept of "real or valid consent", which developed during the *Bolam* case, over the concept of "informed consent", which emerged from the American *Canterbury* case. This preference was justified by considering the "ground realities" of healthcare in

India, acknowledging the contextual differences that influence how consent is understood and applied in medical practice within the country.

In bioethics and legal debates, the preferred standard for consent is typically based on the patient's perspective, with physicians obligated to provide the necessary information that patients require to make an informed decision. This approach prioritizes patients' rights to self-determination, which in turn defines the boundaries of the duty to disclose information (Faden et al., 1986; McLean, 2009). In the UK's *Bolam* case, however, the concept of consent and information disclosure was based on the "medical professional standard", where the judgment relied on the opinions of a reasonable body of medical professionals. This standard was recently overturned in the 2015 *Montgomery* case (Farrell & Brazier, 2016; Harrison et al., 2018; Le Gallez et al., 2022), which marked a significant departure from the long-held reliance on medical opinion. The *Montgomery* ruling recognized that patients' values should be acknowledged, and thus the test for material information disclosure should be based on either a "reasonable person" or the "particular patient" standard. While some scholars have welcomed this shift as a move toward enhancing patient autonomy and reducing medical paternalism (Edozien, 2015; Harrison et al., 2018), others have critically questioned as it demands further exploration (Dunn, 2016; Dunn et al., 2019; Farrell & Brazier, 2016; Ward et al., 2020). The debates surrounding "informed consent" in both law and clinical practice, particularly concerning the standards for information disclosure, are ongoing due to the complexities and nuances inherent in this concept and practice. However, these debates have drawn my attention to the underlying construction of the "patient" in legal and ethical discourse. The way consent is understood and applied not only reflects but also shapes our broader understanding of patient autonomy, agency, and the role of healthcare providers.

Landmark cases such as *Bolam*, *Sidaway*, *Montgomery*, *Schloendorff*, *Canterbury*, and *Rogers* have played a crucial role in setting standards and contributing to the conceptual development of "consent" in medico-legal debates, especially in US and UK, and in certain postcolonial societies. I observe that the fundamental assumptions and concepts surrounding "patients" and the "doctor–patient relationship" have significantly influenced the adoption of certain concepts and standards within legal discourse. The concept of a "patient" as depicted in court judgments and judges' narratives holds substantial weight in the legal context and has the potential to cause a paradigm shift in both legal and bioethical debates. In this section, I will closely examine the narratives and constructs surrounding "patients" that have influenced the preference for the "medical professional standard" in Indian medical negligence cases, particularly regarding consent to treatment and information disclosures. By uncovering the narratives and rhetoric that shape legal reasoning, my goal is to identify the underlying concepts that must be addressed to if one needs to think about legal reform. This analysis aims to shed light on how these narratives affect legal standards and to explore the potential for reshaping the understanding of patient autonomy and rights in the legal and medical discourse.

> Patients in India cannot afford them. People in India still have great regard and respect for Doctors. The Members of medical profession have also, by and large, shown care and concern for the patients. There is an atmosphere of trust and implicit faith in the advice given by the Doctor. The India psyche rarely questions or challenges the medical advice. Having regard to the conditions obtaining in India, as also the settled and recognized practices of medical fraternity in India, we are of the view that to nurture the doctor-patient relationship on the basis of trust, the extent and nature of information required to be given by doctors should continue to be governed by the Bolam test ...It is for the doctor to decide, with reference to the condition of the patient, nature of illness, and the prevailing established practices, how much information regarding risks and consequences should be given to the patients, and how they should be couched, having the best interests of the patient.
>
> (*Samira Kohli* case, p. 15)

The above excerpt captures the broader narratives of "passive patients" and "best interests of the patients", which are frequently invoked to justify the legal reasoning and standards adopted within the Indian legal context. In the *Samira Kohli* case, the central theme was the elevation of the "doctor" through the rhetorical construction of the "passive patient", a concept justified by the "ground realities" of the Indian context. The judgment's significant narrative centered on socio-economic conditions, the "noble" profession of medical doctors, and the importance of nurturing the doctor–patient relationship, which is characterized by "implicit trust". This approach not only reinforces the power dynamics in the doctor–patient relationship but also upholds a paternalistic model of healthcare, where the doctor's authority is paramount, and the patient's agency is often overlooked or diminished.

While much of the legal and ethical analysis in the US and UK engages with patients as "agents" who have the "right" to be informed about treatment decisions, as individuals with the "ability" to participate in medical decision-making, and as "rights holders", this narrative has largely failed to be reflected in Indian court judgments. An examination of the judicial reasoning in the *Samira Kohli* case reveals two dominant constructs that also permeate other contested consent cases: the "passive patient" and the "best interests of the patient". I have explored earlier that these constructs are central to judgments that employ the "medical framework" to issues of clinical interactions, consent, and information disclosure within the Indian context, where physical health and bodily integrity are given precedence (Subramani, 2017). In *Samira Kohli's* case, the justification for applying the Bolam test or the medical professional standard regarding consent to treatment and information disclosure is rooted in the so-called "ground realities" of India, which are characterized by factors such as poverty, illiteracy, and the respect and trust traditionally afforded to doctors. This reasoning suggests that the prevailing socio-economic conditions and cultural norms in India necessitate a different approach to patient rights and autonomy compared to those in other legal systems, such as UK or US. However, this approach also perpetuates a view of patients as passive recipients of care, rather than engaged participants in their health decisions, thus limiting the potential for legal recognition of patient's agency in the Indian context.

In addition to the narrative of poverty and illiteracy, there exists a broader, prejudicial narrative that characterizes patients as individuals who receive "free or cheap" services and do not ask questions because they are illiterate and have "implicit faith" in doctors who act in their "best interests". This perception is pervasive in legal judgments, including those related to consent and medical negligence, where patients are often described as "passive, ignorant, and uninvolved" in the decision-making process. Such descriptions are frequently justified by referencing socio-economic and cultural contexts, as well as the inherently asymmetric nature of the doctor–patient relationship. Another significant narrative in these judgments is the concern with keeping the cost of treatment within affordable limits. The judgment in the *Samira Kohli* case, for instance, argues against adopting American concepts and standards of treatment procedures, including the full disclosure of risks, consequences, and choices, on the grounds that it would lead to a higher cost structure akin to American medical care. The judgment emphasizes the context of "scarce resources" to justify why the "American view" cannot be applied in India. This reasoning reflects a rhetoric that portrays "Indian patients" as having "implicit faith and trust" in doctors, reinforcing the narrative of a "noble" profession that demonstrates care. This perspective not only limits the application of more rigorous standards of informed consent but also perpetuates a paternalistic approach to patient care, where doctors are seen as the ultimate decision-makers and patients as passive recipients of their expertise.

The law constructs narratives that are presented as authoritative, and in this judgment—as well as in other medical negligence cases—the extensive rhetoric surrounding the significance of doctors' roles and the nobility of the medical profession reflects an underlying desire to reinforce the acceptance of "medical authority". Doctors are frequently portrayed as "professional experts" in the court of law, and references to concepts like "doctor knows best" or doctors acting in the "best interest of patients" are rhetorically employed to support the use of the medical professional standard. This standard positions doctors as better suited to make medical decisions than patients, effectively constructing the "passive patient" narrative, which denies patients any meaningful role in the decision-making process.

The excerpt below illustrates how judicial reasoning justifies the constructed narrative of the "passive patient", who is perceived as lacking agency during decision-making processes and is subsumed under the broader concept of "medical authority", where the doctor is always assumed to act in the patient's best interests. This reasoning also reveals the underlying moral judgments made by the judge(s), who validate the doctor's conceptualization of a "patient". Additionally, the statements provide insight into the stereotypical understanding of the status of an "unmarried woman" of a certain age, and how this perception influences the authority exerted over her body and choices.

> The respondent did it in the interest of the appellant. As the appellant was already 44 years old and was having serious menstrual problems, the respondent thought that by surgical removal of uterus and ovaries she was providing permanent relief. It is also possible that the respondent thought that the appellant may approve the additional surgical procedure when she regained consciousness and the consent by appellant's mother gave her authority. This is a case of respondent acting in excess of consent but in good faith and for the benefit of the appellant. Though the appellant has alleged that she had to undergo Hormone Therapy, no other serious repercussions is made out as a result of the removal. The appellant was already fast approaching the age of menopause and in all probability required such Hormone Therapy. Even assuming that AH-BSO surgery was not immediately required, there was a reasonable certainty that she would have ultimately required the said treatment for a complete cure.
>
> (*Samira Kohli* case, p. 23)

The above excerpt illustrates how the construction of the "patient" is rooted in set prejudices within a specific context, particularly in the conception of the doctor–patient relationship where the patient is denied "agency" or "choices" during the decision-making process. For instance, the judge justified the doctor's actions as being performed in "good faith and [for the] benefit" of the patient, based on the cultural presumption that a 44-year-old woman does not need a uterus. This assumption reflects a broader societal belief that women of that age have no reproductive value, thereby undermining their autonomy and bodily integrity. Although the judgment acknowledges the need for specific consent to additional surgery within the framework of "real or valid consent", the rhetoric in the judgment portrays the doctor as acting in the "best interest of the patient", prioritizing what is perceived as "better" health outcomes over the patient's autonomy. The judgment also reinforces the ultimate authority granted to the medical doctor over the patient's body, disregarding the patient's choices or preferences regarding her own body. This landmark judgment defends the doctor's role and authority, emphasizing the "implicit faith" in medical professionals while minimizing the importance of the patient's values, choices, and rights. The judgment justifies this stance by citing the "ground realities" of the Indian context, where socio-cultural factors are often invoked to rationalize paternalistic practices. The concluding remarks of the judgment fail to engage with or reflect on the rights, preferences, and choices of patients, instead focusing on empathizing with the doctor and reinforcing the moral regime of "doctor knows best". This perspective assumes that the doctor's actions were in the "best interest" of the patient, irrespective of the patient's own values and decisions, thus perpetuating a paternalistic approach to healthcare that diminishes patient agency.

The significance of this medical authority over patients is that it reinforces the notion of patients as "passive", lacking the "ability" to participate meaningfully in medical decisions. The judgment fails to consider or engage with patients' values, preferences, and choices regarding consent for treatment or information disclosure. By narrowing the understanding of "information disclosure" to the domain of medicine, the judgment effectively limits the role of the patient and diminishes the importance of their values. The rhetorical emphasis on "doctor knows best" or the idea that doctors act in the "best interests of the patient"—because they are seen as the ultimate authority in medical knowledge and are deemed necessary for the "better health" of the patient—removes the patient's agency and redefines their role as "passive" in the medical decision-making process. This portrayal of the "passive patient" silences the patient's stories, experiences, values, preferences, and choices, which ought to be central to the medical decision-making process. By doing so, the judgment upholds a paternalistic approach that overlooks the patient's right to be an participant in decisions about their own health and treatment.

The *Samira Kohli* judgment provides a deep insight into the concepts of the "patient" and patients' rights as expressed in court judgments. The "patient" constructed within the law is shaped by legal reasoning and justification, and analyzing the narrative and rhetorical elements in judgments can reveal underlying judicial opinions that may not be explicitly stated. The analysis of legal judgments involves unpacking the rhetorical meanings created through political and ethical assessments of the context (Goodrich, 1984a; MacCormick, 2005). Although the language of patients' rights is invoked to support the doctrine of "real or valid consent" within the Indian context, a closer examination of the rhetorical meaning within the judgment suggests that the court actually reinforces the concepts of "medical authority" and the "passive patient" role in medical decision-making. The court's approach privileges "medical authority" by centering the patient's "health" as the fundamental concern of medicine, thereby sidelining the patient's values, preferences, and choices in the decision-making process. The rhetorical choices and narratives in the judgment have profound symbolic effects on the concept of the "patient". The philosophy of "doctor knows best" and the depiction of "passive" patients as unquestioning and incapable decision-makers reveal a view of patients as lacking agency. Rather than recognizing patients as independent agents capable of making their own decisions within the medical framework, the judgment reaffirms the notion of "medical authority" figures acting in the "best interests of the patient", supposedly to protect the patient's health. This perspective also invokes the patients' "socio-economic conditions" and the pursuit of "better health" as justifications for not prioritizing the patient's values in the decision-making process. The result is a legal and ethical framework that diminishes patient autonomy and reinforces a paternalistic model of healthcare.

The rhetoric in the *Samira Kohli* case advances a dichotomy within the "health/choice" approach to patient rights, where the focus is explicitly placed on "physical/bodily health" by recognizing the need for specific consent to additional surgeries, while simultaneously displacing the patient's values, preferences, and choices from the concept of bodily integrity (Subramani, 2017). In Indian law, the concept of bodily integrity is best understood as "a right to be free from physical interference", as articulated in Feldman's work (Feldman, 1993, p. 241). This concept primarily covers negative liberties, such as "freedom from physical assaults, torture, medical or other experimentation, immunization, and compelled eugenic or social sterilization, as well as cruel or degrading treatment or punishment" (Feldman, 1993, p. 241). It also includes some positive duties on the state to protect individuals from interference by others. Here, it is important to distinguish the concept of "bodily integrity" from that of "bodily autonomy". While bodily integrity emphasizes the right to be free from physical interference, bodily autonomy centers on the exercise of choice and decision-making power regarding one's body. In the Indian legal context, case law often prioritizes bodily integrity in terms of physical protection and information disclosure based on medical standards. The culpability for negligence is typically established through deficiencies in service that result in physical or bodily harm. However, this focus on bodily integrity, as framed within the *Samira Kohli* judgment, tends to overshadow the concept of bodily autonomy, where the patient's right to make informed choices about their own body is diminished. The legal reasoning in such cases often reflects a preference for maintaining the status quo of medical authority, where the patient's role in decision-making is limited, and their personal values and preferences are subordinated to the perceived "best interests" as determined by medical professionals. This approach highlights a critical tension between protecting physical integrity and respecting patients' preferences within the broader framework of patient rights in India.

The guidelines provided in the *Samira Kohli* judgment regarding "adequate information" disclosure, the decision to apply the Bolam test, and the acceptance of the UK doctrine of real or valid consent in consent cases related to information disclosure highlight the dominance of the professional standard of disclosure. This analysis reveals that the doctrine of "real or valid consent" primarily serves as a tool to protect the "physical body". In the Indian context, the protection from physical harm based on medical professional standards is regarded as the ultimate protected interest, rather than the patient's right to comprehensive information. This indicates that the foundational legal principle of "real or valid consent" is rooted in the concept of bodily integrity. The patient's entitlement to material information is not given paramount importance unless bodily harm, as defined by medical professional standards, has been established. This demonstrates that the extent to which patients receive material information is contingent upon the physician's adherence to the professional standard of disclosure. As a result, the patient's right to all pertinent information is not a central concern within the legal doctrine, which ultimately places more emphasis on protecting the body from physical harm than on empowering patients with the information necessary to make fully informed decisions about their care. This approach underscores a significant limitation in the legal framework, where patient autonomy and the right to informed consent are often subordinated to the authority of medical professionals.

Although scholarship on autonomy, self-determination, and patient rights has progressed significantly over the decades, legal reasoning in India continues to construct the dominant identity of the "passive patient", often overlooking the intrinsic significance of patients' values and preferences. This reasoning is normatively justified by the rhetoric of "doctor knows best" and considerations of Indian ground realities, including factors such as poverty, the pursuit of "better health", and societal values, holding onto patriarchal and hierarchical norms, of "respect for doctors", "trust", and "implicit faith" in medical professionals. By applying the Bolam principle and upholding the belief that medical professionals act in the "best interests of the patient", the judgment perpetuates the construction of the "passive patient" through its rhetoric and narratives, effectively overlooking the patient's values, preferences, choices, and need for information during clinical interactions. This approach underestimates the capacity of patients to make decisions and disregards their agency. This leads us to important questions: can we justifiably ignore the role of patients' values, preferences, choices, and requirements for information simply because a population is poor, illiterate, and trusts medical professionals? Does being poor and illiterate inherently mean that a person "cannot" make decisions, have "choices and values", or participate in the medical decision-making process? Does it follow that their values, preferences, and right to participate in clinical interactions should not be acknowledged? These questions demand further exploration. Given the scope of this chapter, I will, in the next section, limit my argument to contextualizing this analysis within the current socio-legal context in India and explore how we can move forward to realize patient rights and dignity in this setting.

Reclaiming Patients' Agency

While being critical of judiciary's role and influence over society, I think that the Supreme Court has historically played a crucial role in transforming social concepts and shaping policy debates to some extent (for instance inBasu, 2015; Baxi, 1985, 1986b; Choudhry et al., 2016; Kapur, 2013; Kapur & Cossman, 1996; Mate & Kapiszewski, 2013; Shankar, 2012). Furthermore, evidence suggests that courts can amplify national attention on key policy issues (de Freitas & Martin, 2015; Gloppen, 2008; Shankar, 2012). Many legal scholars who focus on the attitudinal models of judges have noted that court decisions are often influenced by case facts vis-à-vis their ideological preferences and values (Agnes, 2001; Baxi, 1982, 1986b, 1986a; Epstein et al., 2007; Kannabiran, 2013). Given this understanding, I argue that a paradigm shift in the concept of a "patient" as a *person*—who is a situated participant in decision-making processes—and a focus on effective communication within court judgments would significantly advance the push for a culture of patient-centered care in society. Patient-centered care, as I understand it, is care that is respectful of and responsive to individual patient preferences, needs, and values. Many studies have demonstrated that patient-centered care not only improves health outcomes but also enhances the overall quality of healthcare (Dubbin et al., 2013; Mead & Bower, 2000; Tanenbaum, 2015). More specifically, patient-centered care enhances healthcare by reducing social, economic, and demographic disparities between doctors and patients, while also encouraging healthcare providers to be more attuned to their patients' values, beliefs, hopes, and concerns (Beach et al., 2007; Epstein & Street, 2011; Kuehn, 2012). By reshaping the judicial narrative to recognize patients as persons with agency and by fostering better communication in court judgments, we can promote a healthcare environment that truly respects patient autonomy and fosters a more equitable and effective healthcare system.

In this patient-centric approach, the emphasis is on supporting patients by facilitating their understanding of information, rather than dismissing them as individuals who "cannot" comprehend or make decisions. In this chapter, building on earlier works (Honneth, 1995; Subramani, 2019; Subramani & Biller-Andorno, 2022), I extend the concept of *respect for persons* to encompass a broader understanding that a *person* must be recognized as political and social agents with their own values and preferences, which ought to be acknowledged within the legal context. However, the rhetoric and construction of the "passive patient" within the court's medical framework, which upholds 'medical authority', provides a normative justification for adopting the "medical professional standard" in the Indian context. This rhetoric implies that patients are not recognized as 'agents' or 'persons' with values and preferences. Instead, they are viewed as passive recipients of care, with their agency effectively sidelined in the decision-making process. This perspective not only undermines patient agency but also reinforces a paternalistic model of healthcare, where the doctor's authority is prioritized over the patient's right to be an active participant in their own care

Although there is a well-established consensus in both medico-legal and bioethical literature that adult patients should be presumed competent and permitted to be decision-makers unless they are rendered clinically or legally "incompetent", here I have demonstrated that Indian law often constructs and perceives "passive patients" as individuals who lack the ability to make decisions or participate in the decision-making process because of social and political structures such as poverty. I argue that that moral attitudes and behaviors that demonstrate respect within institutions can only be achieved when professionals recognize patients and their families as "respect-worthy" individuals—as persons—and actively work to constrain behaviors, attitudes, and actions that disrespect or disregard them. Additionally, a paradigm shift is necessary within the legal framework to replace the "passive patient" narrative and the health/choice dichotomy with a focus on patient agency and effective communication as core components of health discourse. This approach would cultivate a culture of patient-centered care within the healthcare system. Since the purpose of the law is to protect vulnerable individuals and correct injustices, shifting the narrative to view patients as agents who play an active role in their health and medical decisions would promote both legal and moral progress toward a more respectful and equitable legal and social institutions.

While numerous laws and regulations in India aim to protect patient rights, these rights and patients' dignity can only be fully realized when patients are recognized as active political and social agents. Healthcare discourses, particularly among policymakers, health system researchers, and social scientists, have frequently highlighted how the fundamental right of all citizens to adequate healthcare has not been given the highest priority in India (Baxi, 1986a; Dreze & Sen, 1990; Parmar & Wahi, 2011; Pinto, 2021). One way to understand this lack of commitment and prioritization of the right to health and patient rights is by examining the complex relationship between the portrayal of passive patients in modern healthcare narratives and the legal system. As discussed in previous sections of this chapter, the construction of passive patients is both sustained and normalized in legal judgments through the persistence of colonial and upper-caste-class narratives. The *Samira Kohli* case vividly illustrates how legal judgments, intertwined with the authority of the medical profession, are deeply entangled with hierarchies of gender and class. This entanglement serves to subordinate Indian patients, depriving them of socio-political recognition and agency. The legal system's portrayal of patients as passive reinforces these hierarchies, thereby limiting the realization of patients' rights and dignity of persons within the broader framework of healthcare in India.

Upendra Baxi (1982) identified a profound "crisis" within the Indian legal system, highlighting the urgent need for transformation in its normative, cultural, and social dimensions. He observed, and this remains relevant today, that the system has lost its capacity to envision, plan, and build a future centered on justice, often serving the interests of the elite rather than the marginalized majority in India. In a country marked by deep inequalities and inequities health has not be given priority (Baru et al., 2010; Das & Hammer, 2012; Das, 2015; Dreze & Sen, 1990; Joe et al., 2008). The majority of Indians—particularly the poor, women, queer individuals, Dalits, and lower-caste-class communities—are frequently neither acknowledged nor recognized as agents within the legal framework. Drawing inspiration from ongoing anti-caste and anti-imperial-colonial movements, and my personal and professional anchor to lean on to heal, bell hooks (2015), and other critical scholars works (Ambedkar, 1990; Guru, 2009; Guru & Sarukkai, 2018; Honneth, 1995, 2014; Rodrigues, 2024) who emphasize the importance of recognizing the agency and embodied personhood of marginalized and oppressed communities, it becomes clear that the agency of patients is deeply embedded in power relations and inextricably linked to the socio-political context. Without a fundamental recognition of patients, who are persons, as individuals deserving of self-respect and true dignity—by acknowledging their agency—the right to health and patients' rights in India cannot be fully realized. The transformation Baxi calls for is essential, not just within the legal system, but also in the broader recognition of agency among those who have historically been marginalized, ensuring that they are engaged and active participants in their healthcare and in society at large.

For meaningful change to occur within the Indian legal system, particularly in the healthcare context, judges and legal judgments must cultivate an ethical imagination that focuses on the ideological, political, and contextual mechanisms needed to reimagine "Indian patients" as political agents. Only through such a reimagining can the democratic promise of self-determination be realized. Historically, we have seen how the language and sentiments of the upper-class-caste often manifest in colonial and nationalist laws, policies, and practices, reinforcing harmful stereotypes, such as the depiction of patients as "passive". This is evident to varying degrees, whether through explicit statements labeling "these people" as "poor", "ignorant", or "incompetent", or through more subtle references that suggest non-egalitarian and authoritarian ways of thinking.

These perspectives imply that in a country facing vast challenges, "these people" need to place unquestioning trust in healthcare professionals and institutions, without acknowledging or respecting their agency as individuals. This kind of thinking fails to recognize the capacity and agency of all individuals, regardless of their socio-economic status, to engage as active agents in their own healthcare decisions. To move towards a more just and equitable system, it is imperative that the judiciary and the legal system as a whole shift from these entrenched, hierarchical views and begin to view patients as capable political agents who have the right to participate fully in decisions affecting their health and lives, and acknowledge self-respect and true dignity. Only then can we dismantle the stereotypes and power dynamics that have long marginalized significant portions of the population and advance toward a more inclusive and democratic society.

Way Ahead: Dismantling Passive Patient Rhetoric

> Equality may be a fiction but nonetheless one must accept it as the governing principle. A man's power is dependent upon (1) physical heredity, (2) social inheritance or endowment in the form of parental care, education, accumulation of scientific knowledge, everything which enables him to be more efficient than the savage, and finally, (3) on his own efforts. In all these three respects men are undoubtedly unequal. But the question is, shall we treat them as unequal because they are unequal? This is a question which the opponents of equality must answer. From the standpoint of the individualist it may be just to treat men unequally so far as their efforts are unequal. It may be desirable to give as much incentive as possible to the full development of every one's powers. But what would happen if men were treated unequally as they are, in the first two respects?
>
> (Ambedkar, 12 December 1935 (in Ambedkar 1990))

For scholars familiar with Ambedkar and Periyar's writings and speeches, Dalitbahujan, and critical thinkers, it is well known that the key ethical and political issues are self-respect and true/unique dignity, with an emphasis on how intersubjective spaces and sociality provide opportunities for realizing these values and political commitments—or hindering them, such as social inequalities within interpersonal relationships and institutions. Thus, I would argue that addressing the lack of social and political recognition is essential for realizing any values, as it directly impacts one's self-respect, recognition, and true dignity, which are crucial for nurturing one's agency, especially for those who are marginalized.

On 15 August 2024, even after nearly 77 years of independence, it is evident that Indian institutions, whether in law or medicine, continue to be burdened by their colonial past. This is not an indictment of colonial masters but rather of the elite upper-class-caste values and norms of independent India, as it grapples with colonial legacies. You might ask why I refer to this as colonial or upper-class-caste. I use these terms to describe the colonial ways of thinking and the continuities we observe in the norms, ideologies, values, and functioning of institutions, including the structure of legal norms. This is especially true when the "status quo" is maintained—whether in values or norms—by the elites, through assumptions and justifications that are reminiscent of "culture" or "tradition", or through the sheer "passivity" of perceiving citizens.

As we have seen, the logic, narratives, and rhetoric of the "passive patient", who is deemed ignorant or uneducated, are used to justify certain values, principles, and norms. Is this not colonial? Even if this perspective is not accepted, one cannot ignore or deny the legal and historical context where there is a continuous reliance on the legal systems of the UK and US, as seen in the common law tradition, by judges and the legal system. This reliance is evident in cases like *Samira Kohli*. While judges consider the socio-political conditions and realities of India when deciding rulings and setting precedents, how can these judicial reasonings and judgments create space for possibilities, opportunities, or social change when they entirely ignore, disregard, or fail to acknowledge individuals' agency—in this context, the agency of the patient? The problem is not simply that these values are colonial or Eurocentric and thus require an "indigenized" version, which could be equally problematic if it perpetuates power asymmetries. The core issue is that legal institutions and the elites within them do not center the experiences, voices, and stories of the marginalized, nor do they recognize their agency. When examining 22 court cases that referenced *Samira Kohli*, it becomes apparent that these judgments do not center the voices of the vulnerable and marginalised; instead, they perpetuate the values and norms of upper-class-caste rhetoric and narratives.

While the social and political reality is that the majority of the Indian population is poor and not literate, it is flawed to draw causal relationships between poverty and education and a lack of agency. If the voices of the marginalized were centered, judgments and legal institutions would become more aware of how power asymmetries are normalized and sustained in medical institutions and healthcare encounters. They would also recognize how elites—often upper-middle-class-caste-male individuals—exploit and disregard patients, especially within the increasingly privatized and corporatized healthcare system, rather than demanding trust only in these "elites". Instead, the focus of these judgments and institutions should be on addressing the systemic barriers and hegemonic culture that create vulnerability for the majority of Indian patients. Is it not the goal of any legal institution, regulation, or judgment to protect the dignity and rights of patients, particularly those who are vulnerable and poor (with the understanding that poverty is relative and changes across time, space, and context), by recognizing their agency?

Over the past several decades, the concepts of respect for persons and self-determination have gradually supplanted medical paternalism, driving the shift toward patient and person-centered care and promoting patients as agents (often in the narrative of "active participant") in medical decision-making processes. However, as I have illustrated in this chapter, the rhetorical positions within Indian law have largely upheld the notion of the "passive patient". The constructs of the "passive patient" and "doctor knows best" within legal discourse provide ample justification for critically examining patients' rights. The rhetoric in the *Samira Kohli* case, for instance, failed to acknowledge the voices and experiences of patients and disregarded their agency by excluding their values, choices and preferences during medical decision-making processes, ostensibly to protect their health. This rhetoric creates a false dichotomy between health and choice for the patient, rather than recognizing the equal significance of both for the overall well-being of patients and the integrity of the decision-making process.

The analysis in this chapter underscores the need for critically understanding the "rhetoric" embedded in legal processes, judicial opinions, and rules, and introducing new rhetoric or language into the law. This chapter further illustrates the necessity of rethinking the construction of the "patient" in legal and medical contexts, acknowledging the patient's status as an agentic individual within a particular situated sociocultural context who should be valued and respected during medical decision-making processes. Emphasizing patient engagement and effective communication is essential to cultivating a culture of respect and patient-centered care in society. Breaking away from the systems of power that sustain and normalize the status quo is crucial if we are to envision a society grounded in dignity, respect, and justice. This requires a critical reflection on how institutions—including law and medicine, especially in postcolonial countries—embody and perpetuate colonial pasts, elite values, and norms. As Baxi (1982) pointed out, the Indian legal system often betrays the "broad conception of a socialist society in India by being continuously instrumental in promoting the values of the bourgeois legal order" (p. 30). In a country like India, where the majority of the population comprises social and political minorities, the archetypal image of the "passive patient" illustrates how individuals' subjectivities and agency are systematically denied, particularly when a person assumes the role of a patient. This denial of agency is rooted in elite values, ideologies, and norms, which are further exacerbated by systemic inequalities and inequities. To dismantle the archetype of "passive patienthood", we must center recognition and self-respect by recognizing the true dignity and agency of individuals within relational and situated context.

References

Agnes, F. (2001). *Law and gender inequality: The politics of women's rights in India*. Oxford University Press.

Agrawal, A. (2016). Medical negligence: Indian legal perspective. *Annals of Indian Academy of Neurology*, *19*(Suppl 1). https://journals.lww.com/annalsofian/fulltext/2016/19001/medical_negligence__indian_legal_perspective.4.aspx

Ambedkar, B. R. (1990). *Dr. Babasaheb Ambedkar: Writings and speeches, vol. 2*. Government of Maharashtra, Bombay, 243.

Amsterdam, A. G., & Bruner, J. (2009). *Minding the law*. Harvard University Press.

Anand, S., Peter, F., & Sen, A. (2006). *Public health, ethics, and equity*. Oxford University Press, Incorporated. http://ebookcentral.proquest.com/lib/usyd/detail.action?docID=430350

Baru, R., Acharya, A., Acharya, S., Kumar, A. K. S., & Nagaraj, K. (2010). Inequities in access to health services in India: Caste, class and region. *Economic and Political Weekly*, 49–58.

Basu, S. (2015). *The trouble with marriage: Feminists confront law and violence in India* (Vol. 1). University of California Press.

Baxi, P. (2013). *Public secrets of law: Rape trials in India*. Oxford University Press.

Baxi, U. (1982). *The crisis of the Indian legal system. Alternatives in development: Law*. Stranger Journalism.

Baxi, U. (1985). Taking suffering seriously: Social action litigation in the Supreme Court of India. *Third World Legal Studies*, *4*, 107.

Baxi, U. (1986a). From human rights to the right to be human: Some heresies. *India International Centre Quarterly*, *13*(3/4), 185–200.

Baxi, U. (1986b). *Towards a sociology of Indian law* (Vol. 77). Satvahan New Delhi.

Baxi, U. (2000). Postcolonial legality. In *A companion to postcolonial studies* (pp. 540–555). Blackwell Publishing.

Beach, M. C., Duggan, P. S., Cassel, C. K., & Geller, G. (2007). What does 'Respect' mean? Exploring the moral obligation of health professionals to respect patients. *Journal of General Internal Medicine*, *22*(5), 692–695. https://doi.org/10.1007/s11606-006-0054-7

Beauchamp, T. L., & Childress, J. F. (2013). *Principles of biomedical ethics*. Oxford University Press.

Berg, J. W., Appelbaum, P. S., Lidz, C. W., & Parker, L. S. (2001). *Informed consent: Legal theory and clinical practice*. Oxford University Press.

Burnham, J. C. (2012). The death of the sick role. *Social History of Medicine*, *25*(4), 761–776. https://doi.org/10.1093/shm/hks018

Chattopadhyay, S. (2017). Gendering legal discourse: A critical feminist analysis of domestic violence adjudication in India. *The Journal of Law, Social Justice and Global Development*, *20*(2), 1–17.

Childress, J. F. (2017). Needed: A more rigorous analysis of models of decision making and a Richer account of respect for autonomy. *The American Journal of Bioethics*, *17*(11), 52–54. https://doi.org/10.1080/15265161.2017.1382168

Childress, J. F., & Quante, M. (2021). *Thick (Concepts of) autonomy: Personal autonomy in ethics and bioethics* (1st ed. 2022, Vol. 146). Springer Nature. https://doi.org/10.1007/978-3-030-80991-1

Choudhry, S., Khosla, M., & Mehta, P. B. (2016). *The Oxford handbook of the Indian constitution*. Oxford University Press.

Collyer, F. (2018). Envisaging the healthcare sector as a field: Moving from Talcott Parsons to Pierre Bourdieu. *Social Theory & Health, 16*, 111–126.

Das, J., & Hammer, J. (2012). Health and health care policy in India: The case for quality of care. In *The Oxford handbook of the Indian economy*. Routledge, Oxford University Press.

Das, V. (2015). *Affliction: Health, disease, poverty*. Fordham University Press. https://doi.org/10.5422/fordham/9780823261802.001.0001

de Freitas, C., & Martin, G. (2015). Inclusive public participation in health: Policy, practice and theoretical contributions to promote the involvement of marginalised groups in healthcare. *Social Science and Medicine, 135*, 31–39. https://doi.org/10.1016/j.socscimed.2015.04.019

Dhagamwar, V. (2006). *Role and image of law in India: The tribal experience*. Sage.

Dreze, J., & Sen, A. (1990). *Hunger and public action*. Clarendon Press.

Dubbin, L. A., Chang, J. S., & Shim, J. K. (2013). Cultural health capital and the interactional dynamics of patient-centered care. *Social Science & Medicine, 93*, 113–120.

Dunn, M. (2016). Contextualising consent. *Journal of Medical Ethics, 42*(2), 67. https://doi.org/10.1136/medethics-2016-103381

Dunn, M., Fulford, K., Herring, J., & Handa, A. (2019). Between the reasonable and the particular: Deflating autonomy in the legal regulation of informed consent to medical treatment. *Health Care Analysis, 27*, 110–127.

Edozien, L. C. (2015). UK law on consent finally embraces the prudent patient standard. *BMJ, 350*, 1–2.

Epstein, L., Martin, A. D., Quinn, K. M., & Segal, J. A. (2007). Ideological drift among Supreme Court justices: Who, when, and how important. *Northwestern University Law Review, 101*, 1483.

Epstein, R. M., & Street, R. L. (2011). The values and value of patient-centered care. *The Annals of Family Medicine, 9*(2), 100–103.

Faden, R. R., Beauchamp, T. L., & King, N. M. (1986). *A history and theory of informed consent*. Oxford University Press.

Farrell, A. M., & Brazier, M. (2016). Not so new directions in the law of consent? Examining Montgomery v Lanarkshire Health Board. *Journal of Medical Ethics, 42*(2), 85–88.

Feldman, D. (1993). *Civil liberties and human rights in England and Wales* (Vol. 1993). Clarendon Press.

Fochsen, G., Deshpande, K., & Thorson, A. (2006). Power imbalance and consumerism in the doctor-patient relationship: Health care providers' experiences of patient encounters in a rural district in India. *Qualitative Health Research, 16*(9), 1236–1251. https://doi.org/10.1177/1049732306293776

Frank, A. W. (2016). From sick role to narrative subject: An analytic memoir. *Health, 20*(1), 9–21. https://doi.org/10.1177/1363459315615395

Gangoli, G. (2016). *Indian feminisms: Law, patriarchies and violence in India*. Routledge.

Gatowski, S. I., Dobbin, S. A., Richardson, J. T., Ginsburg, G. P., Merlino, M. L., & Dahir, V. (2001). Asking the gatekeepers: A national survey of judges on judging expert evidence in a post-Daubert world. *Law and Human Behavior, 25*, 433–458.

Gillman, H. (2001). What's law got to do with it? Judicial behavioralists test the "legal model" of judicial decision making. *Law & Social Inquiry, 26*(2), 465–504.

Gloppen, S. (2008). Public interest litigation, social rights and social policy. *Inclusive States. Social Policy and Structural Inequalities, Washington: World Bank*, 343–367.

Goodrich, P. (1984a). Law and language: An historical and critical introduction. *Journal of Law and Society, 11*(2), 173–206.

Goodrich, P. (1984b). Rhetoric as jurisprudence: An introduction to the politics of legal language. *Oxford Journal of Legal Studies, 4*, 88.

Gopichandran, V. (2019). *Dynamics of trust in doctor-patient relationship in India: A clinical, social and ethical analysis.* Springer Nature.

Gubrium, E. K., & Pellissery, S. (2013). *The shame of it: Global perspectives on anti-poverty policies.* Policy Press.

Guru, G. (2009). *Humiliation: Claims and context.* Oxford University Press.

Guru, G., & Sarukkai, S. (2018). *The cracked mirror: An Indian debate on experience and theory.* Oxford University Press.

Hahn, R. A., & Kleinman, A. (1983). Biomedical practice and anthropological theory: Frameworks and directions. *Annual Review of Anthropology*, 305–333.

Harrison, N., Hewitt, H., Pandya, P., & Reisel, D. (2018). How Montgomery is reconfiguring consent in the UK. *The Lancet, 392*(10142), 102–104.

Hoffmann, D. E., & Tarzian, A. J. (2001). The girl who cried pain: A bias against women in the treatment of pain. *Journal of Law, Medicine & Ethics, 29*(1), 13–27.

Honneth, A. (1995). *The struggle for recognition: The moral grammar of social conflicts.* Polity Press. http://ebookcentral.proquest.com/lib/usyd/detail.action?docID=4029984

Honneth, A. (2014). *Disrespect: The normative foundations of critical theory.* John Wiley & Sons.

hooks, b. (2015). Choosing the margin as a space of radical openness. In A. Garry & M. Pearsall (Eds.), *Women, knowledge, and reality* (pp. 48–55). Routledge.

Jacob, K. (2014). Informed consent and India. *The National Medical Journal of India, 27*(1), 35–38.

Joe, W., Mishra, U. S., & Navaneetham, K. (2008). Health inequality in India: Evidence from NFHS 3. *Economic and Political Weekly*, 41–47.

Kannabiran, K. (2013). *Tools of justice: Non-discrimination and the Indian constitution.* Routledge India.

Kapur, R. (2013). Gender, sovereignty and the rise of sexual security regime in international law and postcolonial India. *Melbourne Journal of International Law, 14*, 317.

Kapur, R., & Cossman, B. (1996). *Feminist engagement with law in India.* Sage.

Kotiswaran, P. (2017). A bittersweet moment: Indian governance feminism and the 2013 rape law reforms. *Economic and Political Weekly, 52*(25–26), 78–87.

Kuehn, B. M. (2012). Patient-centered care model demands better physician-patient communication. *JAMA, 307*(5), 441–442.

Kumar, S., Mohanraj, R., Rose, A., Paul, M., & Thomas, G. (2012). How 'informed'is informed consent? Findings from a study in South India. *Indian Journal of Medical Ethics, 9*(3), 180–185.

Le Gallez, I., Skopek, J., Liddell, K., Kuhn, I., Sagar, A., & Fritz, Z. (2022). Montgomery's legal and practical impact: A systematic review at 6 years. *Journal of Evaluation in Clinical Practice*, *28*(4), 690–702. https://doi.org/10.1111/jep.13620

MacCormick, N. (2005). *Rhetoric and the rule of law: A theory of legal reasoning*. OUP Oxford.

Madhivanan, P., Krupp, K., Kulkarni, V., Kulkarni, S., Vaidya, N., Shaheen, R., Philpott, S., & Fisher, C. (2014). HIV testing among pregnant women living with HIV in India: Are private healthcare providers routinely violating women's human rights? *BMC International Health and Human Rights*, *14*(1), 7. https://doi.org/10.1186/1472-698X-14-7

Madhok, S. (2014). *Rethinking agency: Developmentalism, gender and rights*. Routledge India.

Mate, M., & Kapiszewski, D. (2013). Public interest litigation and the transformation of the Supreme Court of India. In D. Kapiszewski, G. Silverstein & R. A. Kagan (Eds.), *Consequential courts: Judicial roles in global perspective* (pp. 262–288). Cambridge University Press.

McLean, S. A. (2009). *Autonomy, consent and the law*. Routledge.

Mead, N., & Bower, P. (2000). Patient-centredness: A conceptual framework and review of the empirical literature. *Social Science & Medicine*, *51*(7), 1087–1110.

Montgomery, J. (2017). Patient no longer? What next in healthcare law? *Current Legal Problems*, *70*(1), 73–109.

Narain, V. (2001). *Gender and community: Muslim women's rights in India*. University of Toronto Press.

Paramasivan, S., Davies, P., Richards, A., Wade, J., Rooshenas, L., Mills, N., Realpe, A., Raj, J. P., Subramani, S., & Ives, J. (2021). What empirical research has been undertaken on the ethics of clinical research in India? A systematic scoping review and narrative synthesis. *BMJ Global Health*, *6*(5), e004729.

Parmar, S., & Wahi, N. (2011). Citizens, courts and the right to health: Between promise and progress. In *Litigating health rights* (pp. 155–189). Harvard University Press.

Parsons, T. (1975). The sick role and the role of the physician reconsidered. *The Milbank Memorial Fund Quarterly. Health and Society*, *53*(3), 257–278. JSTOR. https://doi.org/10.2307/3349493

Pellissery, S. (2008). Social hierarchies, economic inequalities and interpersonal relationships: An overview from India. *Interpersona: An International Journal on Personal Relationships*, *2*(2), 243–259. https://doi.org/10.5964/ijpr.v2i2.27

Pellissery, S., & Mathew, L. (2013). Thick poverty, thicker society and thin state: Policy spaces for human dignity in India. In E. K. Gubrium, S. Pellissery, & I. Lødemel (Eds.), *The shame of it: Global perspectives on anti-poverty policies* (pp. 37–60). Bristol University Press; Cambridge Core. https://doi.org/10.46692/9781447308720.004

Pilnick, A., & Dingwall, R. (2011). On the remarkable persistence of asymmetry in doctor/patient interaction: A critical review. *Social Science & Medicine*, *72*(8), 1374–1382. https://doi.org/10.1016/j.socscimed.2011.02.033

Pinto, E. P. (2021). Health care jurisprudence and health justice: Procedural and substantive justice dimensions. In E. P. Pinto (Ed.), *Health justice in India: Citizenship, power and health care jurisprudence* (pp. 177–218). Springer Singapore. https://doi.org/10.1007/978-981-15-8143-4_4

Rhode, D. L. (2013). Feminist critical theories. In *Feminist legal theories* (pp. 109–130). Routledge.

Rodrigues, V. (2024). *Ambedkar's political philosophy: A grammar of public life from the social margins.* Oxford University Press.

Sakalys, J. A. (2000). The political role of illness narratives. *Journal of Advanced Nursing, 31*(6), 1469–1475. https://doi.org/10.1046/j.1365-2648.2000.01461.x

Sanwal, A., Kumar, S., Sahni, P., & Nundy, S. (1996). Informed consent in Indian patients. *Journal of the Royal Society of Medicine, 89*(4), 196–198.

Schermer, M. (2002). *The different faces of autonomy: Patient autonomy in ethical theory and hospital practice* (Vol. 13). Springer Science & Business Media.

Schneider, A., & Ingram, H. (1993). Social construction of target populations: Implications for politics and policy. *The American Political Science Review, 87*(2), 334–347. JSTOR. https://doi.org/10.2307/2939044

Secker, B. (1999). Labeling patient (in) competence: A feminist analysis of medico-legal discourse. *Journal of Social Philosophy, 30*(2), 295–314. https://doi.org/10.1111/0047-2786.00019

Sen, A. (2001). Health equity: Perspectives, measurability, and criteria. *Challenging Inequities in Health: From Ethics to Action, 69*, 75.

Shankar, S. (2012). The judiciary, policy, and politics in India 1. In B. Dressel (Ed.), *The judicialization of politics in Asia* (pp. 56–76). Routledge.

Shim, J. K. (2010). Cultural health capital: A theoretical approach to understanding health care interactions and the dynamics of unequal treatment. *Journal of Health and Social Behavior, 51*(1), 1–15.

Sircar, O., Kapur, R., & Cossman, B. (2016). The fraught terrain of law and feminism: 20 years of subversive sites. *Socio-Legal Review, 12*, 133.

Subramani, S. (2017). Patient autonomy within real or valid consent: Samira Kohli's case. *Indian Journal of Medical Ethics, 2*(3), 184–189. https://doi.org/10.20529/IJME.2017.038

Subramani, S. (2019). The rhetoric of the 'Passive Patient' in Indian medical negligence cases. *Asian Bioethics Review, 11*(4), 349–366. https://doi.org/10.1007/s41649-019-00106-1

Subramani, S., & Biller-Andorno, N. (2022). Revisiting respect for persons: Conceptual analysis and implications for clinical practice. *Medicine, Health Care and Philosophy.* https://doi.org/10.1007/s11019-022-10079-y

Tanenbaum, S. J. (2015). What is patient-centered care? A typology of models and missions. *Health Care Analysis, 23*, 272–287.

Venkatapuram, S. (2013). *Health justice: An argument from the capabilities approach.* John Wiley & Sons.

Venkatapuram, S., & Marmot, M. (2009). Epidemiology and social justice in light of social determinants of health research. *Bioethics, 23*(2), 79–89.

Walker, R., Kyomuhendo, G. B., Chase, E., Choudhry, S., Gubrium, E. K., Nicola, J. Y., Lødemel, I., Mathew, L., Mwiine, A., & Pellissery, S. (2013). Poverty in global perspective: Is shame a common denominator? *Journal of Social Policy, 42*(2), 215–233.

Ward, J., Kalsi, D., Chandrashekar, A., Fulford, B., Lee, R., Herring, J., & Handa, A. (2020). Shared decision making and consent post-Montgomery, UK Supreme Court judgement supporting best practice. *Patient Education and Counseling, 103*(12), 2609–2612. https://doi.org/10.1016/j.pec.2020.05.017

3 Construction of Incompetent Patient

Stepping Back: Revisiting Competence

As we saw in the last chapter, in the landmark Supreme Court judgment of *Samira Kohli v. Prabha Manchanda* in 2008, the judges stated that the hysterectomy and salpingo-oophorectomy constituted an unauthorized invasion and interference with the patient's body, amounting to a tortious act of assault and battery, and therefore a deficiency in service. However, the doctor was not held negligent, as the procedure was performed "in excess of consent but in good faith and for the benefit of the patient". The doctor was asked to pay compensation of Rs. 25,000.

> What we are considering in this case, is not the duties or obligations of doctors in government charitable hospitals where treatment is free or on actual cost basis. We are concerned with doctors in private practice and hospitals and nursing homes run commercially... Bringing in the American concepts and standards of treatment procedures and disclosure of risks, consequences and choices will inevitably bring in higher cost-structure of American medical care. Patients in India cannot afford them. People in India still have great regard and respect for Doctors. The Members of medical profession have also, by and large, shown care and concern for the patients. There is an atmosphere of trust and implicit faith in the advice given by the Doctor. The India psyche rarely questions or challenges the medical advice. Having regard to the conditions obtaining in India, as also the settled and recognized practices of medical fraternity in India, we are of the view that to nurture the doctor-patient relationship on the basis of trust, the extent and nature of information required to be given by doctors should continue to be governed by the Bolam test rather than the 'reasonably prudential patient' test evolved in Canterbury... *Samira Kohli v. Prabha Manchanda*, 2008, p. 9

From the above quote and a close reading of the narratives in this judgment, one can observe how the judges uphold gendered and class-based norms and values. The narrative assumes a traditional, perhaps authoritative and paternalistic,

DOI: 10.4324/9781003129998-4

dynamic in which doctors are the unquestioned authority figures, while patients are often implicitly positioned as passive recipients of care. The *Samira Kohli* case is not an isolated incident; rather, it exemplifies routine and everyday decisions that frequently discriminate against patients, particularly those from marginalized communities. Similar to the *Samira Kohli* case, there are countless instances in India where doctors routinely make decisions on behalf of patients "in their best interest", influenced by their own values and perceptions of the social categories of patients within specific institutional cultures.

Based on my doctoral fieldwork, which involved listening to doctors, nurses, patients, and family members, it is clear that situations like this are not merely individual problems and/or rare. Learning from other studies from India (Baru et al., 2010; Chattopadhyay, 2018; Das & Hammer, 2012; Das, 2015; Jungari & Chauhan, 2017; Madhiwalla et al., 2018; Ravindran & Gaitonde, 2018; Sen & Iyer, 2012), they are not isolated issues confined to a few select doctors or institutions. I observed how everyday social inequalities are subtly or overtly reproduced within the language of morality and culture in healthcare settings. In this chapter, I illustrate how these routine generalized assumptions expose the underlying politics of everyday disrespect and how patients are often not recognized as agents from the perspective of healthcare professionals. Patients are frequently blamed or disregarded, while doctors and nurses, to varying degrees, obscure the medical decision-making process from the broader socio-cultural and political context in which healthcare interactions and decisions occur. Physicians' judgments and assumptions significantly influence how they perceive patients' needs and consider their values, often shaped by socio-cultural-political assumptions about social identities and categories such as class, gender, caste, religion, profession, geography, and age. These existing social inequalities are exacerbated or reproduced, leading to a failure to respect patients' agency.

By situating the discourse between physicians and patients within their broader social and political contexts, these seemingly incompatible macro and micro approaches are reconceived, revealing how social structure and social interaction are interrelated and mutually reinforcing. This pattern has been evident since the colonial and post-independence eras and persists today, showing how doctors often treat marginalized communities with disrespect. Medical professionals are shaped by the hidden curriculum of their institutions. For instance, a study at the All India Institute of Medical Sciences (AIIMS) in Delhi highlights how social inequalities are reinforced and how power imbalances are maintained in both doctor–patient interactions and the training of medical students (Ruddock, 2021), and in other works we can see how caste-class-gender becomes embedded in medical education and healthcare system (Barua & Verma, 2021; Karpagam, 2021). Many studies, from other countries too, illustrate how physicians' evaluative judgments influence patient health outcomes, often placing marginalized communities at greater risk when patient values and needs are overlooked (Cheston, 2022; Dolezal, 2022; Kelly & Haidet, 2007; Mead & Bower, 2000; Park et al., 2021; Smith-Oka, 2015, 2021, 2022). It is unsurprising that decisions regarding health and illness must account for the broader social and political context, as values and norms are sustained and normalized in ways that, whether consciously or unconsciously, benefit those in privileged positions.

Numerous studies have established that marginalized individuals often experience worse health outcomes and diminished well-being due to inadequate care and systemic barriers to accessing care, including broader issues like insufficient resources allocated to health in general (Baru et al., 2010; Ravindran & Gaitonde, 2018; Sen, 2011). Doctors and nurses often become agents of control and power, deciding whom to share information with, who deserves to know, and whose voice should be heard. As a result, healthcare encounters become sites of social and political power. Research in medical sociology and anthropology has shown how institutional and bureaucratic practices create a web of constraints—whether in terms of time, material, or human resources (Banerjee, 2022; Das, 2006, 2015; Kannabiran, 2013; Majumdar, 2017). In this chapter, I show through narratives and observations how the evaluative judgments and attitudes of healthcare professionals sustain and reproduce the upper-class-caste status quo, shaping everyday healthcare encounters. While many sociological studies have highlighted the impact of paternalistic behaviors and attitudes on interactions between patients and physicians, much of the healthcare ethics debate has distanced itself from the social, cultural, and political realities that shape how patients, especially those from marginalized communities, are often treated with disregard. I hope this chapter illustrates the need to understand the attitudes of doctors and nurses within their socio-political contexts and emphasizes that social and normative discourses, including those in bioethics, cannot detach themselves from this reality.

Similar to what we observed in the *Samira Kohli* case, medical decisions are often structured around evaluative judgments and normative assumptions about what is best for patients, shaped by social, cultural, and institutional factors. However, it is essential to recognize that these healthcare interactions are micro-political. To bring about meaningful social change within institutional culture and ethos, the actions, decisions, and attitudes of doctors and nurses must be critically reflected upon. While judges and healthcare professionals may acknowledge social and political realities—such as the stark divide in healthcare access due to economic constraints—they often endorse a tiered system where comprehensive care becomes a privilege for the affluent rather than a right and dignity-based. References to overburdened government hospitals and patients from lower socio-economic backgrounds accepting whatever care they can get, with financial limitations dictating the quality and extent of their treatment, illustrate how the hierarchical structure is preserved rather than challenged in these judgments.

Over the last few decades, due to various civil rights and patient rights movements, particularly in the US, UK, and Western European countries, there has been a shift from a paternalistic model of patient care towards consumer models, shared decision-making, and patient-centered approaches where patient autonomy is central (Beauchamp & Childress, 2013; Elwyn et al., 2012; Faden et al., 1986; Hoving et al., 2010). In these patient-centered care models, as discussed in Chapter 1, the patient becomes an active and engaged participant—an "ideal patient" who engages in decision-making, seeks information, takes responsibility for their health, and exercises self-control while adhering to doctors' orders. The patient is thus presumed to have the capacity and right to make decisions and to provide informed consent. The medico-legal, ethical, and health services literature emphasizes that for a patient's consent to be valid, they must have adequate capacity (competency), be provided with sufficient information about the proposed treatment(s), and voluntarily agree to and authorize the treatment. Failing to meet any of these conditions not only invalidates consent but also renders the clinical interaction between the doctor and the patient, or their family, meaningless. Labeling a patient as "incapacitated/incompetent" restricts their ability and authority to make decisions, which can have significant moral, social, and legal implications.

The meaning and definition of "capacity" as a decision-making ability and "competence" as a legal term have been widely discussed, with these terms often used interchangeably to describe a person's ability to make decisions (Berg & Makielski, 2014; Bielby, 2005). The concept of capacity/competence is generally understood as an individual's ability to understand, engage with others, and communicate decisions. Scholars have proposed various methods and criteria to assess whether a person is competent (Dunn et al., 2006; Sessums et al., 2011; Torroella Carney et al., 2001; Lamont et al., 2013). Patient competence—the ability of patients to comprehend and make decisions—is considered a crucial prerequisite for the informed consent process and is fundamental to respecting patient autonomy and self-determination in medical decision-making (Faden et al., 1986; Lysaught, 2004). In much of the bioethics and medical ethics literature, patients are generally assumed to possess the competence to make medical decisions and express preferences in clinical settings. Unless an individual is legally or clinically classified as incompetent—such as minors or those deemed mentally incompetent based on legal or clinical evaluations—competence is the standard criterion for determining who can make autonomous decisions. In everyday clinical interactions, physicians or nurses typically hold the authority to assess whether patients are socially and legally "competent or incompetent". When patients' wishes conflict with practitioners' recommendations, the competence of the patient is often scrutinized and further evaluated through legal and clinical assessments. However, these assessments of competence are not absolute; scholars have questioned the foundations and validity of these evaluations (Breden & Vollmann, 2004; Hermann et al., 2016; Tan et al., 2006).

Despite the lack of consensus on what constitutes competency, and the standards required to determine it, physicians routinely assess patients during clinical interactions. However, these assessments are often influenced by social factors such as class, caste, and gender, rather than being based solely on medical conceptions of illness or health, thereby perpetuating societal inequalities. When examining the discourse surrounding the notion of (in)competency, it is crucial to critically consider how it is understood and practiced by healthcare practitioners within hospital settings. Existing studies tend to focus on legal and clinical assessments to define "capacity" and decision-making ability as objective truths (Dunn et al., 2006). Few studies, however, have explored the influence of factors such as values, judgments, and emotions (Hermann et al., 2016). As a result, medical ethics, legal, and medical literature often overlook the subjective and social interpretations and meanings constructed by practitioners that shape their actions. Ignoring these subjective constructions in practitioner–patient interactions can have significant implications for both practice and theory. Treating (in)competence as an objective measure of an individual's capacity or decision-making ability disregards the nuanced and subjective nature of these assessments. This approach pays little attention to the subjective meanings and constructions of competence, capacity, and decision-making. Although the literature acknowledges the lack of consensus on competency standards, there is less focus on how the concept of incompetence is constructed through the subjective interpretations of practitioners, who wield varying degrees of authority in specific contexts.

In clinical practice and ethics literature, medical paternalism is generally understood as a situation where a practitioner interferes with a patient's choices or decisions regarding their treatment in order to protect or promote the patient's well-being or act in their best interests (Bullock, 2018; Groll, 2014). Many studies have highlighted the persistence of paternalistic practices within clinical interactions, hospital settings, and legal contexts. While soft paternalism, applied to children or incapacitated individuals, is not typically considered morally problematic, hard paternalism—where competent patients are restricted or prevented from making their own care decisions—is widely regarded as morally objectionable. However, recent debates have controversially justified paternalism as ethically valid when dealing with marginalized communities, citing socio-economic and cultural factors.

While the relationship between access to healthcare and social categories has been well-established in health services research, and sociological and anthropological studies (Baru et al., 2010; Jungari & Chauhan, 2017; Kowal & Afshar, 2015; Ravindran & Gaitonde, 2018; Subramanian et al., 2008), the role of healthcare professionals' perceptions of patients, particularly in terms of stereotypes, has gained more recent attention. It is crucial to understand how stereotypes sustain, perpetuate, and normalize dominant values and norms within healthcare settings. Some studies on the hidden curriculum in medical education and in hospital settings reveal how medical students learn to become doctors, showing how values and norms are ingrained through everyday perceptions, routines, and rituals (Jeffery, 1979; Joyce & Jeske, 2019; Kelly & May, 1982; Smith-Oka, 2021; Sointu, 2017). I would see these works analyze different categories of patients—such as good, bad, deviant, or unworthy—often linked to the roles patients play within the spectrum of the sick role. For instance, "bad" patients are those who refuse to accept the "sick role", while "good" patients embrace it or accept any characterization of themselves as "ill" (Brüggemann et al., 2022; Dingwall & Murray, 1983; Joyce & Jeske, 2019; Kelly & May, 1982). Scholars critique biomedicine's hidden curriculum along with existing social norms within their context for creating and reinforcing these categories (Campbell et al., 2015; Chuang et al., 2010; Kenison et al., 2017; Sointu, 2017; Steinberg, 2016).

Most of the discourse and studies on the social and cultural capital of health, where stereotypes and categories of patients are closely examined, are often situated within US, UK, or European contexts. Often, these studies explore the conception of the "ideal" patient through critiques of the biomedical model. In this model, the doctor assumes the role of medical authority, with the medical gaze determining what is "normal or abnormal", focusing more on the medicalization of bodies than on the lived experience of illness and health. As a result, the patient becomes decontextualized and disembodied, reduced to an object of the doctor's control. Rather than assuming that patients passively accept medical advice due to a lack of resources or confidence to question it, judges and healthcare professionals should recognize how the system could empower and acknowledge them as situated and engaged agents in their own treatment, deserving of respectful attitudes and practices. In the remainder of this chapter, I will demonstrate that it is not just judges, as shown in Chapter 2, who treat patients as "passive" or "ignorant", but also healthcare professionals who perpetuate the archetypal image of the "incompetent", thus "passive patient", fostering a culture of disrespect in clinical practice.

Construing Incompetent Patient

The subjective meanings that individuals attribute to perceptions, beliefs, and values within a structure are socially constructed through interpretation. In this context, I examine the meanings, perceptions, and actions related to discussions about treatment options and the risks of elective clinical surgery between doctors and patients or their family members. By exploring these interactions, I aim to illustrate how healthcare professionals, doctors and nurses, construct the image of the "incompetent patient" and how this construction influences their interactions and behaviors. Based on my analysis from fieldwork, doctors often assess patients, and their family members, based on their perceptions of the patients' ability to understand information related to treatments, including the available options and associated risks. They frequently categorize patients and family members into two groups: (1) those who are poor, illiterate, uneducated, scared, and/or likely to "run away" (referred to as "incapables") and (2) those who are seen as "troublemakers" or "critical cases" (typically those who ask questions or come from high-risk or medically uncertain situations; these patients are referred to as "cases"). I offer a deeper analysis of the "incapables" category, as it plays a dominant role in the rhetoric and construction of the concept of an incompetent patient. The constructed notion of incompetence is often applied to those patients and family members whom doctors perceive as "incapables", thereby deeming them incapable of meaningful participation in clinical interactions.

When I spoke with a doctor from a government hospital (GH) about his practice in general when sharing information about treatment, he expressed frustration with the lack of time and resources, saying, "These people from such areas just waste our time. They won't improve their lifestyle if they keep smoking and drinking, and half the time they're not really present. Nanag enna panrade [what should we be doing], they are just like that, and we just decide for them what is best". Similarly, another doctor from GH shared his frustration, stating, "These people just want free medicines and attention. Where do we have the time or the resources? They just wait here". In these conversations, the reference to "these people" often implicitly points to individuals from certain lower socio-economic and caste communities. These stereotypes lead physicians to view such patients as undeserving of the necessary attention or time, thereby reinforcing the social and moral marginalization experienced by these communities. This illustrates how doctors often perceive the health issues of individuals from lower socio-economic and caste backgrounds as self-inflicted, holding them responsible for their health problems without acknowledging the broader structural and systemic issues at play.

Many studies have demonstrated how socio-economic status affects communication in clinical settings (Heritage & Maynard, 2006; Smith et al., 2010). Doctors often adopt a less consultative approach with lower socio-economic patients, providing minimal information and emotional support (Richardson et al., 2012; Willems et al., 2005). When discussing the process of informed consent, a surgeon from a government hospital revealed his approach, which is steeped in paternalism and shaped by assumptions about his patients' capabilities. He shared:

> It is a form that will be signed by the patient and family, as part of a routine. Here, they may not understand. Many people may not understand! The best way to ease the issue of informed consent for them [patients and family members] is to tell them what I would have done if I were in their place. I tell them what I would do and how I would accept the complications. This is how I do it most of the time. As they are uneducated, it is not easy to make them understand… also, they mostly say, *Nengale solenga AAyya (you only decide, Sir)*

This quote, from a 41-year-old male general surgeon, encapsulates a common narrative in medical practice where patients from lower socio-economic backgrounds are not seen as agents but as individuals' incapable of understanding the complexities of their health decisions. In the government hospital, amidst the weight of hurried decisions and overburdened system, the surgeon's words echo a troubling sentiment. "These people", he implies, are not worth the time it takes to explain, to engage, to respect. They are viewed through a lens of impatience and prejudice, where their socio-economic and caste backgrounds reduce them to beings undeserving of detailed attention or empathetic communication. This narrative extends beyond one surgeon or one hospital; it reflects a pervasive attitude that devalues the lived experiences of marginalized communities. These stereotypes, deeply embedded in the psyche of medical professionals, perpetuate the social and moral marginalization of patients from these communities. The health issues of marginalized individuals are dismissed as self-inflicted, their struggles overlooked, and their voices silenced. In this context, the process of informed consent becomes a hollow ritual, stripped of its essence of agency.

This narrative also captures how doctors' perceptions of the consent process are dominated by a procedural understanding, where simply completing a form is deemed sufficient. They perceive informed consent as merely a routine procedure that needs to be simplified, particularly for patients in government hospitals, who are often uneducated and unable to grasp the nuances of the informed consent process. Doctors "ease" the process by adopting a "to do" (sign) as "I do" approach, highlighting the implicit expectation that patients place blind faith and trust in their doctors. This is further justified by the patients or family members who say, "You better decide on our behalf". My analysis revealed that practitioners often view informed consent as a mere formality or routine requirement for hospital management. These findings are unsurprising. Doctors in public hospitals tend to tailor their communication with patients based on the patients' education levels and socio-economic backgrounds. However, the tailoring of information in these cases is not intended to help patients understand their situation, decisions, or improve their health despite social inequalities; rather, it utilizes social categories to justify the unfair distribution of time, attention, and information.

Consider the following excerpt from an interview with a surgeon at a private hospital, which encapsulates this approach:

> I believe the way we explain things to patients varies depending on their education and socioeconomic status. For instance, I don't think it's always necessary to be completely transparent with every patient—in fact, I often am not. Take, for example, a patient from a lower socioeconomic background with limited education. If I start detailing the complications associated with cardiac surgery, they might get scared and run away. So, I keep things simple and avoid going into too much detail. On the other hand, there are middle-class patients who come in after doing their own research online. With them, I have to go into more detail because they tend to be more demanding. These patients are harder to deal with, so I often end up asserting my authority as a doctor and insisting they follow my advice without question.

This reflection highlights the intersections of class, education, and power in the clinical settings. It underscores how medical professionals, consciously or unconsciously, navigate these intersections, often reinforcing existing hierarchies. In doing so, they may perpetuate a practice where the less privileged receive less attention, information, and agency in their healthcare decisions, while those with more resources and knowledge demand—and often receive—greater involvement or dismissed. However, when these more informed patients are perceived as "troublemakers", it reflects a defensive practice among medical professionals. This dynamic not only affects the patient experience but also highlights broader issues of inequality within the healthcare system.

Most doctors emphasized that they withhold detailed information from patients and their families, especially if they are perceived as uneducated, unless the case is high-risk. They justify this by claiming that too much information could "scare" the patients. A male neurosurgeon from a public hospital explained, "The best options are, of course, from us, as we know... we do not discuss in great detail because that sometimes scares patients". Doctors tend to be more forthcoming with those they consider troublemakers or those involved in high-risk cases, as these patients are more likely to question and potentially file complaints. Patients from the middle class, particularly those who are educated or use the Internet, are viewed as difficult. One surgeon expressed this sentiment clearly:

> There is a huge difference between patients from the middle class and the very rich and the very poor. Usually, the very rich and the very poor are easy to handle. It's the middle class who have half-baked knowledge; they think they know everything but, actually, they don't know anything. So, it's quite difficult to explain things to those people when the patient has complications. They will say, 'Oh! you didn't tell us this.' No, actually, I didn't, so that you would go ahead with the surgery!

Similarly, nurses in both public and private hospitals often express frustration, perceiving patients as incapable of understanding medical information. A senior nurse from a public hospital remarked, "See, lay people [patients], they don't understand. Even if we explain, they can't grasp it. For example, if something happens post-operatively, even mildly, when we go to treat it, they start asking why it's happening. They should have been informed earlier. Sometimes, it seems like they would understand, but later they'll say, 'If we had known this, we wouldn't have gone through with the surgery; we should have been told.' They say, 'You say one thing and do another... So, even after explaining, we still hear this".

These narratives reveal a troubling dynamic in which medical professionals dismiss patients' capacities to understand and participate in their own healthcare, leading to a paternalistic approach that undermines patient's self-respect, dignity and fosters distrust. With a slight shrug, one of the woman doctors from government hospital remarked, "Sometimes, women from the slums or rural areas come in without any real problem, just seeking attention". The casual observation when doctor shared it with me, was an evaluative judgement that these women, often marginalized by poverty and location, were not seen as individuals with legitimate concerns. Instead, their visits were reduced to a mere nuisance, an unwarranted demand on limited medical resources. For the doctor, these women's concerns seemed trivial, easily brushed off as cries for attention rather than cries for care. The assumptions were, because of their background, their problems couldn't be serious. They were, in her view, exaggerating—perhaps even inventing their discomfort. The weight of their experiences, their pain, and their health anxieties went unnoticed, which we could see how patients and family members share these othering experiences in next chapter. In a system where medical authority often dictates the terms of care, their voices were quietly disregarded, their needs overshadowed by the assumption that their struggles weren't real enough to deserve the respect and care. In this seemingly simple remark, I could feel the structures of domination at work, the way they weave themselves into our everyday language, our interactions, and our institutions. This is how disrespect is normalized, how it is cloaked in the authority of medical knowledge, and how it perpetuates the cycle of exclusion. The doctor's words, in their casual dismissal, stirred in me that deep anger and rage at how easy it is for those in power to disregard the most vulnerable and marginalised.

Similar perceptions extend to patients from certain religions and castes. An obstetrician from a government hospital commented, "No matter how much information we provide, these people will not learn. For instance, yesterday, I had a woman from a particular area (implying she was Muslim), and she has now visited almost 10 times for vaginal infections. These people don't seem to understand cleanliness or hygiene, or maybe they just don't care... (nodding)... Do you think I can sit and explain it to her, and she will understand? Where do I have the time?" Similarly, some nurses in government hospitals often refer to "these people" from marginalized socio-economic groups, suggesting that they need to be "strict" with them to manage their care. For instance, a senior female nurse at the government hospital claimed, "See, these people don't comply if we talk nicely. We have to manage them to provide care". These perceptions, along with stereotypes based on religion, gender, class, and caste, lead to a patronizing attitude that dismisses patients' knowledge, values, social life, and experiences, showing disrespect while ignoring broader systemic problems and structural challenges. These narratives and quotes illustrate how stereotypes based on class, caste, gender, socio-economic status, and cultural background lead to biased medical practices. Such stereotypes and prejudices undermine patient agency, self-respect, dignity, and quality of care, perpetuating the passive and incompetent patient archetype and reinforcing social, moral and political marginalization.

For many doctors in India, queerness continues to be perceived through a pathologizing lens often. Rooted in colonial legacies and rigid biomedical gaze that classified queer experiences and identities as illnesses or perversions, this perception reduces queer individuals to clinical cases rather than full persons. Doctors often approach queer patients with suspicion, pity, or moral judgment, erasing their agency and humanity. As one surgeon remarked, "They come to us asking for impossible things. It's not medicine—I think its social confusion". Medical professionals, accustomed to heteronormative scripts, tend to dismiss or disregard the lived realities of queer communities, such as the social, emotional, and structural violence they endure. For instance, trans and gender-nonconforming patients may encounter blatant discrimination, from misgendering to outright denial of care, justified through paternalistic attitudes that claim to know what is "best" for them. One of the gynecologists while sharing her experiences of how they help patients in private care, mentioned "these days there is some trend, we only see this when I do consultancy in these hospitals (referring to corporate hospital)…Sometimes, these women don't realize what they need. We're helping them". During my fieldwork in a government hospital, I twice observed a security guard and a male nurse treating a transgender person disrespectfully. The security guard, through his bodily gestures, was trying to "get rid" of the person from the premises, and the conversation was extremely hostile toward them. I felt frustrated and angry as I witnessed this, so I approached to ask why the security guard was behaving that way. Even though I was scared at that moment, the guard gave me a look that seemed to say, 'What's your business here?' and dismissively said, "Yenna!" (what?!). I feel guilty for not being more assertive. There have been so many instances where I have failed to stand up for myself and for others in similar situations, as witnessing outright discrimination and suffering while doing fieldwork in hospital settings.

The expectation of passive patienthood within healthcare perpetuates a form of medical paternalism that denies queer patients the right to self-determination. This is reflected not only in clinical practices but also in broader healthcare policies that fail to address health needs of LGBTQ+ individuals. Doctors often refuse to engage with queer patients as partners in their care, choosing instead to reinforce moralistic and hierarchical norms. By reducing queer individuals to their bodies—to sites of deviance, pathology, or shame—doctors strip them of their humanity, their voices, and their ability to advocate for their well-being. As reflected in the quotes, we can see moral habitus and norms, and how passive patient archetype is sustained by paternalism that reinforces structural violence. Many studies have established how the cumulative impact of these practices is devastating. Queer patients, especially those from lower socio-econmic groups, are pushed to the margins of healthcare systems, either avoiding care altogether or enduring systemic violence in healthcare settings. Their mistrust in medical institutions grows, as they internalize the pervasive message that their lives and health do not matter. This cycle of dehumanization not only harms individuals but also reflects a broader failure of healthcare systems, and beyond, to recognize intersectional experiences of those marginalised (Pandya and Redcay, 2020; Raghuram et al., 2024).

Examining how and on what basis individuals assess others helps to uncover the underlying assumptions behind their taken-for-granted understandings. An analysis of the doctors' narratives reveals the assumptions underlying their perceptions of patients and family members as "incapables". These perceptions are often based on factors such as class, caste, gender, level of education, and psychological responses during illness, such as anxiety and fear. Individuals who are poor, illiterate, uneducated, or scared, as well as those who might "run away", are perceived as unable to understand information. As a result, doctors often refrain from discussing alternative treatments and the risks involved in elective surgery with them. These observations align with findings from various health communication studies and health services investigations, which have explored how societal structures and health systems influence clinical interactions across different settings (Basu & Dutta, 2007; Fochsen et al., 2006; Madhivanan et al., 2014; Verlinde et al., 2012).

Individuals act based on the meanings they attribute to practices, and these meanings, in turn, structure their behavior. Doctors' subjective understanding of incompetence shapes their approach during clinical interactions. The assessments doctors make regarding the capacity of patients and their family members—based on perceived circumstantial characteristics such as social and psychological factors—significantly influence their practices and actions. Based on their assumptions and evaluations of the patients' and families' ability to understand information, doctors typically practice in three major ways: (1) they refrain from discussing or engaging; (2) they make decisions on behalf of patients and family members; and (3) they engage in discussion only if it is a critical or high-risk case.

In both government and private hospitals, it was observed that doctors often perceive themselves as acting in the best interest of patients, making decisions based on their medical expertise and knowledge. For instance, a female ophthalmology surgeon from a GH remarked,

> We do things on a routine basis with the best intentions and do whatever we can. There is a difference between patients in GHs and those in PHs. GHs are mostly for people below the poverty line. Most of the patients here are either uneducated or poor. They come here because they don't have any other options. They don't understand the nature and extent of their disease. They just think that if they come here, everything will be resolved through some magic that doctors perform. The doctors are pushed into a situation where they have to play God. So, we can't discuss things with them.

It is evident that doctors perceive patients and family members at government hospitals (GHs) as mostly poor and uneducated, with patients often assigning a "God-like" role to the doctors. Consequently, the power to make decisions without discussion, ostensibly in the patients' best interests, is rooted in the doctors' constructed perceptions of 'passive patients, which is ingrained in hierarchical oppressive systems, due to being poor and/or uneducated. We can observe how poverty rhetoric becomes part of the justification for one's attitudes and behaviors, similar to what is discussed in Chapter 2. Doctors adopt the role of decision-makers and refrain from discussing information with them. As noted earlier, doctors in private hospitals (PHs) exhibit similar behavior, making decisions without discussion when patients and their families are perceived as poor or illiterate. One PH surgeon remarked,

> If they [the patients] are poor or from the lower class, we don't discuss the details with them. We just tell them to get the required things

> done, warning them that they may die if they don't. They can't understand anything! In India, people can't understand. I don't discuss much because I can't afford to waste my time. We decide in their best interests. We are trained to do good for them.

The above statements illustrate how doctors' views and perceptions shape their interaction process. Another female urology surgeon in a GH stated, "If we tell the patients anything, they may get scared. I can't explain to these people and make them understand. They want us to decide for them. So, we do that". This underlying assumption of their role as "powerful benefactor" allows doctors to maintain a position of power in the relationship and during interactions while believing they are doing in patients' best interest. Across both types of hospitals, doctors consistently mentioned that they make decisions for patients because they are expected to do so. As I listened to doctors, it was evident that doctors' perceptions of patients and their families influence their actions, leading them to avoid discussions and make decisions on their behalf. Thus, doctors assume the role of decision-makers for their patients and their families. As noted earlier, middle-class patients and family members, high-risk patients, and those who question or are potential "suers" are often perceived as troublemakers. Many nurses in GHs expressed frustration with administrative tasks and a lack of time. For instance, a senior nurse in the O&G ward remarked, "Madam, we need to shout at them; otherwise, they will not listen. We will take care of them, that's our job. We make sure they get well soon". The nurses viewed themselves as responsible for both caregiving and administrative duties, leaving them with little time to spare. They also held positions of authority and were perceived as such by patients and their families. The nurses policed the wards and acted as strict disciplinarians.

One of the doctors I interviewed, who had a deeper engagement with the issue of information discussion and disclosure, suggested that these practices are influenced by various factors, including education and training. He noted that doctors in India are indoctrinated to adopt an authoritative stance, particularly within the Indian context. Comparing his experience in India with his experience abroad, he described how doctors in Indian medical institutions and hospitals are mentored by their seniors and peers to uphold this authoritative approach.

> I have also worked in the United Kingdom (UK), where I have to sit down and spend at least 15 to 20 minutes to get consent. I have to talk to the patient and get consent for all the patients on the list; only after this will we start surgery/treatment. That is the training I got in the UK. When I try to do the same here, my seniors say, 'Indians are not like that; they listen to whatever you say. Don't give too much information; they will get confused.' That is the mindset of most physicians practicing in India.

Some nurses, both in GH and PH, view their role in communication as being there for patients and providing care, while also acknowledging their position within a hierarchical system where they must act as "bridgers" between doctors and patients. A key aspect of their perception is an awareness of their place in this hierarchy and the need to act accordingly. One nurse commented on the significance of the consent process, illustrating how they see their role and perceive patients: "It is very important. Sometimes we indirectly counter-check—we won't ask directly, so as not to affect the doctor—but we will make sure that the work is done. We ask questions in such a way... Sometimes patients do not understand the seriousness. If anything happens on the [operating] table—side effects of anesthesia, complications of surgery—they will ask questions or even file a case. So, consent is to protect management... Patients should be aware of that. It is their own body, so they have a right to ask".

In the nursing profession, which often involves status anxiety, especially in the Indian context, nurses navigate complex hierarchical systems within the biomedical framework and a gendered institutional culture (Ray, 2016, 2020). This broader social, political, and cultural environment shapes their roles and influences how they perceive the patients they interact with. Often, nurses, like any professionals, perpetuate and reproduce the unequal dynamics of society. However, there are also instances where they resist these norms, demonstrating a shifting perspective. Some nurses mentioned that, being more comfortable with the local language compared to some doctors who are not familiar with it, they often take on the role of translators. A few nurses from private hospitals emphasized that it is their responsibility to provide sufficient information to patients and family members who are in vulnerable positions. The following excerpt from an interview with a nurse in a private hospital illustrates this:

> Definitely care for patients. See, [in the] meantime patients and attenders will be there. But sometimes they tend to forget because of anxiety or tension. So we will be keenly noting down whatever doctors say. So when the patient asks the same question again, we can replace them [the doctors]. It is what I feel. Most of the time, patients or attenders won't or are unable to ask the doctors these questions. Some people will be scared. So when they ask us during that time, we can help. Even if we are not knowledgeable enough, we can give psychological support while talking.
>
> [consent]

As observed in this section, healthcare professionals construct a dominant narrative of the "incompetent" patient who is perceived as incapable of understanding medical information. Consequently, doctors often choose not to share information with these patients, as they do not view them as autonomous agents. Instead, doctors see their ethical obligations as avoiding frightening the patient, ensuring the best treatment is carried out, and making decisions in the best interests of patients and their families. Their assessments of patients' and family members' abilities, influenced by social class and psychological factors, serve as a collective moral and rational justification for these practices. Similar to doctors, most nurses perceive informed consent as a "formality" and part of institutional protocol. Many nurses in private hospitals noted that informed consent primarily serves to protect the management in case of legal action, while also informing patients about the procedure. Except for one nurse, all of them stated that their role in the informed consent process is simply to obtain a signature. This particular nurse mentioned that it is the doctor's responsibility to inform and then obtain the signature from patients and their families, while the nurse's role is to ensure patients are aware by indirectly checking with them. All of the nurses emphasized that their primary role is caregiving, which involves being present for patients and providing clinical care.

A discussion with a senior nurse manager from a private hospital revealed that the ideal role of the nurse is to be present when doctors discuss technical information about treatments, both pre-surgery and post-surgery, with patients and family members. The nurse's responsibility is then to ensure that patients remain aware of this information during their stay at the hospital and at the time of discharge. The frequent reference to following doctors' instructions or orders by nurses during interviews reflects their position within the institutional hierarchy. Aware of the power dynamics between doctors and patients, as well as the patients' state of mind, nurses act as facilitators. They assume that patients "do not understand" and often mention that patients do not read the informed consent form before signing it. Nurses observe that only a few patients ask questions to doctors, with most either blindly accepting the information or raising concerns only if they encounter an issue. According to the nurses from private hospitals, this dynamic leads to a perception that when things go wrong, patients—who are seen as laypeople lacking medical understanding—tend to blame doctors and nurses. The roles of nurses as patient advocates and collaborators are well established within nursing studies (Shannon, 2016; Water et al., 2016). While the majority of nurses in this study distanced themselves from the informed consent process, a few, particularly those in private hospitals, viewed their role as facilitators—clarifying doubts, providing information on post-operative care, and ensuring patients are aware of the significant risks or side effects of their prescribed treatment or surgery. Nurses believe their role includes an ethical obligation to provide care and ensure patients are informed about their decisions. Additionally, they see protecting doctors and management from potential legal battles as part of their duty.

Although these analysis echo observations from other studies on paternalistic practices, this work offers deeper insights into how such constructions, actions, and practices are embedded in clinical practice. Analysis suggest that most doctors view informed consent as primarily influenced by legal and institutional protocols, reducing it to a ritualistic formality within the hospital structure. Many doctors perceive that patients do not place enough importance on informed consent, viewing it as a tool for protecting themselves and the management, particularly in high-risk cases. The findings and analysis indicate that many doctors perceive their role as decision-makers, believing that patients cannot fully understand the information or make informed decisions—a view supported by other studies in India (Banerjee & Sanyal, 2012; Fochsen et al., 2006; Gopichandran, 2019; Kumar et al., 2020; Madhivanan et al., 2014). A common belief among doctors is that patients and their families trust them due to their "position and professional role" and are expected to do so because of the doctors' medical knowledge and expertise. An interesting finding is that while the majority of doctors think it is better not to discuss the treatment plan with patients and their families—citing "medicine being uncertain" and the "lack of risk acceptance" within Indian culture—a few emphasized the importance of discussing information with patients.

If we consider these perceptions within the Indian context, the increasing incidents of violence and anger directed at doctors or in clinics by patients' family members become more understandable, though no less concerning. In India, where there is often a significant power imbalance between healthcare providers and patients, especially in government hospitals, patients and their families may feel marginalized or powerless in their interactions with medical professionals. This imbalance is exacerbated by the common practice of withholding detailed information from patients, as many doctors assume that patients, particularly those from lower socio-economic backgrounds, lack the capacity to understand complex medical details. When patients or their families are not fully informed about treatment plans, potential risks, or the reasons behind certain medical decisions, it can lead to feelings of frustration, helplessness, and distrust. When these expectations are unmet, or when patients feel that they have been kept in the dark, it can result in anger and, in some cases, violence. Of course, we can't overlook the larger social context such as overcrowded hospitals, long wait times, and the perceived lack of empathy from overburdened healthcare professionals. The combination of these elements—perceived indifference, lack of communication, and high stakes—can lead to explosive situations where family members, already under immense stress, resort to violence as a means of expressing their frustration and reclaiming a sense of control in an otherwise disempowering situation. I think it becomes necessary to understand the incidents of violence against doctors can be seen as a tragic outcome of systemic issues within the healthcare system, where the need for better communication, patient education, and a more equitable doctor–patient relationship is urgently needed.

As demonstrated in this section through various narratives, the significance of discussing treatment information with patients and their families is shaped by multiple factors, including education, caste, class, gender, the hospital they stay in, and geography. Doctors in government hospitals (GH) often perceive patients and their families as incapable of understanding complex medical information and making informed decisions. As a result, they tend to view the informed consent process as relatively unimportant for these patients. In contrast, doctors in private hospitals (PH) often perceive certain classes of patients—particularly the educated middle class—as "troublemakers" and consider informed consent to be more relevant for this specific group.

Interestingly, a few doctors highlighted the importance of honesty, open communication, and the development of communication skills for meaningful interactions with patients. They remarked that these aspects are not given the attention they deserve in medical education in India. This suggests a recognition among some medical professionals that the current approach to patient communication could be improved to foster better doctor–patient relationships and ultimately enhance patient care.

The importance of building communication skills and fostering discussions with patients and their families is particularly significant in light of the increasing incidents of violence in hospitals, where patients and their families have lashed out against doctors (Garg & Garg, 2019; Nagral, 2001). It becomes important to understand how the humiliating oppressive healthcare systems contributes to violence and disrespect against both healthcare workers and patients. Thus, understanding the culture of disrespect is key to addressing it. Many healthcare professionals, particularly in government hospitals (GH), equate being authoritative with ethical practice, based on the belief that patients are incapable of making informed decisions or grasping the complexities of medical care. To facilitate decision-making, they often invoke empathy, using phrases like "if I were in your position", which they perceive as fulfilling their ethical obligation. These findings suggest that doctors believe they are acting in the "patients' best interest", while simultaneously holding the authority to define what that best interest is. This presumption of authority raises important moral concerns, as it implies a paternalistic approach that may undermine patient's agency. The ethical implications of this dynamic, including the potential consequences for doctor–patient relationships and the broader healthcare system, will be discussed in the next section.

The Weight of Stereotypes & Bodily Dispositions: The Unspoken Language of Disrespect

As I experience and explored the world of healthcare more deeply, the impact of socio-economic status and other intersecting identities—such as caste, gender, and religion—became undeniably clear in shaping clinical interactions and the quality of care patients received. These factors not only influence how patients are treated but also actively shape the perceptions and implicit biases of physicians, ultimately guiding the entire course of medical interactions. The subtle yet powerful force of these explicit and implicit biases became increasingly evident as I conducted in-depth interviews with doctors about their practices regarding informed consent, information disclosure, and patient discussions.

In these conversations, it became clear that many physicians' perceptions of patients were not merely professional assessments but were deeply rooted in stereotypes. These stereotypes often dictated how doctors interacted with patients and their families, subtly categorizing them based on perceived "worthiness". For instance, doctors often found it more "worthy" to spend time with patients they perceived as educated and upper-class, while the time spent with poorer, less-educated and lower caste patients was seen as less valuable. Less time spent with lower caste and class patients has been observed by few scholars (Das et al., 2022; George, 2019; Shaikh et al., 2018). This moral reasoning, which justifies unequal treatment, is steeped in the paternalistic and authoritative practices, and underlying upper-caste-class-gendered values, that many physicians believe are essential to their role.

One narrative that frequently surfaced among doctors in government hospitals was the belief that their patients were "irrational and incompetent". This perception was not born out of malice but rather from a deep-seated assumption that the patients they served—often from lower socio-economic backgrounds—lacked the capacity to understand complex medical information. As one surgeon bluntly stated, "Here, these people cannot understand... they run away if I tell them anything. I have to save their lives, so they sign. Many people may not understand, so I have to tell them, 'If I don't operate, 100% you may die.'" Such statements reveal an ingrained belief that these patients are incapable of meaningful participation in their own healthcare decisions. Time constraints and the overwhelming nature of work in government hospitals were frequently cited by physicians as reasons for their brusque interaction styles. As one surgeon noted, "You know, if you concentrate on improving [communication], a lot of people won't get care because more resources will be allocated for one person... it's so busy here that we can't just sit and talk". These justifications underscore a deeper issue: the perception that poor patients, who typically seek care in government hospitals, are not "worthy" of the time and resources that might be afforded to those in private hospitals.

The patients themselves are acutely aware of these dynamics. They understand that the care they receive is not solely a product of the medical system but is also shaped by their perceived social standing. A family member of a patient at a government hospital, who was dealing with a post-operative infection, shared her resigned understanding of the situation: "We know what we get here and how we are treated. We understand them [doctors]... I can see that they are busy and have no time for people like us". The phrase "people like us" encapsulates a painful awareness of their place in the social hierarchy—a place that dictates the quality and nature of the care they receive. In private hospitals, the dynamic shifts slightly, but the underlying biases remain. Doctors often view middle-class patients as "troublemakers", individuals who challenge medical authority and question doctors' decisions. One surgeon from a private hospital expressed his frustration, saying, "There's a huge difference between the middle class and the very rich and the very poor. Usually, the very rich and the very poor are easy to handle. It's the middle class who think they know everything but actually don't know anything". This perception of the middle class as "half-baked know-it-alls" highlights the tension between the doctors' desire to maintain authority and the patients' desire to be involved in their care.

Interestingly, doctors in private hospitals often found it easier to engage with "rich" patients, whom they described as "sophisticated" and more receptive to medical advice. These patients were seen as "worthy" of time and effort, not just because of their wealth but because they were perceived as understanding the complexities of medical care. This interaction was not merely about the medical details; it was also about the comfort and ease that came with shared social markers—language, education, and class. One surgeon from a private hospital, who was originally from another region and not fluent in the local language, candidly shared, "I feel comfortable talking to the rich and middle class as they can understand, as mostly we speak English; I don't find much difficulty explaining to them". This preference for patients who spoke English and understood medical jargon reveals a bias towards those who are seen as more "worthy" of the surgeon's time and attention. It underscores how language and perceived intelligence can influence the quality of care a patient receives, which is as much a colonial and upper-caste-class narrative within Indian context.

As I continued my interviews, it became clear that these stereotypes and prejudices were not just characteristics of individual doctors but were deeply embedded in the culture of the hospital itself. Many doctors learned to navigate the consent process and patient interactions by observing and mimicking their peers. One surgeon explained, "I learned to ease the process [interaction] through seeing and doing; if I take more time and talk, they [senior doctors and other professionals] will laugh at me... sometimes even they get angry as we have long queues... anyway, they [patients in GH] are used to it". This quote reveals how deeply entrenched these practices are within the hospital's hierarchical system, making it difficult for any individual to change the status quo. The decisions on how to interact with patients, what information to disclose, and how much time to spend with them were all influenced by stereotypes about the patients' socio-economic status. These decisions were also shaped by structural factors such as time constraints, lack of resources, and the need to conform to the existing culture of the hospital. Over time, these practices became part of the moral habitus—a set of ingrained behaviors and attitudes that sustain asymmetrical interactions and reinforce the moral authority of healthcare professionals. Taking forward habitus framework, and building on the work of Sayer and Ignatow, I conceptualize moral habitus as the "social actor's embodied bodily dispositions of everyday practice and cognitive elements", which aids in understanding moral judgments and actions within specific contexts. I have discussed in detail elsewhere.

The strength of moral habitus lies in its ability to encompass both micro-level bodily dispositions and cognitive habits, as well as meso-level actors, practices, and institutions with which one interacts. It requires careful attention to comprehend how moral judgments, actions, and ethical dispositions contribute to sustaining inequality and fostering disrespectful attitudes and practices. This moral habitus, in turn, creates an environment where vulnerable patients, particularly those from poorer backgrounds, find it nearly impossible to engage in meaningful discussions about their treatment options. The expectation that healthcare professionals should treat all patients as equals, regardless of their social background, is often unrealistic in practice. Numerous studies suggest that the pressures of time and the need to categorize people quickly lead to the use of stereotypes and implicit biases, which then shape the entire course of clinical interactions. Even in encounters where doctors are more attuned to the nuances of their patients' needs, a pervasive stereotype remains: patients—especially those from lower socio-economic backgrounds—are seen as "incompetent". This stereotype not only affects the quality of care but also reinforces social inequalities and undermines the dignity of the patients. The micro-level interactions between doctors and patients, which often reproduce and sustain these inequities, reflect the broader macro structures of society. Ethnographic research has documented how patients experience these interactions, often feeling unrecognized and devalued. The focus on bodily dispositions and communicative practices—such as eye contact, listening, and not interrupting—reveals how these subtle behaviors can either reinforce or undermine a patient's sense of self-worth.

In my earlier exploration of moral habitus (Subramani, 2022), I discussed how stereotypes function as cognitive dispositions that shape moral judgments. In this context, the treatment of patients and their families is heavily influenced by how they are perceived by healthcare professionals. These perceptions are often shaped by visible social markers—such as clothing, language, and demeanor—that doctors use to categorize patients as either "worthy" or "unworthy" of their time and attention. One young woman, caring for her mother in a government hospital, expressed her frustration at being ignored by the doctors: "I keep following them [the doctors] from the ward to their offices and back. They don't even bother to stop for a second and listen to me... As everywhere else, we are made to keep waiting... I feel frustrated to keep asking them and walking behind them as you see here is common". Her words capture a common experience in government hospitals, where patients and their families often feel dismissed and devalued. Many patients in these settings internalize the belief that they are "undeserving" of better treatment because they receive free care. This internalization is reinforced by the way patients are treated by the medical staff, who often fail to recognize or acknowledge their dignity. For example, one family member remarked, "See, we get free [care] here, so we can't expect [to be treated] like in private [hospitals]". This sense of unworthiness is further compounded by the physical distancing behaviors of doctors and nurses, who often avoid interacting with certain patients based on their perceived social status. In contrast, patients in private hospitals often describe the treatment they receive as more respectful and attentive, though still shaped by their social and economic status. They understand that the quality of care they receive is tied to their ability to pay, which reinforces their sense of being "worthy" of the doctors' time and attention. However, even in these settings, underlying biases continue to influence how patients are treated.

One particularly troubling aspect of these biases is the way in which patients are segregated within the hospital based on their perceived worthiness. For instance, patients covered by health insurance are often treated differently from those who are homeless or from marginalized communities. One patient, who was homeless, shared how nurses and doctors rarely visited his corner, saying, "Nurses and doctors don't come to this part often; when they do, they don't even touch the place where it is paining". This segregation within the hospital system mirrors a broader societal tendency to distance oneself from those perceived as socially and morally unworthy. These observations highlight the complex interplay between bodily dispositions, implicit biases, and the moral habitus within institutions. The way doctors and nurses interact with patients—whether through physical contact, eye contact, or verbal communication—sends powerful messages about the patients' worthiness to be treated with respect and dignity. For patients from marginalized communities, these interactions often reinforce their social and moral unworthiness, making it difficult for them to engage fully in their own care.

The cognitive distortions involved in stereotyping patients as "incompetent" carry profound moral implications. These stereotypes not only impact the quality of care but also perpetuate a culture of disrespect and moral othering, where patients are viewed as less deserving of attention and care. The bodily dispositions of healthcare professionals—such as whether they choose to stop and talk to a patient, or avoid eye contact and touch—are deeply intertwined with these cognitive biases, creating a moral habitus that reinforces social inequalities (Subramani, 2022; Subramani & Biller-Andorno, 2022). The implicit biases and bodily dispositions of healthcare professionals significantly influence the quality of care that patients receive. These biases, rooted in stereotypes about socio-economic status and other intersecting identities, contribute to a moral habitus that legitimizes paternalistic and authoritative practices. This habitus not only perpetuates social inequalities but also undermines the dignity and self-worth of patients, particularly those from marginalized communities. Addressing these deep-rooted issues requires a critical examination of the moral and ethical dimensions of healthcare interactions, with a focus on respecting the humanity and dignity of all patients, regardless of their social position.

Imposed Incompetence: The Quiet Justifications for Silencing Patients

In healthcare encounters, the power dynamics between doctors, nurses, and patients reveal a troubling pattern of constructed incompetence. The analysis in the previous section illustrates that incompetence is predominantly shaped and understood by healthcare professionals based on their values and assumptions. Throughout their accounts, it becomes evident that patients are often viewed as incapable of understanding and making decisions. Factors such as educational background, class status, and psychological states like fear are employed as informal metrics to judge a patient's capacity to comprehend and decide. These subjective assessments justify doctors' decisions to bypass discussions with patients and their families, opting instead to act on their behalf under the guise of "best interests".

This paternalistic approach perpetuates the expectation that patients should adopt a passive role, reinforcing a cycle where patients and their families, who are neither legally nor clinically incompetent, are nonetheless treated as such. This pattern of assuming incompetence reinforces paternalistic practices and perpetuates existing inequalities. The construction of the "passive" and "incompetent" patient not only undermines the agency of patients but also sustains an unequal power dynamic, where the authority of the surgeon remains unchallenged, and the voice of the patient is consistently marginalized. To grasp the concept of incompetence outlined in this chapter, as discussed elsewhere, consider the following thought reflection, a method often favored by ethicists: "When asserting that X (in this case, patients and family members) is incompetent to do Y (understand information), it seems we are merely stating that X lacks the ability to do Y, and therefore is not qualified to do Y" (Subramani, 2020). As a result, patients and family members are deemed incapable of understanding information and, consequently, are not considered qualified to participate in clinical decision-making or interactions. Through these subjectively constructed evaluations, doctors justify their paternalistic approach as morally correct, believing they are acting in the best interests of patients and families. They feel morally justified in withholding information, thinking they are "sparing" patients and families from unnecessary burden. This rationalization leads to a paternalistic practice, where doctors engage with patients and families only in exceptional cases—such as high-risk situations—to avoid potential legal repercussions.

Through analysis, I have come to understand that these actions and practices are perpetuated by the healthcare system, as doctors' moral attitudes and actions exist within a framework that promotes the belief that "doctors know best". I observe that hospital environments and clinical interactions are shaped by deeply ingrained moral attitudes, behaviors, and social interaction styles. In the next chapter, taking forward earlier work (Subramani, 2018), I will demonstrate how everyday indignities and othering are normalized within the hospital settings, reflecting dominant attitudes and behaviors that define doctor–patient and doctor–family member relationships from the patients' perspective. This perspective reveals that doctors often assume a dominant role, consciously or subconsciously, by adopting the moral habitus of their specific contexts and institutions. This habitus influences their attitudes, actions, and practices, leading them to behave in particular ways. Within this context, doctors approach patients with the belief that they inherently know what is best—a socially reinforced attitude that has become deeply embedded in both institutional and individual behavior.

Beyond the socially imposed, distorted, default relationship towards certain subordinated individuals common in any hierarchical society, doctors' attitudes and behaviors stem from the social habits of clinical interactions, which are dominated by paternalism in the hospital setting (Crossley & Crossley, 2001; McDonald, 2009). As a result, patients and family members are deprived of the opportunity to participate meaningfully in clinical interactions.

Doctors' perceptions of patients and family members as incompetent drive these paternalistic practices. This socially enforced interaction habit within the hospital context convinces doctors that their actions are both morally and validly justified. While these might be subjective reasons for actions, they do not constitute normative or objective reasons to sustain paternalistic practices. As shown, doctors base their actions and practices on assumptions and beliefs that are perceived as facts and reasons rather than being actual facts or reasons. However, further critical analysis is needed to determine whether these subjective reasons can function as normative reasons for specific practices and whether factual considerations would alter the moral values, positions, and actions of healthcare professionals. As discussed in the first section, within the healthcare context, it is generally assumed that patients should be considered competent unless proven otherwise. However, as I have shown here, patients and their families are often perceived as incompetent due to doctors' subjective and constructed assessments. The findings indicate that doctors frequently refrain from discussing treatment options, alternative therapies, and associated risks with patients and their families based on these assumptions.

Other research has explored how factors such as age, race, caste, gender, ethnicity, intersectional characteristics, social class, and psychological aspects impact clinical interactions (Ahmad & Bradby, 2007; Baru et al., 2010; Jungari & Chauhan, 2017; Richardson et al., 2012). This body of work suggests that socially constructed incompetence significantly influences healthcare interactions, often before considerations of legal and clinical incompetence even arise. This form of incompetence is not evaluated based on medical, biological, or psychological criteria—areas that are also contentious in other studies—but rather on perceived and constructed circumstantial factors such as social class and psychological elements. These constructed assessments thus serve as a foundation for paternalistic practices, providing both moral and practical normative justification for such behaviors. While medico-legal and ethical literature often discusses competence with the assumption that patients are either inherently competent or incompetent, this study demonstrates that informed consent processes, medical decision-making, and clinical interactions frequently proceed under the assumption that patients and their families are inherently incompetent. When perceived as incompetent, patients and family members receive treatment that fundamentally disrespects them, raising significant moral concerns and highlighting the need for further investigation into the implications of doctors' constructed assessments.

Re-Centering Patient's Agency

As shown in this chapter, institutionalized modern medicine, similar to law, becomes a site of upper-caste and middle-class-heteronormative values. These upholds the archetype of the "incompetent and passive patient" through everyday ritualized practices within medical institutions. For instance, this is demonstrated through "getting rid" of patients, making them wait and treating marginalized communities with disrespect—ranging from outright violence such as yelling, scolding, and pinching, to subtle behaviors such as tailing and not making eye contact. The conviction that every person is respect-worthy and treated with dignity, is a fundamental in moral discussions. However, this chapter illustrated that this value is not often practiced in healthcare encounters in India. Promoting attitudes and actions that reflect 'respect for persons' can be achieved by emphasizing the substantive manifestation of moral attitudes and behaviors toward individuals in the hospital settings. I argue that moral attitudes and behaviors of respect within institutions can only be realized when professionals recognize patients and family members as respect-worthy. This involves constraining behaviors, attitudes, and actions that might disrespect or disregard individuals by treating them as "incompetent" and "passive". Nurses, often women, find their work and labor devalued and stigmatized in the postcolonial context of India due to its colonial legacies and caste system, and often doctors are predominantly from upper-caste-class background. In my observations in GH and PH wards, interactions with nurses and doctors revealed that identities and status were frequently contested and negotiated within these interactions. This often reinforced social stratifications based on caste, class, and gender, which were, in turn, reproduced power asymmetry in their interactions with patients and their family members, and upholds the "passive patient" and "incompetent patient" archytype.

Moral and political philosophical literature commonly argues that individuals should be respected and have an inherent right to be treated as persons. In applied ethics debates, this argument is grounded in the claim that every person possesses qualities such as dignity, autonomy, and capacity, which make them worthy of respect (Childress, 2017; Childress & Quante, 2021; Fateh-Moghadam & Gutmann, 2014; Gutmann, 2022; Jacobson, 2007; Henry, et al., 2015; Beach et al., 2007). In this given context, it becomes evident that doctors' attitudes toward patients and their families are justified by their failure to recognize these qualities due to their constructed notion of incompetency. The consequences of this attitude are twofold: first, patients and their families are not regarded or respected as individuals with adequate capacity, and second, they are not allowed to be the primary agents of their treatment decisions. The presumption of incompetence thus serves to justify these attitudes and actions by the doctors. In this chapter, I have demonstrated that through practical normative reasoning and justification, the paternalistic and authoritative practices of doctors have become the moral standard within the Indian context. Discussing information is crucial for obtaining valid consent and ensuring effective communication in the doctor–patient relationship and is central to respectful patient care. However, doctors (and some nurses) often use their constructed knowledge of incompetence—shaped by their stereotypes, prejudices, and perceptions as members of a dominant upper-class-caste-gendered culture—to assess patients and family members as "incompetent".

The prevailing moral norms in healthcare are significantly influenced by a confluence of dominant colonial legacies, upper-class-caste structures, and the biomedical culture. The colonial history, along with hierarchical caste-class and patriarchal medical system, in India has left a lasting imprint on its institutions, including healthcare. During the colonial era, medical practices were often paternalistic and hierarchical, with a clear division between the educated, authoritative colonizer and the subjugated, often deemed "inferior", local population. This legacy has continued to influence the way medical authority is exercised in contemporary India. The colonial mindset, which viewed certain populations as incapable of self-governance or decision-making, persists in how healthcare professionals perceive and interact with patients, especially those from marginalized communities. This entrenched belief system promotes a top-down approach where doctors, seen as the ultimate authority, make decisions on behalf of patients, often without their full involvement or consent. As I showed in this chapter, the upper-class-caste structure in India further reinforces these paternalistic practices; in Chapter 4 and 5, I will elaborate more on this. In a society where social hierarchies are deeply ingrained, the medical profession is often dominated by individuals from privileged backgrounds—those who belong to higher castes and socio-economic classes. These professionals bring with them the biases and prejudices of their social strata, which influence their interactions with patients, and healthcare professionals from marginalized communities endure systemic violence, and sometimes perpetuate the same violence. For instance, individuals from lower castes or economically disadvantaged backgrounds are often stereotyped as being less educated, less capable, or even less deserving of the same quality of care as their upper-caste counterparts. These prejudices shape the moral reasoning of healthcare professionals, leading to discriminatory practices that marginalize patients based on their interesections of caste, class, and gender categories.

The biomedical model, which is predominant in Indian healthcare, emphasizes a scientific and often reductionist approach to medicine, focusing primarily on the biological aspects of disease while neglecting the social, cultural, and psychological dimensions of health. This model tends to prioritize the authority of the healthcare professional over the experiences and voices of patients. Within this framework, the moral norms are directed by a belief in the superiority of scientific knowledge, which further justifies the exclusion of patients from decision-making processes. The biomedical culture, in conjunction with the colonial and upper-class-caste influences, fosters an environment where patients are seen as passive recipients of care rather than active participants in their health decisions. By questioning the capacity or ability (competence) of individuals, healthcare professionals disregard and disrespect the values and preferences of patients and their families, effectively excluding them from meaningful interactions. This practice not only undermines the autonomy of patients but also challenges the ethical and legal foundations of the doctor–patient relationship. Critically examining these influences reveals how they collectively shape a healthcare system that perpetuates inequality and disrespect. The dominance of colonial attitudes reinforces a sense of superiority among healthcare professionals, while upper-class-caste biases further entrench social hierarchies within medical practice. The biomedical model, by emphasizing the authority of the healthcare provider, provides a convenient framework for justifying these power imbalances. Together, these forces create a moral landscape where the dignity, autonomy, and agency of patients, particularly those from marginalized groups, are systematically undermined.

This critical perspective highlights the need for a shifting the moral norms that govern healthcare in India. There is an urgent need to challenge the entrenched hierarchies and biases that continue to shape clinical interactions and to promote a more inclusive and respectful approach to patient care. This would involve not only addressing the explicit practices of discrimination but also confronting the underlying cultural and structural factors that perpetuate these social inequalities. People on the margins are acutely aware of how modern professional values and norms perceive them—whether as "lazy", "stupid", "passive", or "incompetent"—and they resist these labels when opportunities arise. What we see in these narratives, and what I want to emphasize, is that one's embodied capital, or lack thereof, shaped by social identities and markers, is maintained, normalized, and reproduced in healthcare encounters. If we recognize how these factors are central to upholding the institutional culture and values in medicine, we begin to understand that the archetype of the "passive patient" is not surprising. Instead, it is a construct manufactured within this deeply ingrained socially and politically fragmented society. Everyday embodied dispositions and attitudes toward marginalized individuals perpetuate this archetype, reinforcing the power dynamics that marginalize them further. The concept of embodied capital refers to the ways in which one's social identity—be it caste, class, gender, or ethnicity—becomes physically and socially inscribed on the body, influencing how one is perceived and treated in various institutional settings, including healthcare. Those who lack this embodied capital, often due to their marginalized social identities, are systematically positioned as "lesser" or "unworthy" within these settings.

In healthcare, this manifests as a normalization of the idea that certain patients are inherently passive, incompetent, or incapable of participating in their own care. This perception is not an isolated bias but a reflection of broader societal structures that devalue marginalised groups. These attitudes are deeply embedded in the everyday practices of healthcare professionals, who may, consciously or unconsciously, reproduce these stereotypes through their interactions with patients. The construction of the "passive patient" archetype is thus a product of the intersection between professional medical norms and the wider social and political context. It reflects the ways in which systemic inequalities are perpetuated through routine practices and interactions in the healthcare setting. By critically examining these dynamics, we can begin to challenge the assumptions that underpin them and work towards a more equitable and respectful healthcare system that truly values all patients, regardless of their social identity.

Hospitals, whether private or government-run, each have their own distinct culture and are often sites of hegemonic power and anxiety, particularly for patients and family members from marginalized communities. These medical institutions, as centers of hierarchical power both synchronically and diachronically, generate inequalities based on class, caste, and gender. Those in power perpetuate these inequalities to varying degrees, through othering behaviors and attitudes, resulting in marginalized patients and their families bearing the brunt of disrespect, shame, humiliation, and indignation. Through these narratives, we see how social identities become central, and how power is reinforced and reproduced by those in authority. The archetype of the passive and incompetent patient becomes an accepted and justified notion for evaluating patient agency. Moreover, this clearly illustrates how modern professions, such as doctors and nurses, along with their roles, norms, attitudes, and behaviors, are structured by existing social, economic, and political inequalities. Interactions with these professionals and institutions further reproduce these inequalities. The colonial legacies, combined with the existing caste and class system in India, and the professionalization of medical education and nursing training, reflect how norms and values uphold upper-caste-class and heteronormative values. This is explored in depth by few scholars at varied degrees and perspectives within healthcare settings (Arnold, 1993; Kumbhar, 2022, 2023; Ray, 2016, 2020).

As I wrap up this chapter, I can't help but reflect on some personal experiences and memories to better contextualize my analysis—especially if I haven't fully convinced you already why I am engaging through this lens. For those who have lived on the margins in India and experienced government hospitals, it's well-known how caste, gender, religion, and class get reinforced through things like speech, gestures, demeanor, and expected manners. I remember how, throughout my childhood, my dad would compare me to my school friend, who was also our neighbor, saying, "Look, learn how she carries herself with her neat *jade* (braided hair) and *boottu* (bindi)"; or trained me in varied ways: 'in front of them don't just sit like that'; 'We need to learn from these people (referring to Brahmins and upper castes); only then we will be respected.' In Indian communities, becoming a "respectable" person often involves conforming to the caste, class, and gender norms of upper-caste-class communities. These norms are reproduced in every institution—whether in banks, at bus stands, in public spaces, or hospitals—through historically and socially constructed behaviors. As I write this, I am reminded of my entire childhood upbringing, where one key value was ingrained in me day in and day out as a woman from a lower caste community. In Kannada, the saying goes, "ತಿರುಗಿ ಹೇಳಬೇಡ" (don't talk back). This was a constant reminder to tame oneself, not to question elders or those in authority. I often wondered how much this practice permeates various aspects of our life. If we apply this understanding to the context of middle-class values, the "good patient" is one who listens passively and does not ask questions. How can we, in this socio-cultural context with deeply ingrained upper-caste-class values, move towards acknowledging that people have agency and recognizing that they are already exercising it in their everyday lives? My quick answer is that true change happens only when the voices of the marginalized are placed at the center, and recognition, self-respect, and dignity through recognizing one's agency becomes ingrained in society.

References

Ahmad, W. I. U., & Bradby, H. (2007). Locating ethnicity and health: Exploring concepts and contexts. *Sociology of Health & Illness*, *29*(6), 795–810. https://doi.org/10.1111/j.1467-9566.2007.01051.x

Arnold, D. (1993). *Colonizing the body: State medicine and epidemic disease in nineteenth-century India*. University of California Press.

Banerjee, A., & Sanyal, D. (2012). Dynamics of doctor–patient relationship: A cross-sectional study on concordance, trust, and patient enablement. *Journal of Family and Community Medicine*, *19*(1), 12–19.

Banerjee, D. (2022). Provincializing bioethics: Dilemmas of end-of-life care in an Indian ICU. *American Ethnologist*, *49*(3), 318–331.

Baru, R., Acharya, A., Acharya, S., Kumar, A. K. S., & Nagaraj, K. (2010). Inequities in access to health services in India: Caste, class and region. *Economic and Political Weekly*, 49–58.

Barua, M. P., & Verma, A. (2021). Workplace bullying in healthcare facilities: Role of caste and reservation. *Indian journal of medical ethics*, 6(1), 1–7.

Basu, A., & Dutta, M. J. (2007). Centralizing context and culture in the co-construction of health: Localizing and vocalizing health meanings in rural India. *Health Communication*, *21*(2), 187–196. https://doi.org/10.1080/10410230701305182

Beach, M. C., Duggan, P. S., Cassel, C. K., & Geller, G. (2007). What does 'Respect' mean? Exploring the moral obligation of health professionals to respect patients. *Journal of General Internal Medicine*, *22*(5), 692–695. https://doi.org/10.1007/s11606-006-0054-7

Beauchamp, T. L., & Childress, J. F. (2013). *Principles of biomedical ethics*. Oxford University Press.

Berg, J., & Makielski, K. S. (2014). Capacity and competence. In *The Routledge companion to bioethics* (pp. 291–301). Routledge.

Bielby, P. (2005). The conflation of competence and capacity in English medical law: A philosophical critique. *Medicine, Health Care and Philosophy*, *8*, 357–369.

Breden, T. M., & Vollmann, J. (2004). The cognitive based approach of capacity assessment in psychiatry: A philosophical critique of the MacCAT-T. *Health Care Analysis*, *12*, 273–283.

Brüggemann, J., Guntram, L., & Nedlund, A.-C. (2022). The "Difficult Patient"– Dominant logics and misfits in medicine. In *Handbook of social sciences and global public health* (pp. 1–14). Springer.

Bullock, E. C. (2018). Paternalism and the practitioner/patient relationship. In *The Routledge handbook of the philosophy of paternalism* (pp. 311–322). Routledge.

Campbell, C., Scott, K., Skovdal, M., Madanhire, C., Nyamukapa, C., & Gregson, S. (2015). A good patient? How notions of 'a good patient'affect patient-nurse relationships and ART adherence in Zimbabwe. *BMC Infectious Diseases*, *15*, 1–11.

Chattopadhyay, S. (2018). The shifting axes of marginalities: The politics of identities shaping women's experiences during childbirth in Northeast India. *Reproductive Health Matters*, *26*(53), 62–69.

Cheston, K. (2022). (Dis)respect and shame in the context of 'medically unexplained' illness. *Journal of Evaluation in Clinical Practice*, *28*(5), 909–916. https://doi.org/10.1111/jep.13740

Childress, J. F. (2017). Needed: A more rigorous analysis of models of decision making and a richer account of respect for autonomy. *The American Journal of Bioethics, 17*(11), 52–54. https://doi.org/10.1080/15265161.2017.1382168

Childress, J. F., & Quante, M. (2021). *Thick (Concepts of) autonomy: Personal autonomy in ethics and bioethics* (1st ed. 2022, Vol. 146). Springer Nature. https://doi.org/10.1007/978-3-030-80991-1

Chuang, A. W., Nuthalapaty, F. S., Casey, P. M., Kaczmarczyk, J. M., Cullimore, A. J., Dalrymple, J. L., Dugoff, L., Espey, E. L., Hammoud, M. M., & Hueppchen, N. A. (2010). To the point: Reviews in medical education—Taking control of the hidden curriculum. *American Journal of Obstetrics and Gynecology, 203*(4), 316–e1.

Crossley, M. L., & Crossley, N. (2001). Patient'voices, social movements and the habitus; how psychiatric survivors 'speak out. *Social Science & Medicine, 52*(10), 1477–1489.

Das, J., Daniels, B., Ashok, M., Shim, E.-Y., & Muralidharan, K. (2022). Two Indias: The structure of primary health care markets in rural Indian villages with implications for policy. *Social Science & Medicine, 301*, 112799.

Das, J., & Hammer, J. (2012). Health and health care policy in India: The case for quality of care. In *The Oxford handbook of the Indian economy*. Routledge; Oxford University Press New York.

Das, V. (2006). *Life and words: Violence and the descent into the ordinary*. University of California Press.

Das, V. (2015). *Affliction: Health, disease, poverty*. Fordham University Press. https://doi.org/10.5422/fordham/9780823261802.001.0001

Dingwall, R., & Murray, T. (1983). Categorization in accident departments: 'good' patients, 'bad' patients and 'children.' *Sociology of Health & Illness, 5*(2), 127–148.

Dolezal, L. (2022). Shame anxiety, stigma and clinical encounters. *Journal of Evaluation in Clinical Practice, 28*(5), 854–860. https://doi.org/10.1111/jep.13744

Dunn, L. B., Nowrangi, M. A., Palmer, B. W., Jeste, D. V., & Saks, E. R. (2006). Assessing decisional capacity for clinical research or treatment: A review of instruments. *American Journal of Psychiatry, 163*(8), 1323–1334.

Elwyn, G., Frosch, D., Thomson, R., Joseph-Williams, N., Lloyd, A., Kinnersley, P., Cording, E., Tomson, D., Dodd, C., & Rollnick, S. (2012). Shared decision making: A model for clinical practice. *Journal of General Internal Medicine, 27*, 1361–1367.

Faden, R. R., Beauchamp, T. L., & King, N. M. (1986). *A history and theory of informed consent*. Oxford University Press.

Fateh-Moghadam, B., & Gutmann, T. (2014). Governing [through] autonomy. The moral and legal limits of "soft paternalism." *Ethical Theory and Moral Practice, 17*, 383–397.

Fochsen, G., Deshpande, K., & Thorson, A. (2006). Power imbalance and consumerism in the doctor-patient relationship: Health care providers' experiences of patient encounters in a rural district in India. *Qualitative Health Research, 16*(9), 1236–1251. https://doi.org/10.1177/1049732306293776

Garg, A., & Garg, A. (2019). Let the healers heal. *Indian Journal of Medical Ethics, 4*(4), 329–330.

George, S. (2019). Reconciliations of caste and medical power in rural public health services. *Economic and Political Weekly, 54*(40), 43–50.

Gopichandran, V. (2019). *Dynamics of trust in doctor-patient relationship in India: A clinical, social and ethical analysis*. Springer Nature.

Groll, D. (2014). Medical paternalism – Part 2. *Philosophy Compass, 9*(3), 194–203. https://doi.org/10.1111/phc3.12110

Gutmann, T. (2022). Is "Autonomy Talk" misleading? In Childress, J. F., & Quante, M. (Eds.), *Thick (Concepts of) autonomy: Personal autonomy in ethics and bioethics* (pp. 117–133). Springer Nature.

Henry, L. M., Rushton, C., Beach, M. C., & Faden, R. (2015). Respect and dignity: A conceptual model for patients in the intensive care unit. *Narrative Inquiry in Bioethics*, *5*(1), 5A–14A. https://doi.org/10.1353/nib.2015.0007

Heritage, J., & Maynard, D. W. (2006). Problems and prospects in the study of physician-patient interaction: 30 years of research. In *Annual Review of Sociology* (Vol. 32, Issue Volume 32, 2006, pp. 351–374). Annual Reviews. https://doi.org/10.1146/annurev.soc.32.082905.093959

Hermann, H., Trachsel, M., Elger, B. S., & Biller-Andorno, N. (2016). Emotion and value in the evaluation of medical decision-making capacity: A narrative review of arguments. *Frontiers in Psychology*, *7*, 765.

Hoving, C., Visser, A., Mullen, P. D., & Van den Borne, B. (2010). A history of patient education by health professionals in Europe and North America: From authority to shared decision making education. *Patient Education and Counseling*, *78*(3), 275–281.

Jacobson, N. (2007). Dignity and health: A review. *Social Science & Medicine*, *64*(2), 292–302. https://doi.org/10.1016/j.socscimed.2006.08.039

Jeffery, R. (1979). Normal rubbish: Deviant patients in casualty departments. *Sociology of Health & Illness*, *1*(1), 90–107.

Joyce, K., & Jeske, M. (2019). Revisiting the sick role: Performing regimes of patienthood in the 21st century. *Sociological Viewpoints*, *33*(1), 70–90.

Jungari, S., & Chauhan, B. G. (2017). Caste, wealth and regional inequalities in health status of women and children in India. *Contemporary Voice of Dalit*, *9*(1), 87–100.

Kannabiran, K. (2013). *Tools of justice: Non-discrimination and the Indian constitution.* Routledge India.

Karpagam, S. (2021). Caste-washing the healthcare system will do little to address its discriminatory practices. *Indian Journal of Medical Ethics*, 6(1), 1–4.

Kelly, M. P., & May, D. (1982). Good and bad patients: A review of the literature and a theoretical critique. *Journal of Advanced Nursing*, *7*(2), 147–156.

Kelly, P. A., & Haidet, P. (2007). Physician overestimation of patient literacy: A potential source of health care disparities. *Patient Education and Counseling*, *66*(1), 119–122.

Kenison, T. C., Madu, A., Krupat, E., Ticona, L., Vargas, I. M., & Green, A. R. (2017). Through the veil of language: Exploring the hidden curriculum for the care of patients with limited English proficiency. *Academic Medicine*, *92*(1), 92–100.

Kowal, P., & Afshar, S. (2015). Health and the Indian caste system. *The Lancet*, *385*(9966), 415–416.

Kumar, S., Kumar, G., Velu, S., Pardhan, S., Sivaprasad, S., Ruamviboonsuk, P., & Raman, R. (2020). Patient and provider perspectives on barriers to screening for diabetic retinopathy: An exploratory study from southern India. *BMJ Open*, *10*(12), e037277. https://doi.org/10.1136/bmjopen-2020-037277

Kumbhar, K. (2023). Doctor sahab: Doctors and the public in the 'golden era' of the Indian medical profession. *Sociology of Health & Illness*, *n/a*(n/a). https://doi.org/10.1111/1467-9566.13630

Kumbhar, K. S. (2022). *Healing and harming: The "Noble Profession" of medicine in post-independence India, 1947–2015.* Harvard University.

Lamont, S., Jeon, Y. H., & Chiarella, M. (2013). Assessing patient capacity to consent to treatment: An integrative review of instruments and tools. *Journal of clinical nursing*, *22*(17-18), 2387–2403.

Lysaught, M. T. (2004). Respect: Or, how respect for persons became respect for autonomy. *Journal of Medicine and Philosophy*, *29*(6), 665–680. https://doi.org/10.1080/03605310490883028

Madhivanan, P., Krupp, K., Kulkarni, V., Kulkarni, S., Vaidya, N., Shaheen, R., Philpott, S., & Fisher, C. (2014). HIV testing among pregnant women living with HIV in India: Are private healthcare providers routinely violating women's human rights? *BMC International Health and Human Rights*, *14*(1), 7. https://doi.org/10.1186/1472-698X-14-7

Madhiwalla, N., Ghoshal, R., Mavani, P., & Roy, N. (2018). Identifying disrespect and abuse in organisational culture: A study of two hospitals in Mumbai, India. *Reproductive Health Matters*, *26*(53), 36–47. https://doi.org/10.1080/09688080.2018.1502021

Majumdar, A. (2017). *Transnational commercial surrogacy and the (un) making of kin in India*. Oxford University Press.

McDonald, R. (2009). Market reforms in English primary medical care: Medicine, habitus and the public sphere. *Sociology of Health & Illness*, *31*(5), 659–672.

Mead, N., & Bower, P. (2000). Patient-centredness: A conceptual framework and review of the empirical literature. *Social Science & Medicine*, *51*(7), 1087–1110.

Nagral, S. (2001). Doctors and violence. *Indian Journal of Medical Ethics*, *9*(4), 107.

Pandya, A., Redcay, A. (2020). Access to health services: Barriers faced by the transgender population in India. *J Gay Lesbian Ment Health*, 0, 1–26.

Park, J., Saha, S., Chee, B., Taylor, J., & Beach, M. C. (2021). Physician use of stigmatizing language in patient medical records. *JAMA Network Open*, *4*(7), e2117052–e2117052. https://doi.org/10.1001/jamanetworkopen.2021.17052

Raghuram, H., Parakh, S., Tugnawat, D., Singh, S., Shaikh, A., & Bhan, A. (2024). Experiences of transgender persons in accessing routine healthcare services in India: Findings from a participatory qualitative study. *PLOS Glob Public Health*, *4*(2): e0002933. https://doi.org/10.1371/journal.pgph.0002933

Ravindran, T. S., & Gaitonde, R. (2018). Health inequities in India. Springer.

Ray, P. (2016). "Is This Even Work?": Nursing care and stigmatised labour. *Economic and Political Weekly*, 60–69.

Ray, P. (2020). Nursing in Kolkata: Everyday politics of labour, power and subjectivities. *South Asia Research*, *40*(1), 40–57.

Richardson, A., Allen, J. A., Xiao, H., & Vallone, D. (2012). Effects of race/ethnicity and socioeconomic status on health information-seeking, confidence, and trust. *Journal of Health Care for the Poor and Underserved*, *23*(4), 1477–1493.

Ruddock, A. (2021). *Special treatment: Student doctors at the all India Institute of Medical Sciences*. Stanford University Press. https://doi.org/10.1515/9781503628267

Sen, B. (2011). Securing the right to health for all in India. *The Lancet*, *377*(9765), 532–533. https://doi.org/10.1016/S0140-6736(10)62182-4

Sen, G., & Iyer, A. (2012). Who gains, who loses and how: Leveraging gender and class intersections to secure health entitlements. *Social Science & Medicine*, *74*(11), 1802–1811.

Sessums, L. L., Zembrzuska, H., & Jackson, J. L. (2011). Does this patient have medical decision-making capacity? *JAMA*, *306*(4), 420–427.

Shaikh, M., Miraldo, M., & Renner, A.-T. (2018). Waiting time at health facilities and social class: Evidence from the Indian caste system. *PloS One*, *13*(10), e0205641.

Shannon, S. E. (2016). The nurse as the patient's advocate: A contrarian view. *Hastings Center Report*, *46*(S1), S43–S47. https://doi.org/10.1002/hast.632

Smith, S. G., Wolf, M. S., & Wagner, C. von. (2010). Socioeconomic status, statistical confidence, and patient–provider communication: An analysis of the Health Information National Trends Survey (HINTS 2007). *Journal of Health Communication*, *15*(sup3), 169–185. https://doi.org/10.1080/10810730.2010.522690

Smith-Oka, V. (2015). Microaggressions and the reproduction of social inequalities in medical encounters in Mexico. *Social Science & Medicine*, *143*, 9–16. https://doi.org/10.1016/j.socscimed.2015.08.039

Smith-Oka, V. (2021). *Becoming gods: Medical training in Mexican hospitals.* Rutgers University Press.

Smith-Oka, V. (2022). You're joking: Exploring humour and humiliation as forms of shame and obstetric violence within medical encounters. *Journal of Evaluation in Clinical Practice*, *28*(5), 917–923. https://doi.org/10.1111/jep.13741

Sointu, E. (2017). 'Good'patient/'bad'patient: Clinical learning and the entrenching of inequality. *Sociology of Health & Illness*, *39*(1), 63–77.

Steinberg, D. L. (2016). Good patient–bad patient: The ethical imaginary of cancer. In *The ethics of care.* Routledge.

Subramani, S. (2018). The moral significance of capturing micro-inequities in hospital settings. *Social Science and Medicine*, *209*, 136–144. https://doi.org/10.1016/j.socscimed.2018.05.036

Subramani, S. (2020). The social construction of incompetency: Moving beyond embedded paternalism toward the practice of respect. *Health Care Analysis*, *28*(3), 249–265. https://doi.org/10.1007/s10728-020-00395-w

Subramani, S. (2022). Moral habitus: An approach to understanding embedded disrespectful practices. *Developing World Bioethics*, *22*(2), 94–104. https://doi.org/10.1111/dewb.12301

Subramani, S., & Biller-Andorno, N. (2022). Revisiting respect for persons: Conceptual analysis and implications for clinical practice. *Medicine, Health Care and Philosophy.* https://doi.org/10.1007/s11019-022-10079-y

Subramanian, S., Ackerson, L. K., Subramanyam, M. A., & Sivaramakrishnan, K. (2008). Health inequalities in India: The axes of stratification. *The Brown Journal of World Affairs*, *14*(2), 127–138.

Tan, J., Stewart, A., Fitzpatrick, R., & Hope, R. (2006). Competence to make treatment decisions in anorexia nervosa: Thinking processes and values. *Philosophy, Psychiatry, & Psychology*, *13*(4), 267–282.

Torroella Carney, M., Neugroschl, J., Morrison, R. S., Marin, D., & Siu, A. L. (2001). The development and piloting of a capacity assessment tool. *The Journal of Clinical Ethics*, *12*(1), 17–23.

Verlinde, E., De Laender, N., De Maesschalck, S., Deveugele, M., & Willems, S. (2012). The social gradient in doctor-patient communication. *International Journal for Equity in Health*, *11*(1), 12.

Water, T., Ford, K., Spence, D., & Rasmussen, S. (2016). Patient advocacy by nurses–past, present and future. *Contemporary Nurse*, *52*(6), 696–709.

Willems, S., De Maesschalck, S., Deveugele, M., Derese, A., & De Maeseneer, J. (2005). Socio-economic status of the patient and doctor–patient communication: Does it make a difference? *Patient Education and Counseling*, *56*(2), 139–146. https://doi.org/10.1016/j.pec.2004.02.011

4 Everyday Indignities

Institutionalising Passive Patienthood

Stories of Othering and Humiliation

> There is no one to take care of us. He was admitted five days ago. I cannot stay inside the ward for more than the briefest of periods. The senior staff nurse scolds me if she sees me when I visit him. I walk out immediately when she stares at me. It is my fate that I can't take him to a private hospital. Well, this is how we are treated everywhere.
>
> Mary, 41, female, fish vendor, Government Hospital

During my doctoral study, the daily walk to the government hospital became more than just a routine; it was a journey through paths marked by deep-seated inequalities. Having lived all my life in a village and on the outskirts of big city until my master's degree, I had encountered inequalities and inequities in various forms. Having recently moved to the big city of Chennai, each day, I passed through a nearby slum on my way from the MRTS station, and the sights and sounds of that journey have stayed with me to this day. The narrow, crowded lanes, the makeshift homes—some with concrete and a tiny room just big enough to sit in—women cooking next to garbage dump, school children hurrying to school, and concerned mothers feeding their children right next to a ditch—all of these scenes painted a vivid picture of the lives of those who were most often overlooked by society, in urban slums. This is well captured by Veena Das in *Affliction: Health, Disease, Poverty,* where she illustrates how health, disease, and poverty are not merely biological or economic conditions but are deeply embedded in the social and moral fabric of people's lives, as seen through her work in Bhagwanpur Kheda in East Delhi. My own lived experiences, along with daily observations of walkthroughs across slum and government hospital, forced me to confront the stark realities of the structural inequalities at play and how it reinforces each other. I began to reflect critically on how these very structures—deeply embedded in the socio-economic and political fabric of our society—shaped the way marginalized people were treated and evaluated during their encounters with the healthcare system. The hospital, a place that should have been a refuge and a caring environment,

DOI: 10.4324/9781003129998-5

instead became a space where these inequalities were magnified and played out in the most personal and painful ways.

As I spent time within the hospital's physical structure, sitting on the benches, lingering in the corridors, and observing from the lawn benches and canteens, a troubling pattern emerged. Everywhere I looked, I saw interactions steeped in disrespect and even violence. Patients were dismissed, humiliated, and shamed, their concerns trivialized, their dignity stripped away with each passing encounter. There were few moments of love, care, and joy, that filled my heart and retained the dignity, self-respect, and integrity as a bystander. For example, when a caretaker who was a sister was feeding her brother, when Aayya (hospital help and support staff) was patiently listening to worries of family member, when a ward boy was respectfully walking an elderly woman and having a fun conversation about her grandson. These moments, however, were exceptions rather than the norm—brief glimmers of humanity in a system otherwise marred by indifference and neglect.

The very mundane conversations and interactions can become sites of shame, humiliation, violence, due to othering, or of joy, care, love, and respect. Learning from various critical scholars over the years (Ahmed, 2013; Ambedkar, 2020; Fanon, 2010; Guru, 2009; Honneth, 2014; hooks, 2014; Rege, 2014; Rodrigues, 2024; Yancy, 2008; Kaufmann et al., 2010; Paik, 2014, 2022), when I refer to Othering, I mean the process of marginalizing minorities and dehumanizing us/them to reinforce existing hierarchies and power structures, particularly within healthcare interactions. Our shared corporeal vulnerability opens the door to experiences of shame, humiliation, indignation, and violence or otherwise. This Othering, evident in both overt actions and little acts of disrespect, often manifests in the construction of the "passive patient" who is disregarded, dismissed, and denied agency in healthcare settings. These little acts of disrespect and everyday indignities are products of Othering, where behaviors and attitudes diminish the patient's sense of self-respect and recognition. By reducing individuals to passive recipients of care, healthcare systems reproduce power imbalances that strip away the fundamental human need for self-respect, recognition, and a precondition for agency. Self-respect and recognition are crucial if we are to emphasize patient's agency within the oppressive structures. Without addressing these everyday indignities and the role Othering plays in their perpetuation, we cannot fully understand how the subjective and objective dimensions of oppression are intertwined in healthcare interactions.

During my fieldwork, the casual cruelty of these interactions was striking—whether it was a nurse's sharp words, a doctor's dismissive glance, or the indifferent bureaucracy that treated people as mere numbers rather than individuals with stories, experiences, struggles, lives, and agency. The voices of those like Mary, a 41-year-old fish vendor, echo in my memory. Her words are a poignant reminder of how the everyday indignities of patients and their families are laden with an affective injustice—a physical and emotional burden carried with each encounter in these spaces. The stare of the nurse, the harsh words, the unspoken judgment—all these are part of a routine that reinforces the message that people like Mary are undeserving of attention and unworthy of dignity. The daily ritual of degradation becomes a part of one's lived experience, an embodied and affective injustice that seeps into our very being. It is not just the obvious acts of disrespect that wound, but the accumulation of these little acts of disrespect—everyday indignities and othering—that erode a person's sense of self-respect and true dignity. For Mary and others like her, the hospital is not just a place of healing; it is also a site where the deep-seated hierarchies of society are played out in the most intimate and vulnerable moments of their lives.

In this chapter, I will present the dominant narratives that emerged from these observations and experiences—the stories of othering, suffering, and humiliation experienced by marginalized patients and their families. Through their voices, I will reveal the harsh realities of healthcare encounters in this context, where the very structures meant to provide care often perpetuate harm. These narratives are not just about individual experiences but are reflective of a larger, systemic issue—one that underscores the urgent need to address the deep-rooted inequalities that shape our healthcare system and, by extension, our society.

The Silent Burden: Dignity Stripped

In the corridors of the government hospital, where the walls seemed to echo with the weariness of those who walked them, a silent yet pervasive reality was woven into the fabric of everyday interactions: the discrimination, stigmatization, and shaming of those already burdened by poverty. This was a place where the power dynamics between caregivers and patients were not just felt—they were etched into the very air, manifesting in both subtle and overt acts of disrespect that served to reinforce the social hierarchies defining life outside the hospital's doors. For many patients and their families, the experience of seeking care at the government hospital was laced with the bitter taste of shame and humiliation. Poverty, which had long dictated the limits of their lives, now dictated the kind of care they received. They were acutely aware that the free treatment they received came with a hidden cost: the cost of their self-respect and dignity, which we saw in judges's passing remarks too in Chapter 2.

We can observe how people in power perceive individuals from marginalized communities. For instance, when closely reading the Supreme Court judgment in *Samira Kohli v Prabha Manchanda*, the judgment casually reflects a common sense view of how poor patients are perceived: "Many poor patients with serious ailments (e.g., heart patients and cancer patients) have to wait for months for their turn even for diagnosis, and due to limited treatment facilities, many die even before their turn comes for treatment. What choice do these poor patients have? Any treatment of whatever degree is a boon or a favor for them... What choice of treatment can these doctors give to the poor patients? What informed consent can they take from them? What we are considering in this case is not the duties or obligations of doctors in government charitable hospitals where treatment is free or on an actual cost basis". This is not surprising in post-Independence to current day narrative (Arnold, 2000; Guru, 2009; Harrison, 1992; Kumbhar, 2022, 2023). In this judgment, while the judges acknowledge the harsh social reality that poor people are at the mercy of institutional and structural injustice, they seem to miss the opportunity to facilitate conditions where poor patients could exercise agency. Instead, these patients are perceived as "passive patients" who cannot make decisions and are in need of benevolent and paternalistic doctors.

In the last chapter, we observed that it's not just that the staff—overwhelmed and under-resourced—often operated under the assumption that patients who walked through the doors of the government hospital did so because they had no other choice; they were perceived as poor, uneducated, and incapable of understanding the complexities of their own treatment. This perception was compounded by assumptions that patients were "passive" due to class-caste-gender hierarchies, along with the "sick role" expectation of patients. These assumptions translated into a myriad of everyday indignities—subtle, often unspoken slights that underscored the stigma attached to poverty and led to unequal treatment during healthcare encounters. Doctors avoided eye contact, rolled their eyes at questions, and sighed loudly in frustration when interacting with patients they perceived as difficult or ignorant. Nurses, stretched thin by the demands of their roles, often scolded or yelled at patients and their family members—actions that were rationalized as necessary to maintain order in an overburdened system (Ray, 2020). But for the patients, these were not mere inconveniences; they were daily reminders of their social status, of the shame and humiliation that accompanied their reliance on a public health system that saw them as lesser and without "choice".

Vani, a young woman working in a garment factory and caring for her mother in the obstetrics and gynecology ward, spoke of her exhaustion and frustration. Beneath her words lay a deeper lived experience of humiliation. She described how she followed the doctors from the ward to their offices, tailing them, hoping for just a moment of their time, only to be ignored time and again. In this embodied experience of humiliation the message was clear: her concerns, her mother's suffering, were not worthy of attention. "They don't even bother to stop for a second and listen to me," she said, her voice heavy with a sense of powerlessness and voice with rage and humiliation that was all too familiar to her. For Vani, like so many others I spoke to at GH, the experience of being disregarded by those in positions of power was not new—it was an extension of the marginalization she faced outside the hospital, now compounded by class and gender. This sense of invisibility, of being treated as if she were not even there, was not just an emotional response; it was a manifestation of the structural inequalities that pervaded the hospital. The care and recognition Vani and her mother received—or rather, the lack of it—was a reflection of their social positioning in society. They were poor, they were women, and in the eyes of the hospital staff, they were undeserving of anything more than the bare minimum. The doctors and nurses, often without realizing it or due to an embraced hidden curriculum within that institution, reinforced these social hierarchies through their behavior, perpetuating a cycle of shame and humiliation that the patients had come to expect.

Another patient's mother echoed these sentiments. Her son, a 26-year-old mechanic, had been admitted for knee surgery, but the care they received was anything but compassionate. She recounted how the senior nurse scolded her for staying in the ward too long, a reprimand that stung deeply. The stare from the nurse—a look that communicated both authority and disdain—compelled her to leave immediately, a silent acknowledgment of her social status due to class and religion. "It is my fate that I can't take him to a private hospital," she said, resigned to the treatment she received because she had no other option. Her inability to afford better care meant she had to accept the disrespect that came with being a patient at a government hospital.

For those familiar with how government hospitals function and the everyday indignities witnessed there, particularly by women and disabled patients, their experiences reveal not just suffering but also the structural processes that produce passive patients. During one of my visits, I recall sitting quietly next to a woman anxiously clutching her ration card in the corridor. From where I sat, I could see the interactions in a busy, packed consultation room. When her turn came, she rushed in, and I saw how the doctor didn't even look up. The nurses were busy with other routines and talking amongst themselves. The doctor gestured impatiently for her to sit and speak. She started to explain her symptoms hesitantly, but he interrupted, saying, "sekrama" (faster). She lowered her voice, complied, and left the room as quickly as she could. In these busy and rushed encounters, I witnessed how passivity is both expected and performed. One of the women patients from the government hospital told me, "I am so scared to ask anything. Once, the doctor said if you have questions, go to private [hospitals]... Now I am worried they'll scold me, so I just don't say much. They treat me like I'm stupid and just give me prescriptions...but now I don't even know what problem I have in my uterus. They just don't tell me much". For her, silence was a learned survival mechanism. Every interaction taught her that her worth as a patient depended on her compliance. Her voice and her pain—both physical and emotional—were not seen as valuable contributions to the encounter. In that silence, the archetype of the passive patient is sustained. Disabled patients face indignities that further entrench their passivity, often exacerbated by a lack of infrastructural support and care. One patient shared with me how he was forced to crawl up hospital steps because there was no ramp. "What else could I do? I needed to see the doctor, so I crawled". When he reached the doctor's office, breathless and humiliated, the physician barely acknowledged him, speaking instead to the caretaker who had accompanied him. The archetype of the passive patient is not a reflection of the individuals themselves but rather the product of deeply embedded hierarchies—medical, gendered, cate-class and ableist—that normalize disrespect. The expectation of silence is not incidental; it is demanded and enforced through repeated indignities. Women and disabled patients often internalize this passivity not because they believe it to be right but because resisting risks further harm. These everyday moments of humiliation—rushed examinations, lack of explanations, inaccessible spaces, and impatient dismissals—are not aberrations but part of the very fabric of public healthcare. They sustain the archetype of the passive patient, where compliance is mistaken for acceptance, and silence becomes a survival strategy.

Kumar, a sanitation worker who had undergone hernia surgery at the same hospital, expressed a similar resignation. He said, "The operation and all went well. We are happy here. We heard that this is the best among the government hospitals. Where else can people like us go? We don't have money, so we get what we always get". His words were tinged with a sense of inevitability. For Kumar, the treatment he received—free, but devoid of respect—was simply the way things were for people like him. The shame of his social position had long shaped his expectations, so much so that he had internalized the belief that he deserved nothing more than what he was given out of helplessness. His "happiness" with the care he received was not genuine satisfaction but rather a coping mechanism, a way to reconcile the reality of his situation with the persistent humiliation that accompanied it. This normalization of disrespect was not limited to the patients; it extended to their interactions with the medical staff, who, in turn, reinforced these feelings through their paternalistic attitudes. Nurses like Meenakshi, who saw herself as responsible for the smooth running of the wards, rationalized her harsh treatment of patients as necessary. "We need to shout at them; otherwise, they will not listen," she explained, justifying her behavior as a form of tough love. But for the patients, this shouting was not a form of care—it was a reminder of their place in the social hierarchy, a place where their self-respect and dignity were always under threat.

Similar to the previous chapter, even though during my ethnographic work I didn't get to meet as many queer patients, I witnessed situations as a bystander and had conversations with two queer patients. The institutionalization of everyday indignities forces queer individuals to avoid healthcare until absolutely necessary. These experiences range from microaggressions to overt violence, leading to profound mistrust of medical systems. One of them said, "na varvemattee, yappome, avan koda sande podite vule varnu (I never come here; every time, I have to deal with the security guard before I can meet anyone inside!)". Even when I do meet the doctor, "they don't have any conversation, pate peysamattanga, nanga yena cheriya!? (They don't talk to us, don't even make eye contact, as though disgusted by us like a ditch)". Government hospitals in India often magnify the indignities faced by queer individuals due to systemic neglect. Everyday indignities are routine in these spaces—doctors and staff avoiding eye contact, using dismissive or condescending tones, or making unnecessary comments about a patient's appearance or behavior. One queer patient recalled, "The nurse called me 'he' even after I corrected her. She laughed under her breath and said, 'Why are you confusing us?'" Another shared, "When I asked a question about my treatment, the doctor ignored me completely and just spoke to the nurse, like I wasn't even there". These spaces, where patients are already expected to endure long waits and hurried care, become particularly hostile for queer individuals, especially those from marginalized communities.

The doctors, too, played into this dynamic, often assuming the role of benevolent saviors who believed they knew what was best for their patients, whether or not the patients understood or agreed. A vascular surgeon, articulated this view clearly: "I act like a God. I'll try to do the best possible. I may not explain to him, but I will..." His words revealed a profound disconnect between the medical staff's perception of their role and the patients' experience of that role. To the doctors, being "authoritative" was synonymous with being ethical, with acting in the best interest of the patient. But to the patients, this authority was a source of alienation, a barrier that prevented them from feeling respected and valued.

The shame and humiliation experienced by patients and family members, coupled with the doctors' and nurses' disrespectful and paternalistic attitudes, created an environment where patients were not merely treated for their ailments—they were managed, disciplined, and controlled to retain the archetype of the 'passive patient,' which the system both constructs and maintains. Disciplining and controlling patients in clinic is not new to medical sociology and health studies (Foucault, 1977, 2012). The control was exercised through both blatant and subtle means, from scolding and yelling to dismissive glances and unacknowledged questions. The patients, already vulnerable due to their class, caste, gender, geographical location, and religion, found themselves further marginalized within the hospital setting, their self-respect eroded by the very people tasked with caring for them. While no doctors or nurses in this study explicitly referred to caste names or mentioned treating certain caste communities with disdain, it is not surprising that in healthcare settings, the explicit discussion of caste rarely occurs in urban settings. Instead, class and caste often become embodied in how individuals are perceived, stereotyped, and prejudiced in everyday encounters through certain social markers.

One day during my fieldwork at the government hospital, as I sat in the corridor on a bench with other caretakers waiting for the "doctor's rounds" time, I noticed an older woman accompanying an elderly man, who I later learned was her father, for a follow-up appointment. Her father, dressed in a blue and white checkered lungi, without sandals, and wearing a not-so-clean shirt, sat next to me. As we waited, the woman and I observed how the hospital staff interacted with other patients. A man wearing a clean white shirt and lungi did not have to wait and was greeted warmly by the nurse as he walked straight into the doctor's office. He was probably a familiar face to the nurse, who spoke to him in a tone that was respectful, almost deferential and from nearby area. Seemed like they were familiar to each other. When it was the woman's turn, who was sitting next to me, the interaction was markedly different. The same nurse, who had been so courteous to the previous patient, barely looked at the woman or her father and called out to them with a tone of rudeness and irritation, saying,

"*Ye ma, wamma inge*" (hey you, come over here). She spoke to them in a curt manner and seemed impatient as she hurried them along. When I saw them coming out, the nurse said, "*Thirumbi varade, idethokaga, podu*" (just don't come back, just take this, enough), as the woman was trying to ask questions. The woman made her father sit next to me and said, "*Yeppavu idesolranga anna thirumbi thirumbi inge varnu*" (they keep saying not to come back, but we have to return due to the same issue). Feeling frustrated and devalued, she added, "They don't ask or pay attention to us". We couldn't help but notice the stark difference in how they were treated compared to the other patient.

While the doctor and nurse never explicitly mentioned caste, it was clear to the woman that their treatment was influenced by the social markers that identified them as lower-caste and lower-class. The subtle yet palpable prejudice was something she had encountered throughout her life, but it felt particularly acute in a setting where her father's health was at stake. This narrative illustrates how caste and class, while rarely discussed openly, are deeply embedded in everyday interactions within India's healthcare system. The biases that healthcare providers hold often manifest in the quality of care they offer and in the way patients are treated, influenced by the social markers subconsciously associated with a patient's caste, class, or social position. The incident with the woman was not an outlier; perceived social status, along with familiarity or lack thereof, contributed to the dismissive treatment she received—a treatment that was less about medical care and more about the unspoken hierarchies that still permeate Indian society. For many of the patients at GH, the experience of pain—both physical and emotional—was compounded by the indifference and disrespect they encountered. Meenu, a housewife recovering from surgery, expressed this sentiment with quiet resignation: "Here they send us back by making us remember the pain". Her words, tinged with hopelessness, highlighted how everyday indignities she faced in the hospital were part of a larger pattern of devaluation that permeated her life. The pain she spoke of was not just the physical discomfort of her recovery; it was the emotional toll of being treated as less than human, as someone whose suffering was unimportant. This is an affective injustice, as our embodied and emotional experiences demonstrate how unjust interactions target and creates unjust emotions such as shame, humiliation and indignation. These experiences clearly shows how our interactions reproduce power and how certain emotions are reproduced and normalized to retain the power asymmetry.

In the government hospital, the notion of authority was often equated with ethical responsibility. Doctors and nurses, faced with an overwhelming number of patients, rationalized their paternalistic attitudes as a necessary measure to maintain order within the overburdened system. For many of them, particularly at the government hospital (GH), being authoritative was seen as acting in the best interest of the patient—a perception deeply rooted in the belief that patients and their families were incapable of understanding complex medical information or that they did not deserve "to know" or "to be listened to". As we saw in Chapters 2 and 3, this narrative not only shapes the meaning healthcare providers assign to their actions but is also viewed as a common sense norm in Indian society, which is heavily influenced by upper-class-caste values. One of the surgeons, Dr. Nitesh, a 41-year-old general surgeon at the GH, articulated this perspective clearly: "But there is a percentage [of patients], especially on this side [GH/poor], that do not understand, so you have to be very authoritative towards them. I have to tell them to listen to what I say… Suppose, if my dad were in a similar state, what would I do? Like this, we obtain consent". His words reveal a mindset where authority and control are seen as necessary tools to guide patients who are perceived as lacking the capacity to make informed decisions. This paternalistic approach was not unique to Dr. Nitesh; it was a common sentiment among many doctors and nurses at the GH. They often justified their need to "play God" by emphasizing the supposed ignorance and helplessness of the patients they served. The doctors believed their role was to act as benevolent figures, ensuring that patients trusted them implicitly and accepted their decisions without question. This perception of patients as "poor", "illiterate", and incapable of understanding was particularly pervasive at the GH, where the overwhelming majority of patients came from socio-economically disadvantaged backgrounds.

The deep roots of many healthcare concerns and ethical issues can often be traced back to poverty, caste, religion, and gender discrimination, particularly in resource-scarce countries (Chattopadhyay, 2018; Jungari & Chauhan, 2017; Kowal & Afshar, 2015; Sen, 2010, 2011; Sen & Iyer, 2012). As mentioned about poverty-induced shame in the last chapter, we can continue to see how Amartya Sen's (1983) argument that shame lies at the heart of poverty continues to be reflection of inequalities across different institutions (Chase et al., 2014; Gubrium et al., 2013; Pellissery & Mathew, 2013). While the lack of access to essential services such as healthcare, sanitation, and nutrition disproportionately affects those of lower socio-economic status, the impact extends beyond these tangible factors (Dreze & Sen, 1990; Sen, 1983). People living in poverty also experience worse treatment outcomes and face increased risks of illness and death. Although financial barriers to accessing treatment and care are often cited as primary causes of health disparities, research suggests that socio-economic disadvantage alone can lead to poorer health outcomes, even when access to healthcare is equal or universally free. This indicates that the relationship between health and socio-economic status is more complex than simply access to care. Improving access to healthcare is undoubtedly crucial, but it is also essential to examine other mechanisms that contribute to reduced health outcomes.

Many studies has showed how stigma, shame, humiliation, and other negative emotions play a significant role in linking socio-economic-gender disadvantage to poorer health outcomes (Cheston, 2022; Dickerson et al., 2004, 2004; Dolezal & Lyons, 2017; Green et al., 2005; Loughlin et al., 2022; Park et al., 2021). The behaviors, actions, and attitudes stemming from stigmatization, shaming, or disrespect toward low-income individuals have long been documented across various societies. Numerous studies have shown that experiencing poverty-related stigma can have a detrimental impact on health and health outcomes (Inglis et al., 2023; Lund et al., 2010). While some studies report that patients experience stigma, shame, and other self-conscious emotions related to race, caste, gender, disability or specific health conditions, much of the discussion has focused primarily on health and illness (Bromley, 2022; Dickerson et al., 2004; Dolezal, 2015, 2022; Dolezal & Lyons, 2017; Johnson et al., 2022; Scully, 2010). While it is important to understand these emotions from the perspective of illness and health through an intersectional lens, it is equally critical to view them as moral emotions within cultural and political context. These emotions influence the moral standards and behaviors that individuals navigate in their everyday lives. As such, self-conscious emotions play a significant role in healthcare interactions, relationships, and patients' sense of self. These moral emotions lead to self-imposed affective consequences as individuals evaluate the ethics of their behavior or actions, reflecting on their own worth and dignity. As I demonstrated in the last chapters and sections, the moral significance of acts of disrespect and the social construction of incompetence are crucial in understanding how overt or subtle acts and behaviors within the context of social inequalities raise concerns about the dignity and respect afforded to patients and their family members. For instance, evidence shows that some doctors use a patient's socio-economic status to determine what information to share regarding treatment and alternative options, and they are value-laden (Park et al., 2021; Timmermans, 2020; Willems et al., 2005). Moreover, some nurses and doctors treat patients differently during these interactions based on their perceptions of those patients due to social markers.

Poor patients are often seen as "incapable", "incompetent", or "passive", leading healthcare providers to withhold critical information about their treatment. Patients and their families internalize and normalize their sense of belonging—or lack thereof—by reflecting on their socio-economic status during these interactions, which significantly impacts how they act, behave, and engage in healthcare decision-making and encounters. As discussed earlier, for example, a fish vendor caring for her son in a government hospital shared her experience: "There is no one to take care of us. He was admitted five days ago. I cannot stay inside the ward for more than the briefest of periods. The senior staff nurse scolds me if she sees me when I visit him. I walk out immediately when she stares at me. It is my fate that I can't take him to a private hospital. Well, this is how we are treated everywhere". By critically reflecting on the narratives of patients and their family members, we can uncover the processes of moral evaluation that shape their experiences of poverty-induced stigma, shame, and humiliation. These negative self-conscious emotions have profound and pernicious effects, not only on health outcomes but also on the moral self. Having lived much of my life in poverty and experienced its various shades, I have been reminded of my gender, caste, class, and ethnic identity in both personal and professional interactions. These experiences continue to haunt me, serving as a constant reminder of the profound impact that poverty-induced stigma, shame, and humiliation have on people's lives and their moral significance in healthcare interactions and on one's moral self.

In this section, by critically analyzing the experiences of patients and family members, as well as through interviews with doctors and nurses, it became clear that the ideal patient, in the eyes of healthcare professionals, was one who do not question and who accepted their authority without resistance. This expectation of unquestioning compliance was deeply ingrained, and any deviation from it was met with a need to reassert control, often through both blatant and subtle behaviors and actions. The doctors' and nurses' perceptions of patients as "ignorant" and "unable to make decisions" served to reinforce their position of power within the hospital. By assuming the role of the powerful benefactor or benign "God", they could maintain a hierarchical relationship where their authority went unchallenged. This dynamic not only perpetuated the doctors' dominance but also stripped patients of their agency, reducing them to passive recipients of care who were expected to fit into the mold of the ideal, passive, incompetent, and compliant patient.

Listening to these varied experiences, the pervasive sense of being disregarded was a common thread among the patients at the government hospital. This feeling was rooted in their experiences outside the hospital, in a society that often saw them as invisible, and it was reinforced by the treatment they received within the hospital's walls. For them, poverty was not just a socioeconomic condition—it was a form of social and moral suffering that marked them as undeserving of respect and stripped them of their agency. This suffering followed them into every interaction within healthcare spaces. In the end, the shame and humiliation these patients and their family members experienced were not isolated incidents but reflections of a broader societal disdain for the marginalized, who are poor and considered "passive". The hospital, a place that should have offered care, listening, and attention, instead became another arena where their dignity was stripped away; where the shame of poverty was laid bare for all to see. And yet, despite this, the patients continued to seek care there, resigned to the social reality that they had no other choice. For them, the disrespect they faced were simply part of the bargain—a necessary evil in exchange for the care they desperately needed but could never afford elsewhere.

These attitudes and practices echo findings from other studies, where there is asymmetry in doctor–patient relationship (Banerjee & Sanyal, 2012; Fochsen et al., 2006; Gopichandran & Chetlapalli, 2013; Madhivanan et al., 2014; Sen et al., 2018; Subramani, 2022). In the GH, these expectations were not just theoretical; they were enacted daily in interactions where patients and their families were subjected to constant control. Whether through direct commands or more subtle cues, the message was clear: patients were to trust, obey, and not question the authority of the medical professionals, who, in their view, always knew best. These narrative paints a picture of a healthcare system where authority is conflated with care, and where the power dynamics between doctors and patients are skewed to such an extent that the very notion of patient autonomy is rendered almost non-existent—one might even wonder how it could be imagined at all. The belief that patients cannot understand or make decisions leads to a culture where they are not only disrespected but also systematically disempowered, reinforcing a cycle of dependence and submission that ultimately undermines the very purpose of healthcare—to care. I would say, care cannot exist without respect!

Stories of Dismissal: Patients Who Dare to Ask

In the private hospital, the corridors may have been quieter, the conversations more measured, but the invisible threads of class, caste, and authority were woven into its complexity just as they were in the government sector. Here, patients arrived not just with ailments but with expectations, fortified by the social, economic, and cultural capital that their status afforded them. In this private hospital, which was also a charitable institution, while profit-making was not the key motivation, it often attracted upper-class and middle-class patients. The doctors and nurses, trained in the art of politeness and professionalism, navigated these expectations with practiced ease, yet their actions often betrayed the deeper, more insidious forces at play.

A significant theme that emerged from talking to patients and family members was the palpable sense of entitlement and confidence that private hospital (PH) patients and their families exhibited in demanding the respect and quality of care they believed they were owed. Unlike in government hospitals, where patients often felt compelled to accept whatever treatment they were given—and were often told so by state and legal judgments—those in the private sector approached their healthcare experience with a clear expectation: they were paying customers, and as such, they deserved professionalism and respect. Mani, a bank manager, embodied the confidence that came with knowing one's place in the social hierarchy. He said, "Sure, I should know what is happening. How long will I be like this? In general, I have to know. He was kind to tell, because it is totally new. Colonoscopy. It is a new technical term for me. I asked him all my doubts. I asked my son also to know about the treatment. My son discussed everything with the doctor and told me not to worry".

When he recounted his interaction with the doctor, there was no trace of doubt in his voice. "I should know what is happening," he stated, as though it were a given. His son, equally assured, took on the role of intermediary, discussing the treatment in detail with the doctor. For Mani, the colonoscopy was new and unfamiliar, but the respect he was shown was not. It was a respect he had come to expect, one that was inextricably tied to his identity as an educated, middle-class man. For patients like Mani, the relationship with their healthcare providers was transactional, defined by the expectation that respect and professionalism were integral parts of the service they were paying for. This sense of deservingness was deeply rooted in their socio-economic status, which not only gave them access to private healthcare but also shaped their interactions with medical professionals. They approached the hospital not with the deference often expected in public settings, but with the assertiveness of a consumer who knows their rights and is prepared to claim them. This demand for professionalism was not merely about receiving competent medical care; it was about being treated with the respect that these patients felt was their due.

The healthcare providers, in turn, were aware that these patients were not passive recipients of care but active participants who expected—and, if necessary, would insist on—being treated with dignity. The professionalism they demanded was as much about interpersonal interactions as it was about the technical aspects of their care. The patients saw respect, communication, and attentiveness as non-negotiable components of the service they were purchasing, and any deviation from this could be met with dissatisfaction or even complaints. Often, the patients and their families at the private hospital viewed themselves as clients in a service industry, where their socio-economic status afforded them the privilege of not just receiving care but dictating the terms of that care. The doctors and nurses were not merely caregivers; they were service providers whose professionalism was a reflection of the value they placed on their clients. For these patients, respectful treatment was not a bonus; it was an expectation, an intrinsic part of the healthcare package they had paid for, in stark contrast to the government hospital, where respect was often nowhere in sight. Yet, even as Mani felt secure in his right to information, others found their confidence tempered by a lingering sense of vulnerability.

Mangai, a software engineer, spoke with the conviction of someone who knew her worth, but her words were tinged with the memory of past experiences where that worth had been overlooked. She said, "Here the staff are very nice and helpful. They make sure that the patient is comfortable. Based on our friends' opinions and our family doctor's second opinion, we came here. The quality of service is good. My brother has talked to the doctor and discussed everything. They are professional, unlike other private hospitals. Our last experience was very bad, though it was at a big branded hospital, hospital 'X'. They did not bother to talk properly. As of now, here it is not like that. We pay to get good quality service". She asserted this while reflecting and comparing the current hospital favorably to others where her family had been treated with less care. Her recounting of those experiences at "Hospital X" revealed a clear understanding: respect, in the world of private healthcare, was transactional. It was something you bought along with the treatment, a commodity tied to the brand of the hospital and the reputation of the doctors. Like many other patients and family members at this private hospital, Mangai approached her healthcare experience with a clear set of expectations. She believed that respect from care providers was not just desirable but something she was owed as part of the service she had paid for. Her interactions with the hospital staff reflected this belief—respect was a non-negotiable part of the transaction. This sense of entitlement to respect and professionalism was a common thread among the patients and families I spoke with. For them, satisfaction with their care was closely tied to how they were treated, acknowledged, and respected by the healthcare providers. These patients were acutely aware of their rights as consumers in what they saw as a service industry. They recognized their position not just as patients in need of care but as clients paying for a service, a perspective that influenced every aspect of their interactions with the hospital staff.

Before choosing to seek treatment at the private hospital, patients and their families went to great lengths to investigate the hospital's reputation and the quality of care it provided. They saw this as an essential part of their role as informed consumers. However, despite their confidence in demanding appropriate service, many of these patients and their families felt a lingering hesitation when it came to questioning the doctors too assertively. This hesitation stemmed from a fear of crossing an invisible line—of being perceived as too "demanding" and potentially annoying the doctors. The doctors were seen as authoritative figures, holding a certain power that the patients and their families were cautious not to challenge too openly. Maintaining a warm, cooperative relationship with the doctors was important, and there was a sense that pushing too hard or asking too many questions could disrupt this delicate balance.

When I was diagnosed with polycystic ovary syndrome (PCOS), I went to a government hospital in Chennai for a consultation, hoping to get some clarity and guidance. Before the appointment, I had done my homework—reading up on PCOS, trying to understand what it meant, and preparing a list of questions to ask the doctor. I wanted to be informed and involved in my care, but things didn't go as smoothly as I'd expected. As soon as I started asking questions, I could sense the doctor's patience wearing thin. She gave me minimal information, almost as if she were annoyed that I was even asking. Her body language and facial expressions made it clear that my inquiries were not welcome. It felt like she was silently telling me, "How dare you question me?" and "Don't bother me with your "stupid" questions". At one point, she couldn't hide her frustration anymore and snapped, "Is it Dr. Google that you trust?" That comment stung. I wasn't trying to challenge her expertise; I just wanted to understand my condition better. But instead of a conversation, I got a lecture. She quickly prescribed some medicines, rattled off instructions for the dosage, and made it clear that my role was simply to follow her orders without question. I left the consultation feeling dismissed and unheard. It was as if I had stepped into a world where the doctor's authority was absolute, and any attempt to engage or seek more information was seen as a challenge to that authority.

The whole experience left me feeling powerless, as if my concerns didn't matter. Similar to my experiences, I frequently heard stories from diverse patients, each with their own version of feeling dismissed or discouraged when they tried to take an active role in their healthcare. One patient, a young woman in her late twenties at the private hospital (PH), shared how she felt completely shut down during a consultation. "I asked the doctor what my options were for managing my condition, and he just sighed and said, 'Why do you need to know all this? Just follow the treatment plan I'm giving you.' It was like he couldn't be bothered to explain anything to me," she said, her frustration still evident. Another patient, a middle-aged man, recounted how his attempts to ask about alternative treatments for his chronic pain were met with outright hostility before coming to this current surgery. "The doctor looked at me and said, 'Do you have a medical degree? No? Then stop acting like you know better and just do as I say.' I felt so small in that moment, like I wasn't even allowed to question my own care". These stories highlight a recurring theme: patients who try to engage in their healthcare are often met with resistance, as if their questions and concerns are an inconvenience. The dismissive attitudes and condescending responses create an environment where patients feel they have to choose between staying silent or risking being labeled as difficult. It's a dynamic that leaves many feeling powerless and unheard, much like I did during my own experiences.

A similar situation occurred when I was taking care of my dad during his stay at a partially government-funded private hospital in Bangalore, when I was 20 years old. He was scheduled for coronary angioplasty, and naturally, my mom and I were anxious and wanted to stay informed about his condition. As my mom was worried and anxious and couldn't feel comfortable, I, with my broken English, tried to reach out to the doctor during his rounds, as he didn't seem to understand Kannada. He didn't even turn towards me when I was trying to talk to him, and the nurses waved at me to be quiet. Trying to get information or a status update on the surgery from the hospital staff was a real struggle. Every time we approached the doctors or nurses for an update, they seemed to avoid us. When they did speak to us, their answers were curt and lacking in detail, almost as if they were deliberately keeping us at a distance. It felt like they were maintaining an unspoken barrier, ensuring we didn't feel too comfortable asking questions or getting involved in the care process. In these experiences, a clear pattern emerged: asking questions or seeking more information wasn't just unwelcome—it was almost punished.

Patients like me, or caretakers like my mom and me, who tried to engage more actively in the healthcare process, were subtly discouraged from doing so. The message was clear: don't challenge the system, don't question the professionals, just do as you're told. There was an underlying fear that if we pushed too hard, asked too many questions, or seemed too involved, we would be labeled as troublemakers. The perception of troublemakers was quite evident in doctors' narratives when discussing informed consent forms in the last chapter. This dynamic creates a difficult situation for patients. On the one hand, we want to be informed and involved in our healthcare decisions, but on the other hand, we have to be careful not to overstep invisible boundaries that might lead to negative consequences, such as being rushed out of the consultation or receiving even less information. It's a delicate balance, and it often leaves patients feeling like they have to tiptoe around their own healthcare providers, just to avoid being seen as too demanding or difficult. As Kumari, a 55-year-old sister of a patient, explained, "See, we can demand and have the right, but we cannot go beyond some extent. If we ask and they get irritated, then it may be a problem for us".

Kumari's words capture the ambivalence that many patients and families felt in private hospitals—on the one hand, they were aware of their rights and felt justified in expecting high standards of care and respect. On the other hand, they were also acutely aware of the power dynamics at play. The doctors' authority, while not absolute, was significant enough to influence how far they felt they could push their demands. This tension between the patients' awareness of their rights and their cautious deference to medical authority reveals the complexities of the doctor–patient relationship, which is becoming more like a provider–client relationship, in the private healthcare setting. In this environment, respect and professionalism were seen as rights that came with the price of care, but they were also commodities that could be jeopardized if the balance of power was disturbed. Patients' satisfaction was thus a delicate interplay between their role as consumers and the traditional hierarchies of the doctor–patient relationship, where the authority of the doctor could still impose limits on how far their demands could go.

But even in this transactional space, the entrenched hierarchies of caste and class were never far from the surface. In the corridors and outpost next to the doctor's office, where sometimes I could get a glimpse from a distance, the pattern in urbanized hospitals I visited to meet doctors often showed visible distancing. The elderly man in a dhoti found himself on the receiving end of a surgeon's indifference. As the doctor checked his phone, the man's presence was acknowledged only in the most perfunctory way. There was no outright disrespect, but the message was clear: this man did not command the same attention as others. Similarly, the middle-aged woman with her heavy gold chains—perhaps a symbol of old wealth, yet still marked by the rurality of her attire—was cut off mid-sentence by a female manager who had little time for her concerns. These interactions were not anomalies; they were the norm in a system where respect was calibrated according to a patient's perceived social value based on social markers. Even those who outwardly conformed to the expectations of the educated middle class found that their status did not always shield them from subtle dismissals. The postgraduate doctor who sighed and nodded as he half-listened to the questions of a female caretaker illustrated this perfectly. His actions were not overtly rude, but they communicated a clear lack of engagement, a signal that this interaction was not one he deemed worthy of his full attention.

While the asymmetry in the power relationship between healthcare providers and patients is a well-known aspect of medical interactions (Pilnick & Dingwall, 2011), what emerged starkly in the private hospital setting were the instances of disrespect that played out at various levels of caregiving. These subtle, often unnoticed, instances of inequities revealed much about the underlying societal norms that shaped interactions within the hospital spaces. Take the case of Saraswathi, a 51-year-old homemaker whose husband was about to be discharged. When she sought basic information about her husband's postoperative care—asking the nurse what food to give and what medicine to take—her query was met not with the attentiveness one might expect, but with a dismissive gesture. The nurse did not engage with Saraswathi directly; instead, she walked away, stating that she would inform Saraswathi's son, implying that he was the one who truly needed to be informed. Saraswathi recounted this experience in a matter-of-fact tone, but her words hinted at the underlying discomfort she felt. The nurse's action, though subtle, was a clear instance of disregard. Saraswathi herself noted that perhaps the nurse considered her less significant in the decision-making process, assuming instead that the son, as the male family member, was the actual authority. This interaction underscores a critical point: while women are generally perceived as the primary caretakers within families, they are not always recognized as key decision-makers in healthcare contexts, particularly when a male family member is present. This anecdote provides a window into how gender and status within the family structure influence the treatment patients and their families receive from healthcare providers. Despite the general expectation that women, especially mothers or wives, would be the ones receiving information about postoperative care, Saraswathi's experience reveals a different dynamic. The nurse's behavior reflects a deeper societal bias that positions young, working male family members as the default decision-makers, often to the exclusion of women.

Such disrespect is not just isolated incidents; it reflects broader cultural norms that permeate the healthcare environment. The actions of the doctors and nurses at the private hospital were not merely professional responses but were deeply influenced by these societal norms. The same tendencies were observed at the government hospital as well, indicating that this issue was not confined to the private sector but was, in fact, a pervasive aspect of the healthcare system in general. The implications of these instances of disrespect are significant. They subtly reinforce the hierarchical structure within families, where decision-making authority is often skewed towards male members, even in situations where women are the primary caregivers. By disregarding Saraswathi and directing the information to her son, the nurse was not just making a simple logistical decision; she was, in effect, perpetuating a broader cultural narrative that undermines the agency of women within the family structure.

These observations point to the need for a more nuanced understanding of patient care, one that recognizes and addresses the ways in which societal norms infiltrate and influence the healthcare environment. The disrespect Saraswathi experienced is not just a minor inconvenience; it is indicative of a larger, systemic issue that affects the quality of care and the respect afforded to patients and their families. Recognizing and addressing these subtleties is crucial for creating a more equitable and respectful healthcare system. One major insight that emerged was the emphasis placed by most surgeons on providing patients with adequate information before obtaining their signatures on consent forms—a practice largely shaped by the need to protect against potential litigation when discussing patient rights and autonomy. Dr. Sriram, a senior general surgeon at the private hospital (PH), captured this shift in approach with a candid admission: "Things have changed. Here we are professionals who should treat patients as people with rights as consumers. They can sue us if we don't maintain proper records. They come for our time and quality of service, and thus they are entitled to their rights. We treat them well. That is the way it works". Dr. Sriram's words highlight a significant transformation in the doctor–patient relationship within private healthcare. The notion of patients as "consumers" with enforceable rights reflects a broader shift towards a more transactional model of care, where the quality of service is directly tied to the legal and financial imperatives of the hospital. This shift is also echoed in the practices of other healthcare professionals at the hospital.

Ms. Lakshmi, a senior staff nurse, emphasized the hospital's commitment to "quality care" and adherence to strict protocols as part of maintaining their accredited status. "We try our best to provide quality care. We are an accredited hospital and strictly follow the protocols," she stated, underscoring the importance of maintaining professional standards and fostering cordial relationships with patients and their families. These interviews with PH doctors and nurses revealed a consistent perspective: patients and their families were seen as consumers who deserved high "quality of care", and professionalism was expected from healthcare providers. The concept of "patients' rights" was firmly embedded within the hospital's legal framework, ensuring that information disclosure and medical decision-making were handled with a degree of transparency designed to protect both the patient and the institution. However, when compared to the experiences of participants at government hospitals (GH), significant differences in demographics and perceptions of care became apparent. The PH participants, often from higher socio-economic backgrounds, experienced a healthcare environment where respect and professionalism were part of the package they were paying for. While instances of disrespect did exist at PH, particularly along lines of gender, class, and geography, they were less pronounced than in the public sector. The private hospital environment was structured around the concept of the "provider–client relationship". Patients and their families viewed themselves as consumers entitled to demand high-quality service, while care providers saw themselves as professionals obligated to deliver that service within the bounds of hospital protocols and legal requirements. This dynamic generally led to positive perceptions of care among the PH participants, who felt their rights as consumers were being respected. Yet, even in this more polished environment, interactions were not free from the influence of broader societal inequities. Disrespect still surfaced, subtly reflecting larger issues of social hierarchy.

The extent to which these inequities were experienced varied based on factors such as socio-economic status, education level, age, gender, and whether patients came from urban or rural areas. These findings offer an important lens through which to understand the nuanced ways in which disrespect manifests in different healthcare settings. While the private hospital provided an environment where patients' rights were more explicitly recognized and respected, the persistence of subtle inequities suggests that underlying social dynamics continue to shape the experiences of patients and their families, regardless of the setting.

By highlighting different degrees of disrespect across public and private hospital settings, I demonstrate the complex interplay between professionalism, legal obligations, and deeply entrenched social norms that influence healthcare delivery. The archetype of the "passive patient" is not merely a relic of an outdated medical model but a construct reinforced by the pervasive authority and paternalism inherent in the upper-middle-class values of society. Patients in private hospitals may have been educated, confident, and aware of their rights, but they were also deeply aware of the social norms that governed their interactions with healthcare providers. They understood that their ability to actively participate in their care was not only a matter of legal or moral rights but was also influenced by the same forces of power and privilege that shaped their lives outside the hospital walls. This awareness extended to recognizing that they might benefit from or be disadvantaged by these forces to varying degrees.

Ultimately, the "passive patient" was not solely a figure representing those who lacked education or resources. It was a role that even the most privileged patients were sometimes compelled to play—not due to a lack of capacity or desire to engage, but because the system, deeply embedded in societal hierarchies, subtly nudged them into this role. Whether through a dismissive glance from a doctor, the harsh tone of a nurse, unspoken expectations of deference, or the careful navigation of power dynamics, the archetype persisted—shaped, reinforced, and perpetuated by the very structures of authority and paternalism that define society.

The Perfect Patient: Why Medicine Prefers Passivity

One might question the necessity of focusing on everyday indignities when more pressing issues in healthcare exist in India. However, this chapter has aimed to demonstrate the pervasive presence of everyday indignities and to elucidate how it operates and influences healthcare interactions. Disrespectful attitudes and behaviors become normalized and legitimized within the hierarchical structure of hospitals, perpetuating asymmetrical power relationships. This chapter has illustrated how experiences of everyday indignities vary between private and government hospitals, reflecting broader power imbalances that undermine patients' and their families' sense of self-respect and their ability to experience hospitalization with true dignity. The insidious power of everyday indignities lies in its ability to be normalized under the guise of knowledge, professional roles, being experts, and as components of larger systemic inequities within institutions. It is essential to address everyday indignities when discussing broader issues of inequalities and inequities in medicine. Despite its significant impact, everyday indignities are often not considered part of larger issues and thus tends to be overlooked or unacknowledged. Its transient nature and everyday normalization make it difficult to address through protocols or stringent legislation alone. For example, a doctor sighing in exasperation or displaying an inattentive expression while attending to a patient is not something that can easily be reported or formally complained about.

In both government hospitals—where resource constraints are evident—and private hospitals—where the veneer of professionalism can obscure underlying power dynamics—patients and their families often find themselves normalizing their experiences of inequity. This normalization, frequently marked by resignation and fatalism, perpetuates the cycle of passive patienthood and reinforces deep-rooted inequalities within the healthcare system and society at large. The narratives of patients and their families, as well as the perceptions of healthcare professionals in both government and private settings, highlight how caste, gender, and class prejudices are embedded in the healthcare system. These accounts reveal how patients are subjected to shaming and humiliation through moralizing and condescending attitudes, illustrating the extent to which their roles are constructed around notions of passivity and inferiority.

Healthcare providers, often from more privileged backgrounds, may not explicitly mention caste, but their actions and words are imbued with assumptions reflecting deep-seated social hierarchies. Disrespectful experiences and attitudes are part of a broader pattern where the "passive patient" archetype is reinforced through everyday interactions. Moralizing discourse and patronizing advice reassert the superiority of healthcare providers while simultaneously diminishing the agency and choices of patients. Addressing the culture of disrespect in hospital settings is crucial and necessitates self-reflection from healthcare professionals and institutions within their specific social contexts. Achieving ethical clinical practice that upholds dignity and respect for all individuals, regardless of their socio-economic or intersectional backgrounds, is challenging if disrespect is not adequately addressed. These seemingly minor acts of discrimination are significant barriers to forming respectful and equitable relationships between doctors, nurses, patients, and families and to fostering a positive institutional climate in hospital settings. In many Indian hospitals, both government-run and private, the notion that a "passive patient" is a "perfect patient" has become an unspoken rule, deeply embedded in the culture of healthcare. This idea reflects a broader expectation that patients should be compliant, quiet, and accepting of their treatment without question or complaint. For instance, consider the atmosphere in a busy government hospital.

In a busy government hospital, the overwhelming number of patients creates a high-pressure environment where doctors and nurses are stretched thin. In such settings, the perfect patient is who is a "good" patient, is often defined as one who doesn't ask questions, doesn't demand excessive time, and follows instructions without hesitation. A senior nurse may view her role as managing the crowd as much as providing care, and reprimanding a patient who steps out of line becomes part of maintaining order. For patients like Vani, who have come to expect this type of treatment, the idea of being passive—of not raising issues—feels almost natural. "This is just how it is here," she might say, resigning herself to a system where silence seems to result in smoother, if not more compassionate, care.

In private hospitals, where patients are more aware of their rights as consumers, the dynamics are somewhat different, though the underlying expectation remains similar. Patients may anticipate being treated with respect, but they also quickly learn that pushing too hard—by asking too many questions or seeking excessive information—can have negative repercussions. In these settings, the "perfect patient" is one who does not disturb the doctor, who agrees with the treatment plan even when harboring doubts or concerns. The fear of being labeled as difficult or problematic keeps patients in check, reinforcing a passive role that is deemed acceptable. This notion of the passive patient as the ideal patient is deeply problematic. It diminishes patients' agency, discouraging them from actively participating in decisions about their own health and undermining their right to be recognized with dignity during healthcare encounters.

As highlighted in this chapter, the passive role is not merely a result of individual interactions but is perpetuated by the very structure of the healthcare system and the broader societal context. The hierarchical nature of medical institutions' entrenched upper-class-caste-gender norms, the stress experienced by healthcare providers, and cultural expectations surrounding authority all contribute to an environment where passivity is rewarded. Patients, particularly those from marginalized backgrounds, quickly learn that being a "perfect patient" means being a quiet one—someone who does not disrupt the flow or challenge the status quo. The consequences of this are far-reaching. Patients who adopt a passive stance are less likely to seek clarification, question their treatment, or express concerns about their care. This passivity can lead to poorer health outcomes, as critical information may be overlooked or misunderstood. Furthermore, it perpetuates a cycle of disregard, where patients feel increasingly incapable of advocating for themselves within the healthcare system. However, it is important to recognize that patients do resist, question, and exercise their agency. The act of sharing their perspectives and experiences and being aware of the hierarchical structures is itself a form of resistance and a desire for change. Recognizing their social position and acknowledging the need for systemic transformation reflect their agency and push towards reform. Breaking free from paternalistic and authoritative values is crucial for creating a healthcare system where patients are not merely passive recipients of care but active agents in their own health and well-being. More importantly, patients must be treated and respected as individuals with agency and deserving of social recognition in all interactions within institutions, including healthcare settings.

Beyond the Doctor Knows Best: Why Paternalism Fails?

One doctor from PH, while sharing his experiences and perspectives on patient rights and informed consent during my fieldwork, said, "Why bother with all these? We do what is best for them, and they need to trust us and listen to us... It's difficult these days, but these people don't get it, so why try, right?" Having shared how healthcare professionals justify their paternalistic behaviors and in legal reasoning in earlier chapters, factors such as lack of time, literacy, poverty, busy hospitals, limited resources, and larger systemic issues, along with the implicit trust marginalized communities often place in doctors, contribute to this mindset. People are aware of the inequalities and the overburdened system, and "Indian patients" are perceived as not wanting to be involved in their health and medical decision-making due to cultural or social factors. These become social and political realities where disrespecting individuals, especially those marginalized, becomes a conscious or unconscious byproduct. Often, these arguments contain an implicit normative worldview where "poor Indians (patients) don't want to engage or lack the conditions for agency", so "we need to do what is best for them". These assumptions draw on the social and political realities of inequality to justify the archetypes of the "passive patient" and the "incompetent patient".

If we consider either thin (atomistic individualism of personal autonomy) or thick (so-called relational conceptions of autonomy) conceptions of autonomy to make sense of the socio-political conditions and the web of relationships in which patients are situated, the experiences of patients and their family members are often seen as lacking agency due to oppressive conditions. They are perceived as lacking autonomous decision-making capacity or competency due to factors like poverty and education. Much philosophical scholarship argues that oppressive conditions attack self-respect and limit one's agency (Dworkin, 1988; Mackenzie, 2014; Mackenzie & Stoljar, 2000; Meyers, 1989, 2018; Oshana, 2014; Abbott, 2020). Also, drawing from critical scholarship (Anderson, & Honneth, 2005; Honneth, 2007; Collins, 1990; Guru, 2009; hooks, 2014, 2015; Mills, 2005, 2019; Rodrigues, 2024; O'Neill, 1987), who in particular explore how paternalism oppresses women and marginalized communities (Dillon, 1992; Dotson, 2011, 2014; Khader, 2011; Khader, 2020; Narayan, 2018), I would argue that these assumptions and constructions of the passive patient are a moral wrong because dominant narratives, rooted in upper-class-caste gendered norms and values, assume that only people in ideal conditions can exercise agency and retain self-respect. While I agree that social and political realities and inequalities certainly target one's self-respect and restrict one's agency, this perspective misses a key point: marginalized and oppressed people are actively resisting, navigating, and negotiating the oppressive system. We do not need to wait for a perfect world to acknowledge our sense of self-respect, recognition, and true dignity.

The paternalistic attitudes and behaviors of judges and healthcare professionals, as discussed earlier and in this chapter, not only demonstrate how the culture of disrespect and everyday indignities are sustained in embodied encounters, but they also contribute to the assumption that people are poor decision-makers because they are perceived as "stupid, passive, ignorant, arrogant, and/or incompetent". This contributes to epistemic injustice, where marginalized and vulnerable people, such as "Indian patients", are deemed to lack knowledge, thereby increasing epistemic violence by excluding their values, preferences, plans, and beliefs from decision-making, and seeing them as "not knowers", and affective injustice by excluding their varied emotions and affects. For example, as we saw in the *Samira Kohli* case in Chapter 2, these assumptions led to paternalistic outcomes which denied the patient's agency and relational context. Building on this analysis, as well as the analysis from earlier chapters, the next chapter—the concluding chapter of this book—will demonstrate why it is not enough to simply resist paternalism, but also how we can move forward to recognize self-respect and recognition in our oppressive and unequal world.

References

Abbott, O. (2020). *The self, relational sociology, and morality in practice* (1st ed. 2020.). Springer International Publishing. https://doi.org/10.1007/978-3-030-31822-2

Ahmed, S. (2013). *The cultural politics of emotion*. Routledge.

Ambedkar, B. R. (2020). *Beef, Brahmins, and broken men*. Columbia University Press. https://doi.org/10.7312/ambe19584

Anderson, J., & Honneth, A. (2005). Autonomy, vulnerability, recognition, and justice. In Christman, J., & Anderson, J. (Eds.), *Autonomy and the challenges to liberalism: New essays*. Cambridge University Press.

Arnold, D. (2000). *Science, technology and medicine in colonial India*. Cambridge University Press.

Banerjee, A., & Sanyal, D. (2012). Dynamics of doctor–patient relationship: A cross-sectional study on concordance, trust, and patient enablement. *Journal of Family and Community Medicine*, *19*(1), 12–19.

Bromley, E. (2022). Shame as a moral mood in medicine. *Journal of Evaluation in Clinical Practice*, *28*(5), 899–908.

Chase, E., Bantebya-Kyomuhendo, G., Chase, E., & Bantebya-Kyomuhendo, G. (Eds.). (2014). Poverty and shame: The future. In *Poverty and shame: Global experiences*. Oxford University Press. https://doi.org/10.1093/acprof:oso/9780199686728.003.0022

Chattopadhyay, S. (2018). The shifting axes of marginalities: The politics of identities shaping women's experiences during childbirth in Northeast India. *Reproductive Health Matters*, *26*(53), 62–69.

Cheston, K. (2022). (Dis)respect and shame in the context of 'medically unexplained' illness. *Journal of Evaluation in Clinical Practice*, *28*(5), 909–916. https://doi.org/10.1111/jep.13740

Collins, P. H. (1990). *Black feminist thought: Knowledge, consciousness, and the politics of empowerment*. Routledge.

Dickerson, S. S., Gruenewald, T. L., & Kemeny, M. E. (2004). When the social self is threatened: Shame, physiology, and health. *Journal of Personality*, *72*(6), 1191–1216. https://doi.org/10.1111/j.1467-6494.2004.00295.x

Dillon, R. S. (1992). Toward a feminist conception of self-respect. *Hypatia*, *7*(1), 52–69. Cambridge Core. https://doi.org/10.1111/j.1527-2001.1992.tb00697.x

Dolezal, L. (2015). *The body and shame: Phenomenology, feminism, and the socially shaped body*. Lexington Books.

Dolezal, L. (2022). Shame anxiety, stigma and clinical encounters. *Journal of Evaluation in Clinical Practice*, *28*(5), 854–860. https://doi.org/10.1111/jep.13744

Dolezal, L., & Lyons, B. (2017). Health-related shame: An affective determinant of health? *Medical Humanities*, *43*(4), 257–263.

Dotson, K. (2011). Tracking epistemic violence, tracking practices of silencing. *Hypatia*, *26*(2), 236–257. https://doi.org/10.1111/j.1527-2001.2011.01177.x
Dotson, K. (2014). Conceptualizing epistemic oppression. *Social Epistemology*, *28*(2), 115–138.
Dreze, J., & Sen, A. (1990). *Hunger and public action*. Clarendon Press.
Dworkin, G. (1988). *The theory and practice of autonomy* (Vol. 20). Cambridge University Press.
Fanon, F. (2010). The lived experience of the Black man. In Szeman, I., & Kaposy, T. (Eds.), *Cultural theory: An anthropology* (pp. 422–431). John Wiley & Sons.
Fochsen, G., Deshpande, K., & Thorson, A. (2006). Power imbalance and consumerism in the doctor-patient relationship: Health care providers' experiences of patient encounters in a rural district in India. *Qualitative Health Research*, *16*(9), 1236–1251. https://doi.org/10.1177/1049732306293776
Foucault, M. (1977). *The birth of the clinic*. Routledge. https://doi.org/10.4324/9780203406373
Foucault, M. (2012). *Discipline and punish: The birth of the prison*. Vintage.
Gopichandran, V., & Chetlapalli, S. K. (2013). Dimensions and determinants of trust in health care in resource poor settings–a qualitative exploration. *PloS One*, *8*(7), e69170.
Green, S., Davis, C., Karshmer, E., Marsh, P., & Straight, B. (2005). Living stigma: The impact of labeling, stereotyping, separation, status loss, and discrimination in the lives of individuals with disabilities and their families. *Sociological Inquiry*, *75*(2), 197–215.
Gubrium, E. K., Pellissery, S., & Lødemel, I. (Eds.). (2013). *The shame of it: Global perspectives on anti-poverty policies*. Bristol University Press; Cambridge Core. https://doi.org/10.46692/9781447308720
Guru, G. (2009). *Humiliation: Claims and context*. Oxford University Press.
Harrison, M. (1992). Tropical medicine in nineteenth-century India. *The British Journal for the History of Science*, *25*(3), 299–318. Cambridge Core. https://doi.org/10.1017/S0007087400029137
Honneth, A. (2007). Recognition as ideology. In Van den Brink, B., & Owen, D. (Eds.), *Recognition and power: Axel Honneth and the tradition of critical social theory* (pp. 323–347). Cambridge University Press.
Honneth, A. (2014). *Disrespect: The normative foundations of critical theory*. John Wiley & Sons.
hooks, b. (2014). *Feminist theory: From margin to center* (3rd ed.). Routledge.
hooks, b. (2015). Choosing the margin as a space of radical openness. In *Women, knowledge, and reality* (pp. 48–55). Routledge.
Inglis, G., Jenkins, P., McHardy, F., Sosu, E., & Wilson, C. (2023). Poverty stigma, mental health, and well-being: A rapid review and synthesis of quantitative and qualitative research. *Journal of Community & Applied Social Psychology*, *33*(4), 783–806.
Johnson, A. J., Urizar Jr, G. G., Nwabuzor, J., & Dinh, P. (2022). Racism, shame, and stress reactivity among young black women. *Stress and Health*, *38*(5), 1001–1013.
Jungari, S., & Chauhan, B. G. (2017). Caste, wealth and regional inequalities in health status of women and children in India. *Contemporary Voice of Dalit*, *9*(1), 87–100.
Kaufmann, P., Kuch, H., Neuhauser, C., & Webster, E. (Eds.). (2010). *Humiliation, degradation, dehumanization: Human dignity violated*. Springer Science & Business Media.

Khader, S. J. (2011). *Adaptive preferences and women's empowerment.* Oxford University Press.

Khader, S. J. (2020). The feminist case against relational autonomy. *Journal of Moral Philosophy*, *17*(5), 499–526.

Kowal, P., & Afshar, S. (2015). Health and the Indian caste system. *The Lancet*, *385*(9966), 415–416.

Kumbhar, K. (2023). Doctor sahab: Doctors and the public in the 'golden era' of the Indian medical profession. *Sociology of Health & Illness*, *n/a*(n/a). https://doi.org/10.1111/1467-9566.13630

Kumbhar, K. S. (2022). *Healing and harming: The "Noble Profession" of medicine in post-independence India, 1947–2015.* Harvard University.

Loughlin, M., Dolezal, L., Hutchinson, P., Subramani, S., Milani, R., & Lafarge, C. (2022). Philosophy and the clinic: Stigma, respect and shame. *Journal of Evaluation in Clinical Practice*, *28*(5), 705–710. https://doi.org/10.1111/jep.13755

Lund, C., Breen, A., Flisher, A. J., Kakuma, R., Corrigall, J., Joska, J. A., Swartz, L., & Patel, V. (2010). Poverty and common mental disorders in low and middle income countries: A systematic review. *Social Science & Medicine*, *71*(3), 517–528.

Mackenzie, C. (2014). Responding to the agency dilemma: Autonomy, adaptive preferences, and internalized oppression. In *Personal autonomy and social oppression* (pp. 48–67). Routledge.

Mackenzie, C., & Stoljar, N. (2000). *Relational autonomy: Feminist perspectives on autonomy, agency, and the social self.* Oxford University Press.

Madhivanan, P., Krupp, K., Kulkarni, V., Kulkarni, S., Vaidya, N., Shaheen, R., Philpott, S., & Fisher, C. (2014). HIV testing among pregnant women living with HIV in India: Are private healthcare providers routinely violating women's human rights? *BMC International Health and Human Rights*, *14*(1), 7. https://doi.org/10.1186/1472-698X-14-7

Meyers, D. T. (1989). *Self, society, and personal choice.* Cambridge University Press.

Meyers, D. T. (2018). *Feminists rethink the self.* Routledge.

Mills, C. W. (2005). "Ideal theory" as ideology. *Hypatia*, *20*(3), 165–183.

Mills, C. W. (2019). *The racial contract.* Cornell University Press.

Narayan, U. (2018). Minds of their own: Choices, autonomy, cultural practices, and other women. In *A mind of one's own* (pp. 418–432). Routledge.

O'neill, O. (1987). Abstraction, idealization and ideology in ethics. *Royal Institute of Philosophy Supplements*, *22*, 55–69.

Oshana, M. A. (2014). Is social-relational autonomy a plausible ideal? In Oshana, M. (Ed.), *Personal autonomy and social oppression* (pp. 3–24). Routledge.

Paik, S. (2014). Dalit women's education in modern India: Double discrimination. Routledge.

Paik, S. (2022). The vulgarity of caste: Dalits, sexuality, and humanity in modern India. Stanford University Press.

Park, J., Saha, S., Chee, B., Taylor, J., & Beach, M. C. (2021). Physician use of stigmatizing language in patient medical records. *JAMA Network Open*, *4*(7), e2117052–e2117052. https://doi.org/10.1001/jamanetworkopen.2021.17052

Pellissery, S., & Mathew, L. (2013). Thick poverty, thicker society and thin state: Policy spaces for human dignity in India. In E. K. Gubrium, S. Pellissery, & I. Lødemel (Eds.), *The shame of it: Global perspectives on anti-poverty policies* (pp. 37–60). Bristol University Press; Cambridge Core. https://doi.org/10.46692/9781447308720.004

Pilnick, A., & Dingwall, R. (2011). On the remarkable persistence of asymmetry in doctor/patient interaction: A critical review. *Social Science & Medicine*, *72*(8), 1374–1382.

Ray, P. (2020). Nursing in Kolkata: Everyday politics of labour, power and subjectivities. *South Asia Research*, *40*(1), 40–57.

Rege, S. (2014). *Writing caste/writing gender: Narrating Dalit women's testimonies.* Zubaan.

Rodrigues, V. (2024). *Ambedkar's political philosophy: A grammar of public life from the social margins.* Oxford University Press.

Scully, J. L. (2010). Hidden labor: Disabled/nondisabled encounters, agency, and autonomy. *IJFAB: International Journal of Feminist Approaches to Bioethics*, *3*(2), 25–42.

Sen, A. (1983). Poor, relatively speaking. *Oxford Economic Papers*, *35*(2), 153–169.

Sen, B. (2011). Securing the right to health for all in India. *The Lancet*, *377*(9765), 532–533. https://doi.org/10.1016/S0140-6736(10)62182-4

Sen, G., & Iyer, A. (2012). Who gains, who loses and how: Leveraging gender and class intersections to secure health entitlements. *Social Science & Medicine*, *74*(11), 1802–1811.

Sen, G., Reddy, B., & Iyer, A. (2018). Beyond measurement: The drivers of disrespect and abuse in obstetric care. *Reproductive Health Matters*, *26*(53), 6–18. https://doi.org/10.1080/09688080.2018.1508173

Sen, I. (2010). Memsahibs and health in colonial medical writings, c. 1840 to c. 1930. *South Asia Research*, *30*(3), 253–274. https://doi.org/10.1177/026272801003000303

Subramani, S. (2022). Moral habitus: An approach to understanding embedded disrespectful practices. *Developing World Bioethics*, *22*(2), 94–104. https://doi.org/10.1111/dewb.12301

Timmermans, S. (2020). The engaged patient: The relevance of patient–physician communication for twenty-first-century health. *Journal of Health and Social Behavior*, *61*(3), 259–273.

Willems, S., De Maesschalck, S., Deveugele, M., Derese, A., & De Maeseneer, J. (2005). Socio-economic status of the patient and doctor–patient communication: Does it make a difference? *Patient Education and Counseling*, *56*(2), 139–146. https://doi.org/10.1016/j.pec.2004.02.011

Yancy, G. (2008). Elevators, social spaces and racism: A philosophical analysis. *Philosophy & Social Criticism*, *34*(8), 843–876. https://doi.org/10.1177/0191453708094727

5 Toward Self-Respect and Recognition in an Unequal World

Respect in the Shadow of Deference

While outright discrimination and harm are often directed at those on the margins, it's the everyday indignities that many have come to expect as part of daily life in unequal societies. These overt or subtle, yet constant, slights—whether being overlooked, spoken down to, or treated as less than—become woven into the fabric of everyday routines. Over time, these persistent acts of disrespect accumulate, reinforcing a sense of marginalization, oppression, and exclusion. For example, in a country like India, those who are marginalized—whether Adivasis, socio-economically minoritized, Dalitbahujans, women, or queer persons and communities—are often subjected to treatment that convey disregard, humiliation, and shame based on how they look, what they do, where they are, and how they exist. These attitudes are directed at the marginalized by those who are privileged and who, consciously or subconsciously, expect deference due to their unearned privileges. The social order and norms in the current caste-class-gendered oppressive system often dictate that deference and obedience are expected moral values in everyday interactions. In India, ಗೌರವ (*Gaurava*, Respect) is almost synonymous with ಮಾನ್ಯತೆ (deference), as I briefly mentioned in the Introduction regarding the significance of language and context. The term is frequently invoked in both public and private spheres, often not in relation to true dignity or self-respect, but rather as a reflection of social status. However, respect and deference are not absolutes; they are understood within specific socio-cultural and political contexts.

Those indoctrinated into the caste-class-gendered system in India are well aware of how the status quo is maintained and how references to respect or deference keep shifting. For instance, I recall a memory from when I was in 8th standard: I asked my Social Science teacher a question for clarification, and the teacher responded, "Don't question my authority, just respect and listen". Another memory from my early twenties stands out as well. I accompanied my parents to a temple near our village (Rayaru Matta). My mother said, "Let's go and eat prasada," so we sat on the floor to eat with a few others. Just before the food was served, one of the priests came and said, "You all get up and wait; the first panti (serving) is only for Brahmins, as they are in madi" (a concept

DOI: 10.4324/9781003129998-6

of purity, where they had just finished their pooja in wet clothes). My mother, along with others sitting with us, got up and told me to do the same, saying we should give them "ಮರ್ಯಾದೆ", (*Maryāde*, respect). This practice, unsurprisingly, still continues.

I haven't forgotten this incident, as it is one of many memories that resurface when I think about the concept of respect, self-respect, humiliation and true dignity. For me, true dignity is only possible when self-respect is combined with recognition, both of which must be acknowledged within our intersubjective spaces. A similar incident occurred at a clinic where I accompanied my mother for her diabetes consultation. As I asked questions about the diagnosis and sought clarification, the doctor became increasingly frustrated. My mother then said to me, "Don't be disrespectful" in front of of the doctor, and later when we were going back home said, "we need to get our job done. If he gets pissed off, then we have to wait and wait and see his *musser-munjee* (colloquial reference to bitter face)". In both cases, I don't believe it was about disrespect or respect; it was about deference. These experiences are neither surprising nor extraordinary; they are part of everyday life, offering a glimpse into how interactions within and between individuals and institutions are shaped by cultural and social norms rooted in deference.

Those who are oppressed within this system are acutely aware of how it operates—its behaviors, rules, norms, and values—and have learned to navigate it through their speech, body language, gestures, and attitudes. They/we understand how the system disciplines and how vital it is to protect the little dignity and self-respect that can be easily eroded in these interactions. For instance, my mom's way to negotiate the space by emphasizing "we need to get our job done" while being fully aware how the doctor was behaving was not fair. Despite the oppressive system, it is important to remember that Adivasis, Dalitbahujans, women, and other oppressed communities have long resisted the status quo and the expectation of deference, continually striving for respect and dignity in our own ways. Resistance becomes a way of life, a path to liberation. It is through these acts of resistance, no matter how small or subtle, that agency is exercised and existence affirmed. Perhaps, in the future—though not in this book—I/we can contribute to the many ways resistance is practiced, both within health and beyond.

In the last three chapters, I have demonstrated how everyday indignities are perpetuated and normalized within legal and medical institutions, and in healthcare encounters, through the construction of the "passive patient". This archetype is sustained and reproduced by social inequalities and inequities within society, the hidden curriculum of medical institutions, and a biomedical culture that expects patient compliance. While a few scholars in medical sociology and medical anthropology, outside India, have engaged with the concept of patienthood within biomedical culture, incorporating lived, embodied, and social realities (Dingwall & Murray, 1983; Sointu, 2017; Jeffery, 1979; Joyce & Jeske, 2019; Joyce et al., 2020; Brüggemann et al., 2022; Smith-Oka, 2015), most applied ethics discourse often treats the "patient" as a distinct category, isolated from social, historical, cultural, environmental, and political contexts. Notably, Indian scholarship has yet to engage with the archetypes of patienthood and its significance to the discourse on agency. However, some Indian scholars have critically examined doctor–patient communication and the narratives of medical authority through historical, anthropological and health service research lenses (Das, 2015; Das & Hammer, 2012; Kumbhar, 2022; Kumbhar, 2023; Madhivanan et al., 2014; Sen et al., 2018; Chattopadhyay, 2018; Gopichandran, 2019).

In the previous chapters, I aimed to illustrate that the archetype of the "passive patient" is socially constituted. It is maintained and sustained by individuals, institutions, and societal structures. In doing so, I have shown how the "passive patient" archetype is socially constructed, and how power and privilege are reproduced within asymmetrical social and political contexts, becoming institutionalized and normalized in the Indian healthcare system and legal system. I believe I have demonstrated why this understanding of interconnectedness is crucial for addressing social and political injustice at both interpersonal and institutional levels. References to the Indian traditional cultural norm of "implicit trust" in doctors, and poverty frequently appear in court judgments and narratives by healthcare professionals. For instance, as discussed in Chapter 2, legal discourse often advocates for the UK standard, Bolam test—a standard that defers to the prevailing practices of the medical community. This narrative reinforces a more paternalistic approach, rooted in India's historical and cultural values. Such a legal standard perpetuates power imbalances, as patients, viewed through a lens of passivity, are not empowered to act as agents in their healthcare decisions. The alternative "reasonably prudent patient" test, which is more patient-centered, is dismissed as impractical due to poverty and cost concerns, further entrenching the status quo and failing to recognize patient agency.

In illustrating how the archetype of the passive patient is constructed, constituted, and reproduced in the last three chapters, I have also demonstrated how indignities manifest through everyday institutional and individual disrespectful attitudes, behaviors, and actions. This underscores the importance of reflecting on recognition and respect when engaging in doctor–patient–family relationships within healthcare interactions. As captured in Ambedkar's reflections on inequities, where he said, "Man's misery is the result of man's inequity to man" (Ambedkar, 2011, p. 152)—particularly in caste and class conversations, though this understanding can also be situated within the contexts of religion, class, and gender—he highlights how inequality is graded at both interpersonal and institutional levels, focusing on suffering and humiliation. In this chapter, I argue that social and political recognition is an essential precondition for dignity, as it is central to our sense of self and to being part of relationships, communities, and institutions in the socially embedded world we live in.

We cannot fully address what it means to be a patient in India without also discussing what it means to be recognized as a person within the asymmetrical social and political realities where the agency of the oppressed and marginalized is often disregarded. In Chapter 1, I began with the question, "When does a person become a patient?" In this chapter, after illustrating how patients are often not respected or recognized as self-regarding agents—meaning they are not seen as persons in the Indian context, as embodied in the archetype of "passive patienthood"—I will explore the implications of what it means when a patient is not seen as an agent, through everyday indignities and the passive patient rhetoric, and why this recognition matters.

Struggling for Self-Respect: Through Everyday Indignities

> You must abolish your slavery yourselves. It is disgraceful to live at the cost of one's self-respect. Self-respect is a most vital factor in life. Without it man is a mere cipher. To live worthily with self-respect one has to overcome difficulties. It is out of hard and ceaseless struggle alone that one derives strength, confidence and recognition… My life was threatened if I came here to wake you up to the causes of your misery and shame. Man is mortal. Every one is to die some day or other. But one must resolve to lay down one's life in enriching the noble ideals of self-respect and in bettering human life. We are not slaves. We are a warrior clan. Nothing is more disgraceful for a brave man than to live a life devoid of self- respect…
>
> Dr. B. R. Ambedkar, 13 April 1929

> …there were then three problems before them. The first was whether they would be ever given an equal status in Hindu society; the second was whether they would get the proper share of national wealth; and the third was what would be the fate of the self-respect, self-help movement…
>
> Dr. B. R. Ambedkar, 31 December 1937

For those familiar with the works of Dr. B. R. Ambedkar and many Dalitbahujan scholars, self-respect and dignity are central to ethics, politics, and everyday morality. Struggles for self-respect and dignity are part of our daily lives, particularly in an unequal world. In this framework, we experience ourselves and rely on each other to make sense of our self, morality, and identity. As I have shown through my own experiences and those of others in this work, being dismissed, insulted, shamed, humiliated, or conversely, praised, appreciated, and recognized, are instances that demonstrate why we depend on each other and how we are treated—and how we treat ourselves—matters. It is this dynamic between self, others, and the world that makes the concept of recognition so important. Many critical theorists have emphasized the significance of recognition in our struggles for self-respect and respect (Honneth, 1995; Ambedkar, 1990; Rodrigues, 2024; Guru, 2009; Guru & Sarukkai, 2018). Drawing from their insights, and many more who have helped me value learning and being at margins—without exploring into each theorist's specific argument—I will briefly explain why social and political recognition is a precondition for healthcare ethics discourse, particularly in relation to patient autonomy, informed consent, patient centered care and medical decision-making discourses.

Before emphasizing why we must take recognition seriously in health (ethics) discourse, I will first outline briefly, in the next few paragraphs, the context through my personal journey into learning ethical issues within healthcare experiences, why I am addressing this issue, and the specific problems I aim to confront or resist.

It was only when I started my role as a project associate in the Wellcome Trust-funded research project, 'Medical Ideas, Tools, Ethics, and Pluralism in South India', under the sub-project 'Patient Welfare and Patient Autonomy: Reflections on Biomedical Ethics in the Indian Context', that I began familiarizing myself with the bioethics discipline. Later, when I transitioned to full-time doctoral research with the support of a UGC research fellowship, I gained more freedom to explore the concept of informed consent in law and medicine in India in greater depth. Given my background in social research and the interdisciplinary approach I enjoy, I often felt troubled as I started engaging with dominant bioethics texts and concepts. At that time, I lacked the vocabulary to articulate these tensions, but key questions that troubled me were: where is everyday life in these ethical concepts? Where am I, in this ethical reasoning and theory construction? How can I theorize without sounding absolute? How can my embodied experiences—and those of my research participants—be included in this theorization without being reduced to mere "data"? Why is there an inherent assumption that patients are detached and disembodied individuals in ethical theories? Over the last few years, I've reflected on these questions to varying degrees, as part of a process of thinking, learning, and unlearning.

Over time, I have learned from the vast literature that engages with these same questions from different perspectives. I've come to realize that the issues I encountered were not only problems within dominant bioethics discourse but were also pervasive across much of philosophical discourse, particularly as I began engaging with feminist and critical scholarship.

A quick cursory reading of dominant bioethics literature reveals that when scholars discuss decision-making in medicine and doctor–patient communication, the first ethical principles and values they emphasize are patient autonomy and informed consent. These philosophical approaches often advocate for a single principle or value—typically autonomy—through an oversimplified and narrow understanding of ethical, social, and political life. I couldn't help but wonder, isn't it absurd to rely on a single ethical principle without critically reflecting on and engaging with the social, cultural, and political context? Moreover, in these arguments, the patient is often perceived as an able-bodied, atomistic individual—a rational person—without consideration for the social categories we live by, or the context, relationships, and emotions that are integral to our being. If we take seriously the intersubjectivity inherent in our interactions and the way we understand morality and ethics, we must recognize the self as embodied and relational, not detached or disembodied. This approach brings affects, emotions, socialization, and context into the realm of our ethical life. One must not forget that medicine is as much about emotions as it is about reasoning. I want to avoid thinking in binary terms here. For instance, the way we perceive risk plays a crucial role in shaping our understanding of autonomy and decision-making, which I have discussed elsewhere (Subramani, 2022; 2023).

As discussed in Chapter 1 and Chapter 4, the assumptions underlying these debates often portray patients as independent individuals who make choices, act, and live according to what is important to them. In this view, the archetype of the patient is someone who is competent, informed, and capable of making autonomous decisions, with little consideration for the intersubjective nature of the self/selves in the moral and social world. While critical scholarship—especially from phenomenology and feminist epistemologies—has increasingly resisted this dominant discourse by acknowledging social relationships and human communities in discussions of patients' medical decisions and healthcare treatments, social and political recognition is still not often emphasized as a necessary precondition for autonomy. With a few exceptions (see Khader, 2011; Narayan, 2018), most scholars discussing relational autonomy do not fully acknowledge the agency of the oppressed, as they often overlook how oppressive structures act as significant limitations. I have avoided, or at least attempted to avoid, theorizing these concepts in detail here (if you're interested in this, please refer to the many philosophers who have done a great job elaborating multiple, varied conceptions, for example: Abbott, 2020; Anderson & Honneth, 2005; Dillon, 1992; Honneth, 1995; Kaufmann et al., 2011; Khader, 2011, 2020; Meyers, 2018). Rather, I have tried to make sense of these theories and conceptions in our context to resist oppressive structures and acknowledge persons' agency—here, specifically the agency of patients, particularly those who are vulnerable and marginalized.

The aim of health ethics, like many other disciplines focused on healthcare interactions, is to achieve patient-centered care and ethical practice. Key components of this effort include healthcare providers' relationships with patients and their families, as well as effective communication. Over the past few decades, there has been a significant shift in medicine toward a patient-centric approach, moving away from paternalism and recognizing concepts such as (relational) autonomy, agency, capacity, self-determination, and dignity (Childress, 2017; 2020; Childress & Quante, 2021; Armstrong, 2014; Faden et al., 1986; Beach et al., 2007; Lysaught, 2004). In bioethics, the dominant debate has centered around safeguarding patient autonomy in their choices and decisions (Naik et al., 2009; Schermer, 2002), with some emphasizing the need to protect patients from exploitation, respect, and coercion (O'Neill, 2002; Manson & O'Neill, 2007; Macklin, 1999; Millum & Bromwich, 2020; Subramani & Biller-Andorno, 2022). Despite global healthcare debates and bioethics literature's recognition of patients' rights and autonomy, asymmetry and inequity persist in healthcare encounters, both in the so called Global North and the Global South.

Numerous studies on doctor–patient relationships have demonstrated that inequities arise from factors such as language, ethnicity, race, education, class, gender, location, and caste. While these studies provide a macro-perspective on inequality and injustice, I argued elsewhere that disrespect within healthcare interactions not only manifests but also sustains these inequities, raising ethical questions that are often overlooked in healthcare ethics discussions (Subramani & Biller-Andorno, 2022). Understanding everyday indignities and othering within healthcare institutions offers another lens for examining power dynamics and their impact on those affected, and ways the "passive patient" archetype is sustained. We must consider the ethical implications of these everyday indignities, particularly how they affect questions of self-respect and true dignity within specific contexts.

Everyday indignities—small acts of disrespect (previously I referred to it as microinequities)—may or may not be recognized by the privileged and disadvantaged alike. These can include subtle changes in tone of voice, gestures during an interaction, or even silence (Subramani, 2018). As I continued to learn, I wanted to capture the humiliation and normalization inherent in these acts, which is why I now use the term everyday indignities. These actions and behaviors, while not blatant enough to be classified as outright discrimination or the basis for a lawsuit, are nonetheless significant to the person on the receiving end. They are typically unjust and unfair acts inflicted on marginalized individuals based on factors such as ethnicity, gender, religion, sexuality, caste, race, class, location, education, and age. Scholars have devised various classifications to better understand these microaggressions, such as microassaults, microinsults, and microinvalidations (Freeman, 2018; Smith-Oka, 2015; Freeman & Schroer, 2020).

The body of microaggression research predominantly focuses on how bias—whether deliberate or unintentional—manifests in daily interactions, alongside its psychological impact on individuals. This research underscores the importance of understanding the toll microaggressions take on an individual's health and well-being, emphasizing the significance of their cumulative effect. This perspective is supported by a wide range of literature, including recent studies in healthcare, which contribute to a deeper understanding of the complex dynamics at play and their broader implications for both individual health and the larger healthcare institutions.

Building on critical scholarship, I understand microaggressions as a subset of a broader spectrum of everyday indignities that predominantly affect individuals from marginalized communities. Drawing upon seminal works in critical theory (Collins, 1990; hooks, 2014; 2014; Mills, 2019; Fanon, 2010; Yancy, 2008; Guru, 2009; Ambedkar, 1990, 2020) expands the framework to recognize that everyday indignities—acts of disrespect and othering—operate on an intersectional basis. These indignities intersect across various dimensions of marginalization, including but not limited to race, gender, sexuality, class, caste, and ability. These everyday indignities are not random but are systematically patterned, targeting marginalized communities in ways that reinforce existing disparities. This broader understanding highlights the importance of addressing the complex, layered nature of oppression in order to fully grasp the impact of everyday indignities on individuals' health, well-being, and access to opportunities.

For instance, women, Adivasis, lower-caste-class communities, queer communities, and ethnic minorities, and intersectional experiences of those marginalised serve as constant reminders that oppression is multifaceted and cannot be reduced to a singular dimension. These everyday indignities underscore the complexity of oppression, illustrating how various forms of injustice interlock and amplify each other at both structural and experiential levels. For those familiar with Indigenous and Dalitbahujan literature, autobiographies, and many critical scholarships, this is nothing new. However, I want to emphasize here that one cannot overlook how these everyday indignities manifest not only in interpersonal interactions but also within the cultural and institutional fabric of society, affecting the recognition—or rather, misrecognition—of individuals. This misrecognition undermines one's self-respect within the intersubjective space, thereby inflicting moral harm.

Drawing on recognition theorists (Honneth, 1995; 2014; Honneth & Margalit, 2001), I refer to moral harm as the ways in which one's true dignity is attacked and how this affects one's sense of self. The moral language of harm helps us reflect on how individuals interpret specific experiences, their moral understanding, and its interaction with cultural and political contexts. The concept of harm I engage with here is understood as normative harm, where the positive relationship individuals have with themselves is undermined.

For instance, Honneth (1995) notes that disrespectful acts "injure individuals with regard to the positive understanding of themselves that they have acquired intersubjectively" (p. 131). I understand harm and injustice as any act, action, or event that impedes an individual's self-formation within the intersubjective space. Moral harm through everyday indignities is a form of injustice because such acts compromise the positive self-understanding that individuals acquire through intersubjective relation, interactions and spaces. This constitutes a violation of justice, as marginalized individuals are not seen as persons in social interaction. This theoretical framework helps us appreciate the deeper, normative dimensions of harm inflicted by everyday indignities, underscoring the urgent need to address these injustices within the intersubjective space.

As I understand the literature, most scholars agree on the basic conditions that define microinequities, which I understand as everyday indignities (Sue, 2017; 2010; Sue et al., 2007; McTernan, 2018). To summarize, they are: 1) subtle acts or behaviors, often considered innocuous or small harms; 2) these acts may or may not be recognized by either the victim or perpetrator, and are often unintentional; and 3) they are generally perceived as small harms or degradations imposed by dominant groups on oppressed or marginalized groups.

Let me clarify my position on everyday indignities and how I employ the term in my arguments. First, I agree with these scholars that everyday indignities, as they refer to them as microinequities, are subtle and small acts of disrespect, expressed both verbally and non-verbally. For instance, in contexts where HIV stigma is common, a doctor may avoid empathetic eye contact with female patients discussing their HIV status, or make a subtle remark such as, "you people are lazy" (said with a smile) when a lower-class-caste woman consults a doctorabout her weight. In these cases, the person receiving the disrespect may be unsure whether the doctor intended to harm or not, but the experience is morally wrong because the patient perceives it as disrespectful and harmful, which reinforces their status as "the other".

In such situations, the patient may not feel able to directly confront the doctor by asking, "Why aren't you making eye contact?" The doctor might dismiss their actions with a formal excuse such as, "just kidding", or "I'm busy and don't have time to pay attention", or "I didn't realize what I said was wrong; I was just trying to lighten the mood". These scenarios illustrate everyday indignities because marginalized communities often cannot or do not confront people in positions of power, even when the acts are not necessarily subtle. A third party observing the interaction may view it as outright or overt discrimination. However, I concur with Sue and colleagues (2007) that everyday indignities are characterized by acts that are difficult or impossible for the victim to object to, prevent, or confront, and which are often "normalized" as part of their daily lives. It is not the observers or third parties who have epistemic authority over whether an act constitutes overt discrimination or a small harm. Instead, it is the person who experiences the act who holds that authority. However, victims of such subtle acts of disrespect often cannot confront or object, and may even question themselves, which is why these acts become everyday indignities.

Second, a central argument made by most scholars when discussing everyday indignities and their distinction from overt discrimination is that these acts are unintentional. While some scholars describe everyday indignities as "unintentional, with neither the target nor the perpetrator fully aware of the occurrence", my earlier works and the narratives of disrespect presented in previous chapters, as well as other empirical studies (Smith-Oka, 2015; 2022; Cheston, 2022; Keith et al., 2017; Subramani, 2018) suggest that receivers of everyday indignities in hospital settings are often acutely aware of them and have "normalized" such acts in specific contexts. Additionally, perpetrators have internalized certain behaviors as part of social norms, allowing these acts to become embedded in their moral habits. I have discussed the concept of moral habitus in greater detail elsewhere (Subramani, 2022). It refers to the embodied, everyday practices and cognitive dispositions of social actors that sustain inequality and produce disrespectful attitudes and practices. For example, when a male doctor belittles or mocks a patient's body in a hospital, this behavior becomes "normalized" and integrated into the institutional ethos.

Third, in agreement with other scholars, I consider everyday indignities as repeated, patterned small acts that are often directed at individuals from marginalized and oppressed groups. While it may be argued that everyday indignities can happen to anyone and that anyone can experience disrespect, I specifically refer to everyday indignities as experienced by historically and socially disadvantaged groups. Context and setting play a crucial role in shaping these experiences. For instance, an upper-class, upper-caste man from a city may feel disrespected if an administrative staff member in a government hospital in a resource-scarce country does not pay attention to him. However, when a young tribal woman receives the same lack of attention in a public hospital, her experience of disrespect is situated within a broader context of structural and systemic oppression that she, and others from similarly disadvantaged backgrounds, frequently encounter in public institutions and spaces, including hospitals. These acts make individuals acutely aware of their social status or prompt them to question their self-respect and recognition within intersubjective encounters.

In healthcare literature, extensive research highlights the adverse relationship between experiences of shame and stigma and health outcomes, including reduced access to healthcare services (Dolezal, 2015, 2022; Loughlin et al., 2022; Green et al., 2005; Hutchinson & Dhairyawan, 2017; Grue, 2016). While I acknowledge that experiences of disrespect are part of the human condition in unequal systems and can be internalized across societal strata, it is crucial to recognize that for marginalized populations, disrespect is not only more prevalent but also deeply normalized within systemic and structural inequalities, and patterned experience. This exacerbates the negative effects on health and well-being, and calls for greater attention to the moral wrong of everyday indignities, especially when moral recognition is central to human experience.

The key question that compels me to emphasize social and political recognition as a precondition for engaging with any ethical values is this: When individuals are not treated as social and political agents by default, revealing a culture of disrespect, how can we meaningfully discuss concepts such as autonomy or informed consent in medical decision-making without considering unequal context and oppressive conditions? This requires us to situate the discourse within a broader social and political context. In other words, how can we simply adopt a narrow understanding of autonomy and informed consent without recognizing the socio-political realities of how individuals are evaluated as moral and political agents in India? This calls for a rethinking of the underlying assumptions behind the archetypes of active and passive patients, or other archetypes. In the next subsections, I will first briefly discuss the dominant assumptions surrounding these patient archetypes and then explain why they are morally problematic.

The Silent Harm: Reclaiming Self-Respect

Becoming a 'patient' is not merely about seeking care—it is about stepping into a role that often strips individuals of one's power, agency, and dignity often. For many, this transition is shaped not just by illness or pain but by the weight of social and cultural realities that hover silently, dictating how one is seen, heard, and treated. As shared in earlier chapters, my own and family experiences, and many who shared their experiences spoke about pain not as something they fought but as something they carried, heavy and silent. Their stories were not full of protest or rage. They had learned to expect disregard, learned that their voices were not to be trusted. I would ask about consent—about whether they understood the choices being made for them—and they would laugh softly, bitterly, as though the question itself were absurd sometimes. To expect choice, to expect to be heard, that was a privilege. This was the normalization of everyday indignities and sustains the "passive patient" archetype and culture of disrespect. The insidious way marginalization—of caste, religion, ethnicity, class, gender—gets folded into everyday encounters, into the smallest gestures, the briefest exchanges. It is the doctor who does not meet your eye, the nurse who speaks to you harshly, the system that makes you wait for hours without explanation. And when you sit in that waiting room, you know that your worth has already been measured, weighed, and found lacking. Then, the hospital is a site of authority, and you are expected to submit. The doctor knows best. The system knows best. Your pain, your body, your story—none of it matters when it conflicts with their truth.

For the marginalized, especially those at the intersections, this erasure feels like something they were born into. When we/they become patients, passivity is already a practice, something they have perfected. But I reject the idea that this passivity is natural. It is imposed. It is the product of systems—medical, cultural, political, historical—that rely on hierarchy and domination. It is the product of a world that teaches some to believe they are more valuable, more deserving of care, while others are taught to expect neglect. In healthcare, this manifests as epistemic and affective violence—when patients' knowledge and embodied experiences of their own bodies is denied, when their pain is doubted, when their words are silenced. To honor their stories is to challenge the structures that silence them. It is to imagine a different kind of healthcare—one where power is shared, where care is not paternalistic but rooted in self-respect and recognition. It is to remember that the role of 'patient' need not be one of submission, that the body is not passive, and the voice is not weak.

In the Indian context, the social and political recognition of persons, particularly those who are marginalized and vulnerable, is profoundly shaped by the intersection of class, caste, religion and gendered norms and values. These intersecting identities often dictate how individuals are treated and recognized—or more accurately, not recognized—within society. The deeply entrenched social hierarchies, rooted in the caste-class system, continue to perpetuate inequalities that influence every aspect of life, including social status, economic opportunities, and access to healthcare, and dignified life. Upper-caste-class values, which are often synonymous with privilege, dictate the norms of deference and respect that are expected in everyday interactions.

These values reinforce a social order where individuals from marginalized communities—Adivasis, Dalitbahujans, lower-class-caste persons, women, and queer communities—are systematically denied the recognition that is readily granted to their upper-caste-class counterparts. Respect in this context is often conditional, based on one's conformity to the social-political categories and norms dictated by those in positions of power. This conditional respect frequently manifests as a demand for deference, where marginalized individuals are expected to demonstrate submissiveness and obedience in their interactions with those of higher social status. Gender further complicates this dynamic, particularly those from lower-caste-class backgrounds who face compounded forms of discrimination and marginalization. They are often denied agency, both within the private sphere and in public life, where their voices and experiences are frequently silenced, dismissed or ignored. This lack of recognition not only strips one's dignity but also reinforces one's vulnerability.

In this system, the marginalized are often rendered invisible. One's struggles, contributions, and humanity are overlooked, as the social and political frameworks are designed to maintain the status quo. This lack of recognition and respect within interpersonal encounters is not just a matter of social etiquette; it has profound implications for access to resources, justice, and opportunities that are critical for improving health and wellbeing. In medicine and law as we saw in earlier chapters, for example, the archetype of the "passive patient"—a concept that often aligns with upper-caste, male-dominated values—further marginalizes and disregards one's agency in healthcare encounters. Marginalized individuals are less likely to be seen as capable of making decisions about their own health and care, and are more likely to be treated with paternalism or outright neglect. This lack of recognition in healthcare reflects broader societal attitudes that devalue the lives and experiences of marginalized communities. Addressing these deep-rooted issues requires a fundamental shift in how social and political recognition is granted. It involves challenging the upper-caste, class, and gendered values that underpin the current system and advocating for a more inclusive approach that recognizes the dignity and worth of all individuals, regardless of their caste, class, gender, or social standing. Only by acknowledging and addressing these systemic inequities can we begin to create a society where everyone is truly recognized and respected as a person.

The construction of the "passive patient" is morally problematic because it denies agency, self-respect and true dignity. Also, as shown in the last chapters, it shows how it is deeply rooted in colonial, upper-caste, class, and gender hierarchies that continue to reproduce injustice and shape the Indian healthcare and legal systems. These hierarchies intersect to perpetuate a form of paternalism that privileges certain social groups while marginalizing others, particularly along the axes of caste, class, and gender. Historically, colonial medical and legal systems in India were designed to serve the elite, while subordinating the majority of the population (Arnold, 1993; 2000; Harrison, 2009; Kumbhar, 2022, 2023; Ruddock, 2021; Baxi, 1982; 2000).

The colonial institutions, which prioritized the authority of the doctor and the state, treated patients, especially those from lower castes and marginalized classes, as passive recipients of care rather than as agents in their own health decisions. This system was structured to maintain control over the bodies of objectified subjects, with an emphasis on order and discipline rather than recognizing them as persons and respecting. These colonial legacies persist in contemporary healthcare practices and legal judgments, which often fail to recognize the agency of patients. As we saw, the upper-caste-class-gender dimensions of this problem are particularly salient in the Indian context, where gender, caste and class hierarchies continue to influence both access to healthcare and the way patients are treated within the system. They are frequently viewed as lacking the knowledge or capacity to engage in decision-making, reinforcing their presumed passivity. This dynamic reflects the broader social inequalities that permeate Indian society, where caste, gender, and class privilege dictate not only social mobility but also the respect and dignity afforded to individuals in everyday encounters.

Gender, along with intersectional oppressive structures, further complicates this issue, as women and queer communities, especially from lower-caste and lower-class backgrounds, face additional layers of marginalization. The presumption of passivity is often more pronounced in the treatment of female and queer patients, who are viewed not only as lacking decision-making capacity but also as subservient to male authority figures, whether they be doctors or family members. The intersection of caste, class, and gender hierarchies means that patients from marginalized communities are doubly or triply disadvantaged, as they are denied both respect and the ability to advocate for themselves within the healthcare system. Their experiences are often overshadowed by the authority of medical professionals who may not take their concerns or preferences into account, leading to poorer health outcomes and a dehumanizing experience of care. Legal judgments in India often reflect these entrenched social hierarchies, upholding the authority of the medical profession while reinforcing the passive role of the patient, particularly when the patient belongs to a marginalized caste or class. The *Samira Kohli* case, for instance in Chapter 2, illustrates how legal narratives sustain and normalize the idea of the passive patient, entangling medical authority with hierarchies of caste, class, and gender. In this case, the court's judgment effectively subordinated the patient's autonomy to the presumed superior knowledge of the medical professional, thereby perpetuating a framework in which the agency of marginalized patients is disregarded as well as due to social and political conditions, self-respect was targeted.

Building on the works of Ambedkar and Periyars' self-respect movements, and learning from Dillon (1997; 1992) and Honneth (2014), when I refer to self-respect, I acknowledge that each of us has a unique set of desires, values, needs, abilities, concerns, and projects, shaped by different histories and initiatives. There is no generic or abstract notion of personhood here, as affectivity plays an essential role in our relationships with ourselves and others. Being aware of ourselves in relation to others and our communities, and understanding our intersubjectivity, we realize our sense of self and identity through recognition by others. When I say self-respect is targeted, I mean that oppressive conditions threaten our sense of self and integrity, making it difficult to maintain true dignity. Marginalized individuals are acutely aware of their social position and how oppressive structures make retaining self-respect a challenge. Yet, we navigate, resist, and negotiate these conditions to retain self-respect, which I see as exercising agency and being conscious of the systemic barriers they face.

Everyday indignities and the passive patient archetype sustain, normalize, and contribute to broader inequalities, thereby perpetuating a culture of disrespect across institutions. I view this as both epistemic and affective injustice, as it affects an individual's self-respect and true dignity, while also reinforcing systemic oppression. This makes those from historically and systemically marginalized groups acutely aware of their social positioning. When scholars discuss everyday indignities, a key argument they emphasize is the need to understand that even a seemingly isolated incident or small harm is part of a larger pattern of repeated harms targeting individuals or groups—harms that must be given moral significance in ethical theory and debates.

As Ambedkar emphasized, self-respect is central to resistance and liberation from oppressive structures. I argue that, given the interconnectedness of dignity and self-respect, perpetrators of everyday indignities target their victims, affecting their sense of self and undermining their self-respect. The way respect is shown to others as worthy human beings is intimately connected to one's self-respect, and it is crucial for individuals to feel morally recognized, both epistemically and affectively. Influenced by critical philosophers (Honneth, 1995; Fanon, 2010; 2016; Guru, 2009; Guru & Sarukkai, 2018; Rege, 2014; Ambedkar, 2020; Rodrigues, 2024; hooks, 2014), I believe that everyday indignities—along with the passive patient archetype that sustains oppressive norms and values—lead to social disrespect, where individuals experience self-conscious emotions such as shame and humiliation. This, in turn, targets one's self-respect, causing marginalized individuals reflect on one's true dignity.

In closely examining these narratives and interactions, we can see how they undermine people's self-respect and perpetuate disrespect. For instance, in Chapter 3, I illustrated the story of a young woman, the caretaker of her mother who underwent surgery in a government hospital. She describes her experience: "I keep following them from the ward to their offices and back," providing readers with a clear sense of how disrespect is felt by its victim. The subtle feeling of being ignored, of having to please people in power by "tailing them", and her statements "they don't even bother to stop for a second and listen to me" and "we are treated like this everywhere", reveal how her self-respect is at stake in her everyday experiences. Whether the doctor intended it or was genuinely "busy" with justifications for his actions, the young woman recognized the embodied, lived experience of disrespect. The act of "tailing" in any space, particularly within hospital settings, highlights the power asymmetry. While "tailing" and being subtly ignored may not constitute overt discrimination, they are small acts of harm that sustain and contribute to broader inequality and inequity. Crucially, these acts disregard the individual's self-respect.

Let me illustrate another example: when I, in my early 20s, due to having severe chronic pain (I labeled my issue as shifting pain as it kept moving from one joint to other! Still no idea what it is!), had multiple visits to different doctors, but no one, except one female doctor took me seriously, which took several years. When I visited government hospital in Bangalore with my dad which is supposed to be top in field, after traveling for two and a half hours from my home, the doctor said, by addressing to my dad, "she just needs attention", and gave prescription of Ibuprofen for one month. Such experiences are not new to people with chronic pain. This conversation sheds light on how being ignored and disregarded is quite common in our healthcare interactions. The moral wrong of being "othered" by stereotyping, through insults from a position of gender, caste, age, class, and professional privilege, through experience of humiliation and shame one disrespects one's self-respect and dignity in healthcare interactions. The interaction, in which the caretaker suggests nobody cares about "people like us" and that one's pain is disregarded by saying she just needs attention, illustrates how uncertainty is created within the patient, caretaker and threatens one's self. These acts, behaviors and attitudes are effective at undermining self-respect because they operate at an affective level. Unless we consider the emotional and epistemic impacts of everyday indignities, we miss a crucial part of their moral wrong. As we saw in the illustrations, everyday indignities target a person's sense of self and her status as both a knower and a moral agent. Further, everyday indignities are not only epistemic injustice because a person's epistemic credibility is not acknowledged, but also affective injustice because they shame and humiliate the person. By making someone feel "ignorant or incapable" due to intersectional factors, you project unwanted affects on them. Shame and humiliation are experienced and the desire for recognition is reflected in these narratives.

I argue that marginalized and vulnerable individuals' narratives reveal their desire for moral recognition in their interpersonal relationships and interactions, and the desire to receive moral recognition from those withholding is a form of affective injustice. As we examine the narratives of patients from marginalized communities, we can see how they carry or suppress emotions such as anger, shame, humiliation, helplessness, frustration, and isolation. Many studies on discrimination and implicit bias indicate that when such emotions are expressed, they are ridiculed or discounted by the privileged. Everyday indignities, passive, and incompetent patient rhetoric create epistemic uncertainty for the targeted individuals, but the uncertainty extends beyond epistemic injustice to affective injustice as well. Its effectiveness is due to the sense of shame and humiliation it conveys inducing doubts about one's own abilities, knowledge, beliefs, and judgments. Consider, for instance, the young woman who was "tailing" behind the doctor or the female patient or how me being dismissed by male doctor. What is interesting about these instances are that those who are disrespected are made to feel like they are "dumb", "ignorant", or "incompetent". They are successful on both an emotional and affective level when the target feels the need to be acknowledged and morally recognized. In particular, affects play a crucial role. It won't be possible to be successful unless they reach the affective dimension. As I illustrated, in Chapters 3 and 4, disrespectful experiences produce self-conscious emotions such as shame and humiliation. While in the future one needs to explore how shame and humiliation relate and influence one's sense of self, for my argument here we can state that these emotions harm one's self-respect and dignity. As I discussed already, marginalised patients are often disregarded in a culture where disrespect has become normalized in the given context, making it difficult to resist feelings of shame and humiliation. Thus, it becomes associated with one's identity and social categories we live by, whether it is caste, gender, or class, as we saw in earlier chapters.

Several feminist scholars discuss the moral wrong of epistemic and affective harm (Fricker, 2007; 2017; Bernstein, 2005; Wiinikka-Lydon, 2019; Whitney, 2018), particularly when discussing the stereotypes of marginalized individuals that reinforce negative identity-prejudicial stereotypes. Similarly, as I have illustrated in earlier chapters, how socio-economic and cultural contexts, roles and power asymmetry between healthcare professionals and patients and their family members, shape clinical interactions, and how these power dynamics are sustained and normalized in this context through everyday indignities. In other words, everyday indignities and the archetype of passive patient target one's self-respect through disrespect like joking, winking, teasing by perpetrators, and certain actions by victims like "tailing", microinsults, submissive body postures, etc, and through perceiving one as "incompetent", "passive", or "ignorant" due to social and political factors.

As noted earlier in Chapters 3 and 4, as well as in similar research, poverty-induced stigma, shame, and humiliation can distort one's self-image, making individuals feel "inferior" to others, particularly the dominant group, thereby affecting their self-respect. It is crucial to recognize that flourishing as social and moral agents depends on meaningful relationships rooted in recognition. The absence of moral recognition reinforces power imbalances and disrupts positive self-relations within intersubjective spaces, which are essential in healthcare encounters. Thus, I argue that the passive patient archetype, coupled with everyday indignities, constitutes a moral wrong by damaging self-respect and perpetuating power asymmetries. These dynamics highlight the urgent need for social respect and have significant implications for healthcare ethics, particularly in relation to patient autonomy, informed consent, and justice.

The moral implications of these intersecting colonial, caste, class, and gender structures and process are profound. They contribute to a healthcare system that not only produces health disparities and reinforces broader inequalities, but disregards patients' agency and one's self-respect. The presumed passive patient becomes a reflection of the ways in which power and privilege operates in Indian society, with those at the intersections of caste, class, and gender oppression being most vulnerable to dehumanizing treatment. This system fails to respect the inherent dignity of all individuals and perpetuates the marginalization of the very groups it should be caring and serving. Moving beyond this construction requires a transformative shift that not only respects persons, here who become patients, but also addresses the structural injustice that sustain these hierarchies, recognizing all persons as moral and political agents, regardless of their social position and need to acknowledge the diverse differential social positioning which puts one in unearned disadvantage. Thus, I would argue that within health discourse, social and political recognition becomes a precondition for any patient rights and patient autonomy discourse, which often healthcare ethics discourse does not recognize or takes it for granted. In the next sections, before illustrating why we need to take social and political recognition seriously in healthcare and (bio)ethics discourse, I will briefly discuss the limitations of the dichotomous understanding of active and passive patient archetypes.

Critique of Archetypes: Passive v. Active Patients

When we start critically engaging with the archetype of passive patient, we will inevitably reflect on the understanding of self and self-respect, as briefly discussed in last section. I hope through last four chapters, I have showed how the notion of patient is shaped by our understanding of the social, moral and political world, and how persons navigate within everyday realities. I would argue that this not only opens up the personal, social, and political engagement but can also become limitation to our ethical imagination. For instance, the archetype of passive patient which illustrated how structures shape autonomy as I have illustrated. In Chapter 1, I briefly discussed on how "active patient", who makes free choice, who has full control and rational, narrative is dominant in Anglo–American moral and political philosophy. In dominant bioethics discourse the idea of self underlying this assumption is isolated from social and personal context, and relationships. There, of course, have been scholars who have critiqued this assumption of self (Taylor, 1989; Dillon, 1992; 1997; Meyers, 2018). I don't want to reiterate the whole story or summarise these discussions. Learning from many critical scholars I would emphasize that the archetype of patients, whether it be active or passive, is based on the notion of self we ascribe. I take it that self is socially, politically and historically situated, and that means it is not static and our social interactions, decisions and actions are influenced by one's social and political categories, such as caste, class, religion, gender, and many varied intersectional factors. If I have not made it clear already, to be explicit, the reason why we should pay close attention to these archetypes is that it shows us how we can recognize and overcome the oppressive structures, norms, attitudes, and practices.

In much of dominant bioethics' discussions, which has its roots of liberalism, as I see, the archetype of active patient (in a thin conception of self), is that individual often presumed as isolated from context and social relationships. Building on the work of feminist and critical scholars, there has been a growing focus on the concept of relational autonomy (Childress & Quante, 2021; Gutmann, 2022; Childress, 2017; 2020), which emphasizes the centrality of social relationships and human communities in shaping individual agency and selfhood. Rather than viewing autonomy as isolation or independence, this perspective recognizes that personal identity and decision-making are deeply intertwined with the social contexts and relationships in which individuals are embedded. Here the reference to archetype of active patient is not in its thin version but as thick conception of self and acknowledging social embeddedness. In tracing the genealogy of patient autonomy discourse, particularly in the US and Western Europe, it becomes clear that the primary aim of promoting patient autonomy and informed consent is to resist paternalism, exploitation, oppression, rights violations, and coercion (Faden et al., 1986; Beauchamp & Childress, 2013; O'Neill, 2002; Manson & O'Neill, 2007; Schermer, 2002; Naik et al., 2009). For more in-depth discussion, you can refer to these texts on the subject.

Ethical arguments for patient autonomy and informed consent, dominant thin version, often construct the figure of the "active patient" in ways that reveal certain assumptions about the self: 1) the self is portrayed as separate from others and detached from interpersonal relationships, 2) the self is seen as having a unified and stable identity, and 3) emotion and affect are distanced from autonomy, as they are seen as inauthentic to the true self. I see that this "active patient" archetype is often shaped by an underlying framework of abstract individualism. On the other hand, the archetype of passive patient as illustrated in the last chapters, reflects certain underlying assumptions about the self, rooted in hierarchical and paternalistic structures. These assumptions, shaped by historical and socio-political narratives, construct a passive patient archetype. The figure of the "passive patient" in the Indian healthcare and legal context is shaped by deeply entrenched assumptions about the self, rooted in hierarchical structures. Unlike the "active patient" who is imagined as autonomous and self-directed, the passive patient is portrayed as dependent on authority figures. Their identity is constructed in relation to medical professionals, who are seen as the sole arbiters of decision-making, leaving little room for the patient's agency or involvement in their own health and well-being, and highly deterministic account of social and political conditions.

This archetype of the passive patient is also marked by an underlying assumption of incompetence. Patients are not granted the presumption of being capable decision-makers but are instead viewed as lacking the necessary understanding to engage in medical choices, as they are perceived as "not knowers". This assumption often intersects with broader socio-cultural hierarchies that equate class, caste, and gender status with competence, portraying those from marginalized communities—such as the poor, women, and lower-caste individuals—as inherently less capable of being agents in their healthcare. Furthermore, the passive patient is reduced to a biological or medical entity, with their embodied social self and personhood secondary to their physical condition. The focus of the medical and legal systems is on the body's needs, to heal, with little regard for the patient's subjective experiences, values, or cultural background as interconnected to health experience. In this construction, the patient's emotional, social, and personal dimensions are minimized, reinforcing the idea that they are objects of medical intervention rather than persons with complex lives and preferences. This passivity is also tied to broader socio-political hierarchies, where power dynamics rooted in class, caste, and gender shape who is seen as worthy of respect and recognition.

The healthcare and legal systems, by adhering to these hierarchical norms, further entrench the idea of the passive patient, normalizing their exclusion from decision-making processes. In this sense, the passive patient is not just passive by nature but is made passive by systems of authority that diminish their agency. Finally, the passive patient is framed within a context of submission and silence. Their lack of verbal expression or resistance is often interpreted as consent, reinforcing the expectation that they should quietly accept whatever treatment is offered. This portrayal erases any possibility for the patient's emotions, affect, or agency to influence the course of their care, thereby normalizing a one-sided, paternalistic dynamic in the doctor–patient relationship. These assumptions about the passive patient reflect broader dynamics of power and subordination in Indian society, where colonial legacies, caste-based discrimination, and patriarchal norms continue to shape how patients are treated within healthcare systems.

While aiming not to sound reductive in discussing the dichotomous understanding of active v. passive patients, I want to briefly explain why, despite its limitations, this framework helps us critically engage with the concepts of self-respect and recognition in healthcare ethics discourse. As discussed, dominant mainstream (thin versions) theories of patient autonomy often place significant emphasis on the conditions that obstruct individual agency—focusing on paternalism, authoritarian interventions, or coercive forms of social control. The passive patient is constructed within this framework as the quintessential archetype who is subject to these external constraints, while the active patient is positioned as someone who successfully resists them and exercise agency in ideal conditions. However, this binary tends to reduce agency to a simplistic struggle between external control and individual resistance, obscuring the social dimensions that feminist critiques and critical scholars have long emphasized. Critical scholars have challenged this narrow focus on external impediments, pointing out that autonomy cannot be fully understood outside of the social relationships and structures in which individuals are embedded (Khader, 2011; 2020; Dillon, 1992; Narayan, 2018). Mainstream autonomy theories, even when they recognize social influences, often do so without sufficiently challenging the individualistic framework at their core. For me, looking through this, helps to show how the archetypes of the active and passive patient reveal these limitations. The active patient is presumed to exercise autonomy in isolation, as a figure detached from the relational and affective contexts that shape real-life decision-making. This archetype embodies an abstract individualism that treats autonomy as a purely rational, self-sufficient act, while downplaying the social and political conditions, and relationships necessary for autonomy to be realized. Meanwhile, the passive patient is portrayed as merely subject to paternalistic control, reinforcing the idea that their lack of autonomy stems primarily from external forces, rather than from a complex interplay of social, economic, and interpersonal factors.

In contexts like India, as shown in last four chapters, where caste, class, and gender deeply influence healthcare interactions, this dichotomy between passive and active patients is especially problematic. The passive patient archetype, constructed as dependent, incompetent, and incapable, obscures the ways in which social hierarchies shape patients' agency. It fails to account for how patients' seeming passivity may be a reflection of the socio-political conditions that limit their agency, such as caste-based oppression or economic precarity. At the same time, the active patient archetype, which is often implicitly based on notions of abstract individualism, may overlook the relational and contextual understanding of decision-making. The assumption that agency is an individual achievement, detached from social conditions, neglects how care, dependency, and relationality are integral to the exercise of agency in these settings. Contemporary mainstream autonomy theorists have increasingly acknowledged the importance of the social context and relationships in realizing agency, yet these discussions often remain rooted to primacy of (often white) women's oppression within patriarchal, upper-caste and racial hierarchical system (Moreton-Robinson, 2021; Narayanan, 2018; Collins, 1990; Paik, 2022; hooks, 2014), and detached from the lived realities of those who are double or tripled marginalized by systems of power such as in India. While mainstream bioethics debates on autonomy, including relational autonomy, worry about the obvious social horrors of paternalism, they often fail to grapple with the more insidious ways that social and political conditions—like poverty, and caste-class-gender based discrimination—shape individuals' interaction with healthcare professional and how one can exercise agency or negotiate. The passive patient, as constructed in by healthcare professionals in Indian healthcare and legal contexts, is often a product of these conditions, yet mainstream autonomy frameworks do not fully account for the ways these social forces operate to limit agency, disregard self-respect and true dignity not just through overt paternalism but through more structural forms of oppression.

Thus, the critique of the passive v. active patient archetypes must go beyond the narrow focus on agency and autonomy. Instead, it requires an understanding of agency as fundamentally relational and shaped by the social conditions in which individuals are embedded, and that marginalized communities are already resisting, negotiating and navigating the system, and this needs to be supported. Feminist and critical scholars have long advocated for this broader conception, arguing that agency is not simply the absence of interference, but the presence of agency in the given social and material conditions that allow individuals to make meaningful choices for them. In this light, both the passive and active patient archetypes fall short, as they fail to capture the complexities of agency (and autonomy) as it is lived by patients, especially those marginalized by class, caste, gender, and other intersecting systems of power. To acknowledge these complexities, especially given that the archetype we are working with in India is, unfortunately, the presumed passive patient, I would argue that we need to center self-respect and recognition as the precondition for true dignity. In the next section, I will discuss why, before concluding with how the "situated patient" archetype, which centers self-respect and recognition, could help us reimagine healthcare institutions.

Recognition, Self-Respect and Agency

When we examine the assumptions behind the archetype of the passive patient, as shown in earlier chapters, we uncover narratives and experiences of healthcare professionals and judges that justify the failure to recognize a person as a social and political agent (extending to the patient). For instance, referring to statements like "Indian patients are passive, and incompetent" or "these people cannot understand". By listening to the perspectives and experiences of patients and family members, we can see how "agency" becomes a key justification for normative dispositions and attitudes, such as whether a person is treated with respect, recognized as an agent, and their decisions taken seriously. Thus, it is important to engage with agency (and autonomy) as socially embedded concepts, rather than detaching them from the social and embodied world.

A relational understanding of autonomy considers the interdependent and socially embedded contexts of persons and selves in any discussion about self, others, and society. Since our social identities are shaped by the socio-political contexts we inhabit and the relationships we have with ourselves, others, and society, agency is always relational to these contexts and relationships. In simpler terms, drawing from various relational conceptions of agency and autonomy, our sense of self is inherently social. Much of the philosophical debate surrounding relational conceptions of autonomy focuses on either resisting the individualistic account of autonomy and agency, or examining whether autonomy and agency, from a social perspective, can still be considered autonomous behaviors. For instance, this includes engagement with self-reflection, authentication, competence, preferences, and identity (Piper, 2016; Terlazzo, 2016; Holroyd, 2010; Meyers, 1989). In the context of decision-making, certain self-regarding attitudes are often required of agents, such as self-discovery, self-respect, or self-worth (Dillon, 1997, 1992; Mackenzie, 2014; Meyers, 1989).

In much of the narrow liberal tradition of autonomy and agency discourse, particularly in the US, UK, and Australia, both relational and non-relational frameworks often overlook the socio-political realities and conditions. These frameworks frequently fail to acknowledge how many marginalized communities and individuals already resist and exercise agency in explicit and implicit ways within oppressive conditions. Of course, there are some exceptions (Galeotti, 2015; Khader, 2011; Dillon, 1992). While some scholars in these debates reflect on the internal and external conditions that restrict one's agency—such as how oppressive social environments hinder marginalized communities from exercising their agency—others critique the idea that being autonomous is primarily about having authentic values. However, the challenge for us, in the context of the passive patient archetype, is not that marginalized communities cannot exercise agency, nor that they lack the ability to determine how they live, but lack of acknowledgment of their agency and self-respect.

Building on Ambedkar's philosophy of the self-respect movement, I argue that the assumption underlying the passive patient archetype, as explored in the last four chapters, risks undermining self-respect and agency. This assumption suggests that, due to oppressive conditions—such as poverty, lack of education, insufficient resources, and cultural values—patients in India cannot be agents or competent decision-makers, leading to their being treated with disrespect. However, just because someone is poor or illiterate does not mean they are incapable of exercising agency in their everyday life, because they are already resisting, negotiating, and navigating as discussed in earlier sections. If we consider the existing disparities and structural injustices in India, shaped by casteism, sexism, classism, and communalism, we see how caste-based discrimination marginalizes Dalits and lower-caste communities, limiting their access to education, healthcare, and economic opportunities. Sexism perpetuates gender inequality, curbing women's autonomy and participation in the workforce. Classism entrenches poverty, benefiting the wealthy while restricting upward mobility for lower-income groups. Communalism, driven by religious divisions, fuels inter-religious violence and discrimination, particularly against Muslims. These "isms" collectively reinforce systemic oppression, deepening disparities in opportunities, rights, and resources for marginalized communities. To break free from these oppressive structures—whether based on caste, class, gender, or ethnicity—the first step toward liberation is the recognition of one's subjectivity, self-respect and agency. It is through this that we begin to respect ourselves and one another, not just in our intimate lives, but within the institutions that seek to define and contain us. This recognition is the starting point for dismantling systems of domination and oppression, for only when we honor the fullness of our humanity can we create spaces of true justice and equality.

Influenced by critical scholarship on the concept of recognition, it's not enough to merely profess moral equality; the challenge lies in how we recognize each other as equals, particularly in a way that acknowledges our social and political conditions, as well as our subjectivity, selfhood, and agency in intersubjective encounters and institutional settings. As I have illustrated in the context of law and medicine, patients are often not recognized as agents. By examining how experiences of othering manifests through everyday indignities, we see how patients are not treated as agents in both law and medicine. Additionally, we observe the struggles for recognition, where patients and their families resist and navigate the system, often exposing the humiliations one endures. Until recognition is acknowledged in both interpersonal encounters and institutional practices, it is impossible to genuinely practice ethical concepts such as patient autonomy or informed consent.

Without getting into the complexities of various conceptions of recognition, I will briefly clarify what I mean by the term and why it is relevant to resisting the passive patient rhetoric. Drawing from Honneth (1996), I argue that recognition is a precondition for agency and autonomy, as it is essential for the development of a positive relationship with oneself, fostering self-respect, identity, and integrity. Recognition is crucial for shaping our social identities and relationships. In the context of the passive patient archetype in India, the concept of recognition highlights a form of misrecognition embedded within both medical and legal frameworks. In Indian law and healthcare, recognition goes beyond simply acknowledging someone as a patient; it often reflects deeper layers of socio-political identity. The passive patient, as constructed in these systems, is a figure that is seen but not fully recognized as an agent. Rather, they are often regarded merely as a "subject of care", defined by a hierarchical, paternalistic dynamic between healthcare professionals and the patient. This represents a significant form of misrecognition, where individuals are not seen as full participants in decision-making processes concerning their own bodies, values, and health.

The archetype of the passive patient in the Indian context can be understood as a form of misrecognition that aligns with Axel Honneth's (2014) analysis of social pathologies. This construction reflects entrenched hierarchical relationships within medical practice, shaped by caste, class, and gender dynamics. Both legal and medical systems often reinforce a paternalistic model that frames patients as incapable of meaningful participation in decisions about their own health. This narrative not only perpetuates a sense of alienation but also denies individuals the opportunity for meaningful engagement in decisions concerning their own body, values, and health. Honneth (1995) argues that recognition is essential for the development of a person's identity, and this process unfolds across three spheres: love (affective care), rights (respect and equality), and social esteem (self-respect). In the context of the passive patient archetype, misrecognition occurs across all these spheres. Marginalized patients, in particular, are often denied affective care when their pain or suffering is dismissed. Their rights to autonomy and self-determination are subordinated to medical authority, and they are treated with disrespect, which undermines their self-respect. Moreover, they are not afforded the self-respect that acknowledges them as agents.

The archetype of the passive patient in India, shaped by oppressive structures, resonates with Honneth's critique of social alienation. Reading Ambedkar and critical scholarship through the lens of social pathologies, we see how this archetype erodes the conditions necessary for self-respect, stripping patients of the possibility to be recognized as agents. The paternalism embedded in Indian medical and legal discourse represents a form of reification, where the patient is treated as an object rather than a person capable of meaningful engagement, decision-making, and deserving of self-respect. This misrecognition creates a divide between the authority of the medical professional and the diminished role of the patient, reinforcing entrenched social hierarchies, norms, and power structures.

While Axel Honneth (2003) suggests that mutual recognition is an "anthropological constant", the reality in Indian healthcare shows that this recognition is not symmetrical. Patients are viewed through a lens of medical authority, where their ability to engage in decision-making is undervalued. Instead of being recognized as contributors to the decision-making process, they are often relegated to the role of passive recipients of care, stripped of their voice and agency. This misrecognition is deeply tied to socio-political structures, such as caste, gender, and class hierarchies, which further diminishes the possibility of reciprocal, meaningful recognition in clinical settings and legal judgements. Taking forward scholarship in recognition and misrecognition (Giladi & McMillan, 2022; Venkataraman, 2020; Fraser & Honneth, 2003; Anderson & Honneth, 2005), I see the misrecognition of patients in this context parallels the notion of "ideological recognition", where the passive patient is constructed through a particular ideological framework that upholds the authority of the medical professional, for instance what we saw in Chapter 2 through medical professional standard in legal judgements. The archetype of the passive patient in the Indian healthcare system, where patients are often seen as incapable of making informed decisions, echoes the broader social pathology of misrecognition, where individuals are denied the recognition necessary for developing and sustaining a positive self-relation that underpins autonomy. The doctor–patient relationship is not one of mutual or symmetrical recognition, as it is typically framed in Western liberal philosophies of patient autonomy debates, where it is taken for granted often in "active patient" narrative, but one marked by power asymmetries within social-political conditions. In India, this hierarchical recognition is perpetuated by a colonial legacy, combined with ongoing caste and class distinctions, where the voice of the patient—particularly from marginalized backgrounds—continues to be silenced.

In much of bioethics discourse, patient autonomy, and informed consent, the socio-political conditions are often not engaged with, but I would argue that these concepts are deeply dependent on intersubjective recognition within interpersonal relationships and institutional structures. Patients are often subjected to forms of subordination and marginalization within medical and legal systems, which not only disregard their agency but also erode their capacity for self-trust, self-respect, and self-esteem—three critical elements of autonomy identified (Anderson & Honneth, 2005). The passive patient archetype in India represents a form of structural misrecognition, where the healthcare system and its legal counterparts fail to recognize the patient's need for respect and recognition. This misrecognition illustrates how it is a deeper issue and how recognition preconditions are undermined. For patients, disrespecting through everyday indignities, and the seeing them as presumed incompetent to participate in decision-making about their treatment results in humiliation and degradation, further weakening their sense of self-respect. This denial of agency reflects the power hierarchies ingrained in Indian society, where caste, class, and gender inform the dynamics between healthcare providers and patients.

This recognition view invites a critical rethinking of how the Indian healthcare system constructs the passive patient and the institutional structures that perpetuate this misrecognition. Thus, centering recognition and self-respect is about transforming the social relationships and institutional frameworks that shape healthcare interactions. Much of bioethics debates, especially patient autonomy and rights-based approaches neglects the affective and relational dimensions of recognition. And I hope, I have illustrated how legal and institutional recognition is insufficient without addressing the broader social and political conditions that shape patient-doctor interactions. Recognizing patients as agents in their own care and respecting within intersubjective and institutional structures is not just a moral imperative but a necessary condition for a healthcare system that promotes true dignity. Incorporating recognition into the healthcare system would involve addressing the psychological and social dimensions of patient care, particularly by ensuring that patients experience self-respect within their interactions with healthcare professionals and legal structures. This, in turn, requires a structural transformation of the healthcare system, where recognition becomes a core principle guiding both medical practice and legal frameworks, recognizing patients' agency within an otherwise hierarchical, paternalistic and oppressive system.

In this chapter, I have tried to show how the passive patient archetype in India speaks to a more significant failure of recognition—how institutions and systems, so profoundly rooted in hierarchy, fail to see patients as persons within social-political realities. To change this narrative, we need more than just institutional reforms. We need a transformation in how society sees the person itself, especially in healthcare. Recognition is not just a matter of seeing people; it is about honoring one's agency, self, subjectivity, and dignity to shape one's life within the web of social relationships and political realities. As discussed in earlier chapters, misrecognition in India frequently occurs through institutions and interpersonal interactions that fail to adequately serve patients. Both the legal and medical systems continue to rely on paternalistic attitudes, treating patients as passive, incapable, and unable to take part in decisions about their own bodies. This kind of misrecognition is a failure that strips people of their agency, subjectivity, and self-respect. This failure of recognition is even more complicated for those who exist at the margins and intersections of caste, class, and gender. For example, a Dalit patient or a Muslim or Adivasi woman might walk into a hospital already carrying the weight of societal oppression. They may be ignored, their voices silenced, their dignity undermined. Healthcare, instead of being a place of healing and care, becomes yet another arena where their value as a person is denied. This misrecognition compounds the exclusion they experience outside the hospital walls, in law and life. So, the passive patient archetype is not just a failure of the Indian healthcare system. It is a mirror reflecting how deeply ingrained our hierarchies are and how the legal and medical frameworks continue to see certain bodies as less worthy of respect and care. What is needed here is a shift—a radical shift—in the way we think about patients. We must move away from viewing persons who are patients as passive subjects and, instead, honor their agency and as respected as agents in their health and well-being.

Challenging this narrative means we must advocate for a deeper, more robust understanding of recognition in law and medicine. It is not just about giving patients the right to routine bureaucratic informed consent forms—it is about seeing them as social and political agents with their values, hopes, and desires. In the Indian context, moving away from the passive patient archetype would require both the medical and legal systems to embrace the diverse experiences that persons/patients bring with them, acknowledging not just their physical care needs but their social and political identities and realities, and respect and recognize them as agents—as "situated patient". This shift would not just change the way we treat patients. It would mark a transformation in the ethical fabric of society itself, where we treat each other with self-respect and true dignity, which is central to social justice. Healthcare would become a space where everyone—acknowledging the *multiplicity and poly-stability of everyday indignities* stemming from one's social and political positioning related to caste, religion, body, class, or gender—can be recognized as a person deserving of self-respect and recognition. Only then can we begin to move beyond the hierarchies, oppression, and exclusions that continue to haunt our systems, and only then can we create a world where every person is truly seen.

Way Forward: Centering the Situated Patient

While much scholarship on epistemic harms has been part of moral philosophy (Alcoff, 1995; Carby, 1982; Davis, 1991)mostly taking forward Fricker's conceptions of epistemic injustice—there has been increasing scholarship on epistemic and affective injustice and violence, especially within health spaces. However, no attention has been given to how archetypes of patienthood sustain or resist these injustices. Given the *multiplicity and poly-stability of everyday indignities*, which uphold the passive patient archetype and a culture of disrespect in law and medicine in India, we need to aspire toward acknowledging these realities and moving toward a culture of respect, where self-respect and recognition are at the core. I wish not to create a category for the sake of "categorization", fully aware of how tempting it is for an academic to create one. Yet I hope that reflecting briefly on aspiring toward a situated patient archetype is to dream of a different kind of institutional ethical imagination—one where patients and family members are not seen as empty vessels to be filled with medical expertise, but as knowers, as holders of stories, as people whose embodied realities teach us to resist and sustain a culture of respect. As I mentioned in the Introduction regarding the approach of this work as a critical philosophical ethnography, this dream does not emerge from abstraction. It grows from my very own experiences, the very corridors and rooms where I have sat with many who are dismissed, who are told their pain is not real, and from the quiet rage of patients who know their bodies and experiences, but are silenced because their suffering does not fit the language of control, power, and diagnosis and is thus disregarded.

When I think of this archetype—this figure of the 'situated patient'—to aspire toward a situated patient archetype instead of the "passive patient" archetype is to undo this silencing within the larger social and political conditions. It is to demand that institutions see patients as situated knowers, as people who come to medical spaces with their own truths and interpretations of their bodies and their lives. It is to recognize that their knowledge is not secondary, but primary—where care must begin. What does this look like in practice? It looks like a doctor who sits with a patient, not as an authority to be revered, but as a listener who trusts the patient's words. It looks like a hospital that is reflexive, that asks itself hard questions: whose voices are missing here? Whose suffering do we fail to name? Whose knowledge do we dismiss as irrelevant? It looks like a system where patients—particularly those whose social identities have historically been marked as unworthy—are not treated as objects of care, but as situated participants in their own healing. In this archetype, patients do not come empty-handed or with blind trust, as assumed in the "passive patient" archetype. They bring their stories, their struggles, their situated knowledge, and they refuse to let these be erased. Their testimony becomes part of the institutional fabric—it reshapes diagnosis, treatment, and care itself. The patient's voice does not simply add to knowledge; it disrupts and transforms the very structures that have worked to silence them. But for this dream to become real, institutions must change. They must become spaces of radical openness—where the limits of current systems are not defended by law and medicine, but questioned. Where those in positions of power are humble enough to say: "We do not know everything. We are willing to learn from you". This requires the kind of courage that shakes the roots of epistemic and affective violence, that unsettles the arrogance of expertise, and insists on building new ways of knowing and being together. Only then, through practices of recognition and self-respect, can we establish a precondition for any discourse of justice within healthcare spaces.

For patients from marginalized communities autonomy is often weaponized, invoked to protect systems rather than people. When a Dalit man refuses treatment because of the humiliation he anticipates at a government clinic, or when a rural or Adivasi woman signs a consent form she cannot read, autonomy becomes a farce. The system insists that a choice was made, but whose choice is it when self-respect is already shattered? When the relational world that sustains dignity and recognition is so ruptured that silence feels safer than speech? These are not abstract questions. They come from the very real violence of hospitals in India, where hierarchical systems mirror the social oppressions outside their walls and fold them into the patient experience. The liberal conception of autonomy that underpins medical ethics in many institutions is woefully inadequate. It imagines the patient as an isolated individual, capable of making decisions without constraint, coercion, or fear. It assumes that autonomy can exist in a vacuum, as though histories of caste-based humiliation, gender-based silencing, and structural poverty do not shape a patient's ability to act or speak. It is a version of autonomy that erases context, a version that refuses to see how power operates in patient-provider relationships. Even relational autonomy—praised as a corrective—falls short when it fails to account for the profound disempowerment that marginalized patients carry with them. Relational autonomy, in its current articulation, acknowledges dependence on others but risks romanticizing relationships that are deeply fractured by domination. What does relational autonomy mean for those who experiences violence in both one's home and in hospital? For a those whose religion is weaponized against when they seek care? The promise of relationality cannot deliver justice unless it confronts the inequities embedded in the very relationships it celebrates. The situated patient archetype is not about asking for permission to be seen or heard. It is about claiming space. It is about saying, *we are here, we have always been here, and it's time we are listened to. We know what our bodies carry, and our lived experiences. We know what the system does to us.* It is a call for institutions to shift, not just in small ways, but in the very foundations of how we/they *see* patients, how we/they *listen*, and how we/they perceive, understand, and relate to ourseleves/patients/persons.

Healthcare systems must develop practices that allow them to identify and respond to multiple, intersecting forms of oppression. This is not about creating tidy ethical, principled frameworks—it is about being willing to listen for connections that may initially appear unrelated. It is about recognizing that a patient's experience of caste-based exclusion, for example, cannot be separated from the way her gender or class shapes her pain. Institutions must move beyond single-axis understandings of care that focus solely on symptoms or protocols. They must engage with patients in ways that make room for their situated experiences and agency. Imagine a hospital where doctors are trained not just to diagnose but to listen—where a woman's pain is not dismissed because it is "normal", and where the knowledge she carries of her body is seen as legitimate. Imagine a ward where a marginalized patient is not spoken to harshly, and where their experience of caste oppression is recognized as part of their health reality. Imagine a migrant patient who does not have to shrink in shame because her language is different, because her suffering cannot be translated neatly into institutional terms. These are not isolated visions; they are fragments of a broader possibility—a reimagining of patienthood that begins with respect and recognition. To aspire to this archetype is to imagine a world where patients are not diminished. It is to see the patient not as passive but as someone who speaks, clearly and courageously,. And it is to believe that when institutions learn to listen, when they learn to honor the situatedness of every patient—given the multiplicity and poly-stability of everyday indignities, which is a reality that is never singular, never stable, always appearing differently depending on where you stand. One that feels inevitable but is deeply shaped by social and political conditions, often oppressive for marginalized communities. To become a patient is to enter a space where your vulnerabilities are heightened, where oppression manifests not only through systems but also through experiences that twist, shift, and accumulate in ways that are often invisible.

To create space for the situated patient archetype, institutions must confront their own complicity in perpetuating epistemic oppression. They must learn to see how domination is reproduced not only through explicit disrespect but through the quiet ways knowledge is devalued, silenced, or erased. This is not easy work. It demands that institutions sit with discomfort, that they question the very foundations of their authority. The multiplicity and poly-stability of everyday indignities require us to resist simplistic narratives, to leave space for understandings that are still emerging. Broadly, I see three levels of the multiplicity and poly-stability of everyday indignities that sustain the "passive patient" archetype, and how systems would need to change so they no longer harm patients and family members, particularly those from marginalized communities. At the first order, othering arises in the operation of an epistemic system within law and medicine, where patients are preemptively deemed ignorant, incapable, or unreliable. Such first-order othering can be understood as relatively "passive" insofar as it results from the system's lack of recognition of the patient's voice. Second-order othering runs deeper. It involves structural gaps in the epistemic and affective system that consistently fail to recognize or address the needs of patients, especially those in marginalized communities. The problem is not simply that patients/individuals are being ignored; it is that the system itself was never developed with their standpoint in mind. While the system may not actively direct harm at these patients, its incomplete conceptual resources mean that their concerns cannot be adequately recognized, understood, or addressed. The system focuses more on a "doctor knows best" approach. From a situated patient perspective, patients are neither entirely passive nor fully active agents; rather, they navigate a system whose very structure is incomplete, forcing them to work around conceptual voids never meant to accommodate their experiences. By contrast, third-order othering signifies a scenario where the entire epistemic system is ill-suited to meet the needs of patients and, in fact, actively misdirects attention and inquiry. These exclusions are not merely gaps or oversights; they are features of a system so deeply entangled with structures of domination that it cannot be reformed simply by adding new concepts or filling in missing pieces.

In a caste-class-heteronormative biomedical environment, for instance, the entire framework of diagnosis and treatment might be oriented around assumptions that uphold certain bodies, genders, and cultural backgrounds as the norm. Patients from historically oppressed groups may find that the system directs medical attention away from the root causes of their suffering (e.g. the ongoing legacies of colonial violence or entrenched caste-based discrimination) and channels it into treatments that fail to address underlying injustices. This is an "active" form of othering: the system doesn't just fail to see these patients, it trains its gaze in a way that ensures their embodied and epistemic contributions and health realities remain obscured. In these situations, the situated patient may find no meaningful way to "fit" into the existing system, no matter how creatively or persistently they try. Instead, entirely new epistemic frameworks—ones that center their experiences and challenge taken-for-granted norms—are required. To center the situated patient archetype in healthcare and apply ethics through self-respect and recognition as a precondition is to confront the thin, fragmented versions of autonomy that have been used to define patienthood for far too long. It is to move beyond a version of agency and dignity defined by protocols, signatures, forms, and half- or non-explained decisions—one that ignores histories of caste, class, gender, age, and religion and the messy realities of how marginalized communities in India experience care. This version of autonomy is not freedom. It is not respect. It is not care. It is abstraction masquerading as ethics, a hollow nod to choice that does not ask who gets to make choices and under what conditions.

I think it is here that the 'situated patient' archetype emerges as a radical intervention. To center this archetype is to recognize that autonomy or any ethics discourse in healthcare spaces cannot exist without self-respect and recognition. These are not lofty ideals—they are preconditions for ethics in practices itself, for the possibility of any meaningful practice of autonomy, informed consent, shared decision-making, and dignity in healthcare. For example, we know dominant practices, especially as they exist in many Indian hospitals, function as rituals of bureaucracy. For marginalized patients, it often feels like yet another act of erasure. The system insists that autonomy, patient rights, and consent have been upheld because a signature was secured. But what does consent mean without understanding? Without trust? Without respect? The situated patient archetype transforms informed consent from a box to be checked into a process of mutual recognition. It demands that healthcare providers engage with patients' lived realities—the fears, the histories, the silences that shape their experiences of care. It insists that consent is not just about information but about understanding—an understanding shaped as much by experiences and relationships as by words. In this framework, medical decision-making becomes dialogic, collaborative. The doctor does not stand as the sole authority. The patient's voice is not ignored. This is not an abandonment of expertise, but an expansion of it. Patients' embodied knowledge—of their pain, their histories, their social worlds—becomes part of the process. Thus, self-respect and recognition from healthcare institutions or professionals are not acts of charity; they are ethical responsibilities. Autonomy in healthcare does not fail because patients lack the ability to choose; it fails because the conditions that make choice meaningful—recognition and self-respect—are systematically denied. Recognition is not simply about seeing a patient; it is about acknowledging their humanity, their agency, their situated knowledge as valid. It is about creating space for patients to speak and to be heard, without fear of dismissal or retaliation.

To restore self-respect, institutions must engage in practices of recognition—seeing patients as embodied knowers, as moral agents, as human beings whose dignity is non-negotiable. This recognition must go beyond words. It must take shape in structural reforms. The situated patient archetype demands this kind of recognition because it insists that patients are situated—their identities and experiences shaped by complex social worlds. To center the situated patient archetype is to reclaim the humanity of those who have been erased—those whose suffering has been rendered invisible, whose knowledge has been devalued. It is to insist that autonomy cannot exist without self-respect, and self-respect cannot exist without recognition. For the marginalized patient in India, this shift is not merely theoretical. It is survival. It is the difference between being seen and being silenced, between care that heals and care that humiliates, between autonomy as abstraction and autonomy as true dignity. For many critical scholars, liberation begins with self-respect and recognition, – with the refusal to let systems of power define who we are and what we deserve. To center the situated patient archetype is to take seriously the voices that have been excluded and resist embodied and epistemic violence. It is to insist that autonomy cannot exist without self-respect and recognition—preconditions for ethical healthcare that cannot be overlooked. Self-respect, as I argue in my book, is deeply relational. It is not a personal attribute but a product of how one is treated, how one is seen, and how one's knowledge and dignity are valued in the social world. Without recognition, there can be no self-respect. And without self-respect, there can be no autonomy. It is to build a healthcare system that does not simply offer treatment but restores self-respect and true dignity. It is to believe that health itself is relational, that justice in care cannot exist without justice in self-respect and recognition within.

I hope, I have demonstrated that the passive patient archetype invites a shift in perspective, from looking at individual wrongdoers or isolated acts of harm to considering how entire epistemic and affective systems shape what counts as knowledge, who gets to contribute it, and whose interests are served or not. I have also shown the importance of taking a situated patient perspective, briefly—one that attends to how people navigate oppressive conditions on the ground, rather than focusing solely on abstract ideals of agency or justice. Healthcare systems should connect seemingly unrelated experiences of oppression, building richer, more complete understandings of how marginalization works. In healthcare, this means listening for connections—seeing how caste humiliation intersects with poverty, how gender-based silencing intersects with epistemic violence, how a Muslim woman's fear of judgment intersects with her inability to voice her pain. Take, for example, a Dalit woman who avoids antenatal care because she knows she will be shamed for her "ignorance" and "uncleanliness". At first glance, this may appear as a failure of access. But when we see deeper layers of injustice—her knowledge of her own body dismissed, her dignity denied, her fear rooted in generational caste trauma—we begin to understand the full picture. The situated patient archetype, which centers self-respect and recognition, forces us to connect these threads. It compels institutions to ask: why does this woman remain silent? What histories shape her silence? What does recognition look like for her? The situated patient archetype answers this challenge by demanding that we stand with the most marginalized, that we listen to their voices, that we recognize their knowledge as vital to the ethical healthcare system and beyond. In doing so, we move closer to a healthcare system that does not simply treat bodies but restores self-respect, fosters agency, and builds the trust required for caring.

I hope that by showing the seemingly taken-for-granted notion of the presumed "passive patient" archetype and everyday indignities, I have illustrated how oppressive systems have historically and socio-politically formed and continue to operate. Attending to these oppressive formations helps us see why some systems must be radically reimagined or replaced rather than simply tinkered with. It also suggests that, in contexts shaped by patriarchal structures with colonial legacies, along with biomedical gaze, certain strategies for resisting embodied and epistemic harms—like encouraging individuals to become better listeners or more virtuous knowers, as tick-box excercies or bureaucratic rituals—may be insufficient. Such strategies can too easily leave oppressive systems intact. Instead, from a situated patient perspective, we are encouraged to consider how patients themselves navigate, resist, and sometimes subvert these systems, even when they cannot entirely escape or transform them. This might involve recognizing that the embodied knowers are themselves situated within systems that advantage some groups over others. Understanding how these environments work, and how they actively produce harm, may be essential to imagining forms of knowledge production, morality and values that genuinely serve those who have long been ignored, excluded, or misrepresented. This is the promise of culture of respect in India's healthcare landscape—and a key step toward democratizing the very systems that, for too long, have ignored patients who deserve self-respect, genuine recognition, and true dignity.

References

Abbott, O. (2020). The self, relational sociology, and morality in practice (1st ed.). Springer International Publishing.

Alcoff, L. (1995). The problem of speaking for others. Who can speak? Authority and critical identity. In J. Roof & R. Wiegman (Eds.), Champaign, IL: University of Illinois Press.

Ambedkar, B. R. (1990). *Dr. Babasaheb Ambedkar: Writings and speeches, vol. 2.* Government of Maharashtra.

Ambedkar, B. R. 2011. The Buddha and his dhamma. Aakash Singh Rathore & Ajay Verma (Eds.). New Delhi: Oxford University Press.

Ambedkar, B. R. (2020). *Beef, Brahmins, and broken men*. An Annotated Critical Selection from The Untouchables. Columbia University Press. https://doi.org/10.7312/ambe19584

Anderson, J., & Honneth, A. (2005). Autonomy, vulnerability, recognition, and justice. In *Autonomy and the challenges to liberalism: New essays*. Cambridge University Press.

Armstrong, D. (2014). Actors, patients and agency: A recent history. *Sociology of Health & Illness, 36*(2), 163–174. https://doi.org/10.1111/1467-9566.12100

Arnold, D. (1993). *Colonizing the body: State medicine and epidemic disease in nineteenth-century India*. University of California Press.

Arnold, D. (2000). *Science, technology and medicine in colonial India*. The New Cambridge History of India. Cambridge University Press.

Baxi, U. (1982). *The crisis of the Indian legal system. Alternatives in development: Law*. Stranger Journalism.

Baxi, U. (2000). Postcolonial legality. In *A companion to postcolonial studies* (pp. 540–555). Blackwell Publishing.

Beach, M. C., Duggan, P. S., Cassel, C. K., & Geller, G. (2007). What does 'Respect' mean? Exploring the moral obligation of health professionals to respect patients. *Journal of General Internal Medicine, 22*(5), 692–695. https://doi.org/10.1007/s11606-006-0054-7

Beauchamp, T. L., & Childress, J. F. (2013). *Principles of biomedical ethics*. Oxford University Press.

Bernstein, J. M. (2005). Suffering injustice: Misrecognition as moral injury in critical theory. *International Journal of Philosophical Studies, 13*(3), 303–324. https://doi.org/10.1080/09672550500169117

Brüggemann, J., Guntram, L., & Nedlund, A.-C. (2022). The 'Difficult Patient'–Dominant logics and misfits in medicine. In *Handbook of social sciences and global public health* (pp. 1–14). Springer.

Carby, H. (1982). White women listen! Black feminism and the boundaries of sisterhood. In *The empire strikes back: Race and racism in the 70s in Britain*, Centre for Contemporary Cultural Studies. London: Routledge.

Chattopadhyay, S. (2018). The shifting axes of marginalities: The politics of identities shaping women's experiences during childbirth in Northeast India. *Reproductive Health Matters, 26*(53), 62–69.

Cheston, K. (2022). (Dis)Respect and shame in the context of 'Medically Unexplained' illness. *Journal of Evaluation in Clinical Practice, 28*(5), 909–916. https://doi.org/10.1111/jep.13740

Childress, J. F. (2017). Needed: A more rigorous analysis of models of decision making and a richer account of respect for autonomy. *The American Journal of Bioethics, 17*(11), 52–54. https://doi.org/10.1080/15265161.2017.1382168

Childress, J. F. (2020). Respecting personal autonomy in bioethics: Relational autonomy as a corrective? In J. F. Childress & J. F. Childress (Eds.), *Public bioethics: Principles and problems*. Oxford University Press. https://doi.org/10.1093/med/9780199798483.003.0002

Childress, J. F., & Quante, M. (2021). *Thick (Concepts of) autonomy: Personal autonomy in ethics and bioethics* (1st ed. 2022). Vol. 146. Philosophical Studies Series. Springer Nature. https://doi.org/10.1007/978-3-030-80991-1

Collins, P. H. (1990). *Black feminist thought: Knowledge, consciousness, and the politics of empowerment*. Routledge.

Das, J., & Hammer, J. (2012). Health and health care policy in India: The case for quality of care. In *The Oxford handbook of the Indian economy*. Routledge Oxford University Press New York.

Das, V. (2015). *Affliction: Health, disease, poverty*. Fordham University Press. https://doi.org/10.5422/fordham/9780823261802.001.0001

Davis, A. Y. (1981). *Race, Women, and Class*. New York: Random House.

Dillon, R. S. (1992). Toward a feminist conception of self-respect. *Hypatia, 7*(1), 52–69. https://doi.org/10.1111/j.1527-2001.1992.tb00697.x

Dillon, R. S. (1997). Self-respect: Moral, emotional, political. *Ethics, 107*(2), 226–249.

Dingwall, R., & Murray, T. (1983). Categorization in accident departments: 'Good' patients, 'bad' patients and 'children.'" *Sociology of Health & Illness*, 5(2), 127–148.

Dolezal, L. (2015). *The body and shame: Phenomenology, feminism, and the socially shaped body*. Lexington Books.

Dolezal, L. (2022). Shame anxiety, stigma and clinical encounters. *Journal of Evaluation in Clinical Practice, 28*(5), 854–860. https://doi.org/10.1111/jep.13744

Faden, R. R., Beauchamp, T. L., & King, N. M. (1986). *A history and theory of informed consent*. Oxford University Press.

Fanon, F. (2010). The lived experience of the Black man. In *Cultural theory: An anthropology* (pp. 422–431).

Fanon, F. (2016). Black skin, White masks. In *Social theory re-wired* (pp. 394–401). Routledge.

Fraser, N., & Honneth, A. (2003). *Redistribution or recognition?: A political-philosophical exchange*. Verso.

Freeman, L. (2018). Micro interactions, macro harms: Some thoughts on improving health care for transgender and gender nonbinary folks. *IJFAB: International Journal of Feminist Approaches to Bioethics, 11*(2), 157–165. https://doi.org/10.3138/ijfab.2018.05.29

Freeman, L., & Weekes Schroer, J. (2020). *Microaggressions and philosophy*. Routledge.

Fricker, M. (2007). *Epistemic injustice: Power and the ethics of knowing*. Oxford University Press.

Fricker, M. (2017). Evolving concepts of epistemic injustice. In *The Routledge handbook of epistemic injustice* (pp. 53–60). Routledge.

Galeotti, A. E. (2015). Autonomy and multiculturalism. In *Authenticity, autonomy and multiculturalism* (pp. 45–65). Routledge.

Giladi, P., & McMillan, N. (2022). *Epistemic injustice and the philosophy of recognition*. Taylor & Francis.

Gopichandran, V. (2019). *Dynamics of trust in doctor-patient relationship in India: A clinical, social and ethical analysis*. Springer Nature.

Green, S., Davis, C., Karshmer, E., Marsh, P., & Straight, B. (2005). Living stigma: The impact of labeling, stereotyping, separation, status loss, and discrimination in the lives of individuals with disabilities and their families. *Sociological Inquiry, 75*(2), 197–215.

Grue, J. (2016). The social meaning of disability: A reflection on categorisation, stigma and identity. *Sociology of Health & Illness, 38*(6), 957–964.

Guru, G. (2009). *Humiliation: Claims and context*. Oxford University Press.

Guru, G., & Sarukkai, S. (2018). *The cracked mirror: An Indian debate on experience and theory*. Oxford University Press.

Gutmann, T. (2022). Is 'Autonomy Talk' misleading? In *Thick (Concepts of) autonomy: Personal autonomy in ethics and bioethics* (pp. 117–133).

Harrison, M. (2009). Medical experimentation in British India: The case of Dr Helenus Scott. In H. Ebrahimnejad (Ed.), *The development of modern medicine in non-western countries* (pp. 37–55). Routledge.

Holroyd, J. (2010). Substantively constrained choice and deference. *Journal of Moral Philosophy, 7*(2), 180–199.

Honneth, A. (1996). *The struggle for recognition: The moral grammar of social conflicts.* Polity Press. http://ebookcentral.proquest.com/lib/usyd/detail.action?docID=4029984

Honneth, A. (2014). *Disrespect: The normative foundations of critical theory.* John Wiley & Sons.

Honneth, A., & Margalit, A. (2001). Recognition. *Proceedings of the Aristotelian Society, Supplementary Volumes, 75*, 111–139.

hooks, b. (2014). *Feminist theory: From margin to center* (3rd ed.). Routledge. https://doi.org/10.4324/9781315743172

Hutchinson, P., & Dhairyawan, R. (2017). Shame, stigma, HIV: Philosophical reflections. *Medical Humanities, 43*(4), 225–230.

Jeffery, R. (1979). Normal rubbish: Deviant patients in casualty departments. *Sociology of Health & Illness, 1*(1), 90–107.

Joyce, K. A., James, J. E., & Jeske, M. (2020). Regimes of patienthood: Developing an intersectional concept to theorize illness experiences. *Engaging Science, Technology, and Society, 6*, 185–192.

Joyce, K., & Jeske, M. (2019). Revisiting the sick role: Performing regimes of patienthood in 21st century. *Sociological Viewpoints, 33*(1).

Kaufmann, P., Kuch, H., Neuhaeuser, C., & Webster, E. (Eds.). (2010). Humiliation, degradation, dehumanization: Human dignity violated (Vol. 24). Springer Science & Business Media.

Keith, V. M., Nguyen, A. W., Joseph Taylor, R., Mouzon, D. M., & Chatters, L. M. (2017). Microaggressions, discrimination, and phenotype among African Americans: A latent class analysis of the impact of skin tone and BMI. *Sociological Inquiry, 87*(2), 233–255. https://doi.org/10.1111/soin.12168.

Khader, S. J. (2011). *Adaptive preferences and women's empowerment.* Oxford University Press.

Khader, S. J. (2020). The feminist case against relational autonomy. *Journal of Moral Philosophy, 17*(5), 499–526.

Kumbhar, K. (2023). Doctor sahab: Doctors and the public in the 'Golden Era' of the Indian Medical Profession. *Sociology of Health & Illness*, n/a(n/a). https://doi.org/10.1111/1467-9566.13630

Kumbhar, K. S. (2022). *Healing and harming: The "Noble Profession" of medicine in post-independence India, 1947–2015.* Harvard University.

Loughlin, M., Dolezal, L., Hutchinson, P., Subramani, S., Milani, R., & Lafarge, C. (2022). Philosophy and the clinic: Stigma, respect and shame. *Journal of Evaluation in Clinical Practice, 28*(5), 705–710. https://doi.org/10.1111/jep.13755

Lysaught, M. T. (2004). Respect: Or, how respect for persons became respect for autonomy. *Journal of Medicine and Philosophy, 29*(6), 665–680. https://doi.org/10.1080/03605310490883028

Mackenzie, C. (2014). Responding to the agency dilemma: Autonomy, adaptive preferences, and internalized oppression. In *Personal autonomy and social oppression* (pp. 48–67). Routledge.

Macklin, R. (1999). *Against relativism: Cultural diversity and the search for ethical universals in medicine*. Oxford University Press.

Madhivanan, P., Krupp, K., Kulkarni, V., Kulkarni, S., Vaidya, N., Shaheen, R., Philpott, S., & Fisher, C. (2014). HIV testing among pregnant women living with HIV in India: Are private healthcare providers routinely violating women's human rights? *BMC International Health and Human Rights, 14*(1), 7. https://doi.org/10.1186/1472-698X-14-7

Manson, N. C., & O'Neill, O. (2007). *Rethinking informed consent in bioethics*. Cambridge University Press.

Margalit, A., Goldblum, N., & Riley, J. (1996). *The decent society*. Vol. 1. Harvard University Press.

McTernan, E. (2018). Microaggressions, equality, and social practices. *Journal of Political Philosophy, 26*(3), 261–281. https://doi.org/10.1111/jopp.12150

Meyers, D. T. (1989). Self, society, and personal choice. Cambridge University Press.

Meyers, D. T. (2018). *Feminists rethink the self*. Routledge.

Mills, C. W. (2019). *The racial contract*. Cornell University Press.

Millum, J., & Bromwich, D. (2020). Respect for persons. In A. S. Iltis & D. MacKay (Eds.), *The Oxford handbook of research ethics*. Oxford University Press. https://doi.org/10.1093/oxfordhb/9780190947750.013.12

Moreton-Robinson, A. (2021). *Talkin'up to the white woman: Indigenous women and feminism*. U of Minnesota Press.

Naik, A. D, Dyer, C. B., Kunik, M. E., & McCullough, L. B. (2009). Patient autonomy for the management of chronic conditions: A two-component re-conceptualization. *The American Journal of Bioethics, 9*(2), 23–30.

Narayan, U. (2018). Minds of their own: Choices, autonomy, cultural practices, and other women. In *A mind of one's own* (pp. 418–432). Routledge.

O'Neill, O. (2002). *Autonomy and trust in bioethics*. Cambridge University Press.

Paik, S. (2022). *The vulgarity of caste: Dalits, sexuality, and humanity in modern India*. Stanford University Press.

Piper, M. (2016). Achieving autonomy. *Social Theory and Practice*, 767–792.

Rege, S. (2014). *Writing caste/Writing gender: Narrating Dalit women's testimonies*. Zubaan.

Rodrigues, V. (2024). *Ambedkar's political philosophy: A grammar of public life from the social margins*. Oxford University Press.

Ruddock, A. (2021). *Special treatment: Student doctors at the all India Institute of Medical Sciences*. South Asia in Motion. Stanford University Press. https://doi.org/10.1515/9781503628267

Schermer, M. (2002). *The different faces of autonomy: Patient autonomy in ethical theory and hospital practice* (1st ed.). Kluwer Academic.

Sen, G., Reddy, B., & Iyer, A. (2018). Beyond measurement: The drivers of disrespect and abuse in obstetric care. *Reproductive Health Matters, 26*(53), 6–18. https://doi.org/10.1080/09688080.2018.1508173

Smith-Oka, V. (2015). Microaggressions and the reproduction of social inequalities in medical encounters in Mexico. *Social Science & Medicine, 143*(October), 9–16. https://doi.org/10.1016/j.socscimed.2015.08.039

Smith-Oka, V. (2022). You're joking: Exploring humour and humiliation as forms of shame and obstetric violence within medical encounters. *Journal of Evaluation in Clinical Practice, 28*(5), 917–923. https://doi.org/10.1111/jep.13741

Sointu, E. (2017). 'Good' patient / 'Bad' patient: Clinical learning and the entrenching of inequality. *Sociology of Health & Illness, 39*(1), 63–77.

Subramani, S. (2018). The moral significance of capturing micro-inequities in hospital settings. *Social Science and Medicine, 209*(July), 136–144. https://doi.org/10.1016/j.socscimed.2018.05.036

Subramani, S. (2022). Moral habitus: An approach to understanding embedded disrespectful practices. *Developing World Bioethics, 22*(2), 94–104. https://doi.org/10.1111/dewb.12301

Subramani, S. (2023). Emotions and affects: The missing piece of the Jigsaw Puzzle of understanding risk attitudes in medical decision-making. *Journal of Medical Ethics, 49*(11), 746. https://doi.org/10.1136/jme-2023-109374

Subramani, S., & Biller-Andorno, N. (2022). Revisiting respect for persons: Conceptual analysis and implications for clinical practice. *Medicine, Health Care and Philosophy.* https://doi.org/10.1007/s11019-022-10079-y

Sue, D. W. (2010). *Microaggressions and marginality: Manifestation, dynamics, and impact.* John Wiley & Sons.

Sue, D. W. (2017). Microaggressions and 'Evidence': Empirical or experiential reality? *Perspectives on Psychological Science, 12*(1), 170–172. https://doi.org/10.1177/1745691616664437

Sue, D. W., Capodilupo, C. M., Torino, G. C., Bucceri, J. M., Holder, A., Nadal, K. L., & Esquilin, M. (2007). Racial microaggressions in everyday life: Implications for clinical practice. *American Psychologist, 62*(4), 271.

Taylor, C. (1989). *Sources of the self: The making of the modern identity.* Cambridge University Press.

Terlazzo, R. (2016). Conceptualizing adaptive preferences respectfully: An indirectly substantive account. *Journal of Political Philosophy, 24*(2).

Venkataraman, P. (2020). Identity and recognition in the case of 'Dalits.' *Contemporary Voice of Dalit, 12*(2), 132–137.

Whitney, S. (2018). Byproductive labor: A feminist theory of affective labor beyond the productive–reproductive distinction. *Philosophy & Social Criticism, 44*(6), 637–660.

Wiinikka-Lydon, J. (2019). Mapping moral injury: Comparing discourses of moral harm. *The Journal of Medicine and Philosophy: A Forum for Bioethics and Philosophy of Medicine, 44*(2), 175–191. https://doi.org/10.1093/jmp/jhy042

Yancy, G. (2008). Elevators, social spaces and racism: A philosophical analysis. *Philosophy & Social Criticism, 34*(8), 843–876. https://doi.org/10.1177/0191453708094727

Afterword

With Rage, Resistance, and Hope: A Culture of Self-Respect

For those who are part of, and familiar with, the self-respect discourse and movement in India, and elsewhere, and who are resisting oppressive systems, even by showing awareness of indignation and how one negotiates and embodies one's body, voice, speech, and attitude—how one navigates the inherent hierarchical system—this demonstrates that people are already exercising their agency and retaining their self-respect and true dignity given the oppressive conditions. When this agency is not recognized, and with the denial of self-respect, it becomes sites for authoritative, paternalistic and oppressive attitudes, behaviors, and practices, which are smothering us in India. The culture of disrespect in law and medicine—sustained by passive patient archetype and reinforced through everyday indignities—does not emerge by accident. It is a product of a moral reasoning that justifies subjugation, a reasoning and practice that must be named, confronted, undone. As we have seen in previous chapters, the constant reference to "these people"—who supposedly can't make decisions, who are poor, blindly trust, or are passive or ignorant—due to colonial and upper-caste-class-gendered assumptions and biomedical gaze, perpetuates a culture of disrespect that fails to recognize the self-respect and true dignity of individuals in one's embodied and epistemic struggles.

Drawing on critical scholars, I find myself asking, for countries like India and beyond—what normative role should concepts like recognition, self-respect, and true dignity play in a world where everyday indignities and othering have become part of living and being? And what does this reveal to us? What does this work dare and hope to do? Doing philosophy and doing theory is about engaging in ethical imagination to envision a world of possibilities, a world where we recognize how oppressive structures sustain injustice for those who are marginalized and see ways we can dismantle it. We learn to envision a better world only when we dare to sit with the discomfort of the non-ideal, the fractured, the imperfect. It is in the fissures, in the brokenness, in the sites of injustice and suffering, that the demand for something better emerges.

If any philosophy or so-called normative theory fails to take into account the lived experiences, emotions and affects of those who are marginalized, whose voices have been silenced, disregarded, and misrecognized, then that philosophy and those normative theories should not matter. As hooks (1991, p.1) said, "theory as intervention, as a way to challenge the status quo", and I see that those who have challenged the status quo, those who make us aware of it, align with my argument: we need to recognize agency—in our case, the situated patient—as an intervention, an archetype, to challenge the pervasive culture of disrespect, authoritarianism, and paternalism within medicine and law. I won't explore into the details here—perhaps that is a discussion for the future—given the purpose of my focus in this work. However, to conclude this Afterword, I turn to the words of hooks (1991, p. 2): "Theory is not inherently healing, liberatory, or revolutionary. It fulfills this function only when we ask that it do so and direct our theorizing towards this end". I hope that by illustrating the othering, suffering, and humiliation experienced through everyday indignities by patients and their family members in the Indian healthcare and legal system, and elsewhere, and by theorizing to emphasize recognition, self-respect, and agency, the conception of 'situated patient', I demonstrate resistance to the dominant status quo of upper-caste-class-gendered-racialized values, which normalize and reproduce disrespect towards those marginalised in our interpersonal relationships and become part of our institutional ethos.

Most patients in India, especially those who seek care in public healthcare systems, are acutely aware of how we are treated. Many choose to go along with it because they know that questioning a healthcare professionals might result in being mistreated or pushed out of the hospital. As we have seen in both law and medicine, these reasoning patterns are used to justify paternalistic and authoritarian practices and decisions. To conclude, if we seek social change, we must acknowledge the voices of the marginalized—those who are suffering, those who are humiliated—and learn how often oppressive institutions such as law and medicine in India practice authoritarianism and paternalism, rooted in ingrained hierarchical values and norms, and resist them. The silent suffering, this forced endurance, is the heartbeat of paternalism in law and medicine, where control and power are justified through a narrative of care, a twisted story that says, "We know what's best for you".

To suggest that people in India, or patients in India, need to be "rescued" is nothing but a colonial and upper-caste-class lie, a moral failure. It is the height of arrogance to assume that because someone lives within a political and social reality shaped by inequalities, they somehow "don't *know* better", or "that they listen out of blind trust". This narrative, this paternalistic savior complex, does nothing but reinforce the very systems of oppression we should be dismantling. The truth is, the oppressed know. We know better than anyone. It is the privileged, the so-called educated authorities and experts, who need to learn. We/they need to unlearn the comfort of power and authority, and instead, sit in the discomfort of listening. We, who are privileged, must learn to listen, engage with, and recognize the voices of those at the receiving end of disrespect in order to bring about social change. This will help us all move towards a respectful, patient-centered culture where we recognize one's agency, retain self-respect, and respect true dignity.

I hope this theorization, as discussed in earlier chapters, becomes liberatory for those who are marginalized, allowing us to resist and acknowledge one's agency, finding a vocabulary to locate and express explicitly, and for those positioned with unearned privilege to resist the culture of disrespect through recognition in everyday encounters and in institutional protocols, guidelines, and policies. Furthermore, I hope it encourages the creation of opportunities and spaces that recognize situated patients with self-respect and agency, and provide structures that stop blaming the Indian population by labeling us as "passive", "ignorant", or "incompetent". These labels justify a perceived lack of agency due to social and political conditions such as poverty, lack of education, and so-called "culture", which refers to dominant values and norms. These justifications and reasoning merely blame individuals without addressing the oppressive structures and conditions. But as we see, these very structural conditions might limit one's agency, but that doesn't mean we blame individuals for it or not address structural issues which limits one's agency. This narrow view casts patients in India as "incapable" of making decisions and choices, thereby limiting the possibilities for creating conditions that nurture one's agency and overall health and well-being.

For those familiar with Amartya Sen's capabilities approach to health and well-being, and Jean Drèze's extensive work on healthcare in India, what I am discussing here is nothing new. Health is central to our well-being, yet it remains one of the least prioritized areas our Indian politics. I attribute this to how dominant, privileged individuals, communities, and institutions disdain the basic needs and values of marginalized communities. The "passive patient" archetype is a symptom of this system. We must not forget to center self-respect and agency, alongside the politics of health, in the pursuit of social justice.

The passive patient archetype serves as a powerful lens through which we can uncover and illuminate the often overlooked and unquestioned assumptions of passivity ingrained in the rhetoric of our institutions. If I have motivated you thus far to consider the significance of self-respect and agency, then you already know that I am directing this to those privileged individuals and institutions, urging them not to dismiss these ideas as impractical in India. It would be a mistake to conclude that we must distance ourselves from patients' decisions or, in other words, practice non-interference, based on social and political realities such as poverty, an overburdened system, or what we refer to as a "culture" of deference, burnout among healthcare professionals, or the idea that "these people" can't make decisions and simply trust us, so we must act in their best interests. I ask you to take those same social realities and contexts into account and recognize that people are already living their lives and exercising one's agency in day-to-day experiences. Paternalism, driven by a culture of disrespect, exacerbates oppressive conditions for the marginalized by stripping away one's self-respect and agency.

If we truly want liberation—if we want social change that is fierce, radical, and lasting—then we must listen to the silenced. We must hear the voices of the marginalized, those suffocating under the weight of humiliation, those dismissed as less-than-human in systems designed to oppress. We must recognize the violence of these institutions—medicine, law—that claim to serve but instead wield power like a weapon, keeping those at the bottom—the poor, the sick, the voiceless—in *their* place.

Let us rage against these oppressive forces, love with the kind of fierceness that demands justice, and fight for a liberation that is born from truly centering the marginalized voices, experiences, and emotions. Let us build a world where agency, self-respect, and true dignity are centered. Because until we do, we will all remain complicit in the harm we claim to want to end.

Reference

hooks, bell. 1991. "Theory as Liberatory Practice." Yale JL & Feminism 4:1.

Appendix

Table 1 Details of Surgeons Profile

Sl. No.	*Specialty*	*Trained*		*Hospital*			*Age*	*Gender*
		Abroad	India	Govt	Private	Both/Consultant		
1	Vascular		X	X			58	M
2	Urology		X		X		37	M
3	Urology	X	X			X	45	M
4	Ophthalmology		X	X			38	F
5	Cardiac	X	X		X		49	M
6	Neurosurgery		X		X		56	M
7	Obstetrician & Gynaecology (O&G)	X	X		X		59	F
8	General Surgery	X	X		X		55	M
9	Urology			X			52	F
10	Plastic		X		X		47	M
11	Obstetrician & Gynaecology	X	X		X		39	F
12	Obstetrician & Gynaecology		X	X			48	F
13	General Surgery (GS)		X	X			41	M
14	Urology	X	X			X	50	M
15	Neurosurgery	X	X		X		54	M
16	Orthopaedic		X		X		42	M

Table 2 Details of Government Hospital Patients' Profile

No	*Specialty/ Ward*	*Number**	*Age*	*Gender*	*Work*	*Education*
1	O&G	0	42	F	Household job	Elementary School
2	O&G	1	37	F	Household job	High School
3	Ortho	0	57	F	Retired Teacher	Secondary School
4	O&G	1	38	F	Homemaker	Secondary School
5	O&G	0	35	F	Small Business	High School
6	Ortho	0	39	M	Hotel work	High School
7	GS	0	38	M	Sanitation worker	Elementary school
8	O&G	0	29	F	Household job	Secondary School
9	Ortho	0	55	F	Homemaker	High School
10	GS	1	42	M	Mechanic	High School
11	GS	0	26	F	Homemaker	Secondary School
12	GS	0	51	M	Small Business	High School
13	GS	0	46	M	Sanitation worker	High School
14	GS	0	45	F	Small Business	Elementary school
15	O&G	0	37	F	Household job	High School
16	GS	0	39	M	Sanitation worker	Secondary School

* Number of individuals present during interview
0-None, 1-Patient and one family member

Table 3 Details of Government Hospital Patients' Family Members' Profile

Sl. No.	*Specialty/Ward*	*Age*	*Relationship*	*Work*
1	GS	45	Wife	Homemaker
2	Ortho	32	Wife	Homemaker
3	O&G	27	Sister	Housekeeping job In small company
4	GS	29	Sister	Household job
5	Ortho	41	Mother	Fish vending
6	O&G	42	Mother	Homemaker
7	GS	29	Sister in law	Small company job
8	O&G	22	Daughter	Garment factory worker

Table 4 Details of Private Hospital Patients and Family members Profile

Sl. no.	*Specialty/ Ward*	*No**	*Age*	*Gender*	*Education/Work*	*Patients' Family member(s)/Relation*	*Age*	*Work*
1	Ortho	1	64	F	Homemaker	Son	38	Software engineer
2	GS	1	26	F	BCA(UG)/ Homemaker	Mother	53	Homemaker
3	GS	0	51	M	Bank Manager			
4	GS	1	59	M	Supervisor in company	Wife	55	Homemaker
5	GS	1	31	M	Sales manager	Mother	59	Homemaker
6	O&G	1	51	F	BCOM(UG)/ Homemaker	Sister	55	Lecturer
7	O&G	1	32	F	High School teacher	Mother	59	Homemaker
8	Ortho	1	69	F	Homemaker	Daughter	31	Software engineer
9	GS	2	72	M	Lawyer	Wife Sister-in-law	67, 62	Social work activities
10	GS	2	49	F	Homemaker	Husband; Sister-in-law	45, 39	Hotel Manager, Software engineer
11	GS	0	45	M	Business			
12	O&G	1	35	F	Software engineer	Mother	59	Homemaker

Table 5 Details of Nurses' Profile

Sl.no	*Specialty*	*Hospital Trained/Nurse Name*		*Working Hospital*	*Age*	*Gender*
		Govt.	*Private*			
1	O&G	X		Govt	42	F
2	GS	X		Govt	51	F
3	GS	X		Govt	42	F
4	Ortho	X		Govt	31	F
5	GS	X		Private	24	F
6	GS	X		Govt	27	F
7	GS		X	Private	25	F
8	O&G		X	Private	29	F
9	GS		X	Govt	31	F
10	GS		X	Private	28	F
11	GS		X	Private	41	F

Index

www.ingramcontent.com/pod-product-compliance
Lightning Source LLC
LaVergne TN
LVHW021128300926
849160LV00010B/914